CHAOTICS

Recent Titles in
Praeger Studies on the 21st Century

CHAOTICS

An Agenda for
Business and
Society in the
21st Century

Georges Anderla
Anthony Dunning
Simon Forge

Westport, Connecticut

PRAEGER

Published in the United States and Canada by Praeger Publishers,
88 Post Road West, Westport, CT 06881.
An imprint of Greenwood Publishing Group, Inc.

Printed in the United States of America

The paper used in this book complies with the
Permanent Paper Standard issued by the National
Information Standards Organization (Z39.48–1984).

10 9 8 7 6 5 4 3 2 1

English language edition, except the United States and Canada,
published by Adamantine Press Limited, Richmond Bridge House,
417–419 Richmond Road, Twickenham TW1 2EX, England.

First published in 1997

Library of Congress Cataloging-in-Publication Data

Anderla, Georges.
    Chaotics : an agenda for business and society in the 21st
century / Georges Anderla, Anthony Dunning, and Simon Forge.
      p. cm.—(Praeger studies on the 21st century, ISSN 1070–1850)
    Includes bibliographical references and index.
    ISBN 0–275–95691–1 (alk. paper).—ISBN 0–275–95882–5 (pbk. :
alk. paper)
    1. Management. 2. Economic forecasting. 3. Business forecasting.
4. Social prediction. 5. Chaotic behavior in systems. 6. Twenty-
first century—Forecasts. I. Dunning, Anthony. II. Forge, Simon,
1946– . III. Title. IV. Series.
HD30.27.A53   1997
302.3′5—dc21   96–37727

Library of Congress Catalog Card Number: 96–37727

ISBN: 0–275–95691–1 Cloth
      0–275–95882–5 Paperback

For my part I wish to dedicate this agenda for the new times to the memory of Professor Vickrey of Columbia University, who was my first teacher in economic analysis and modelling. William Vickrey passed away just three days after receiving the 1996 Nobel prize for economics.

Over 30 years ago, Professor Vickrey encouraged me to write a book on 'Einsteinian Economics', even though he thought it was not really an appropriate subject for the PhD dissertation I was then working on. Some of the ideas from those days have seeped into the present work.

G.A.

To Wendy

A.D.

To Bénédicte, who really does sustain me in the complexity and chaos I choose to call life.

S.C.F.

CONTENTS

LIST OF FIGURES

LIST OF TABLES

LIST OF BOXES

PREFACE

As we move into the 21st century, all our notions about what is sound in business, economics and society, even how we view reality, are poised for redefinition.

In this book we take complexity and chaos as tangible forces for good as well as bad, but with a strong plea to try to understand them and use them creatively. Applying their concepts offers us new perspectives on our many traditional problems—since they are an inevitable part of those problems. For instance, looking through the lens of 'chaotics' we see that the major threat to the US economy is not the thrust of Japanese competition—or indeed that of any outside economy —but the internal challenge of rebuilding the shattered cultural frameworks of its marginalized millions.

All sciences, business and sociology are invariably taught according to a set of rules. Here, we set out to contest many of those basic rules, the value systems and traditional guidelines. We bring together a mix of new ideas and some very ancient wisdom, some from pre-Roman sages, some from the predecessors of Adam Smith, as much as from the latest non- or anti-classical economics school just now emerging from the failure of conventional economics to explain today's business environment and economy in the USA.

In the penultimate Appendix we try to apply some of these concepts to a specific case study—robust computer systems.

PART I

FOUNDATIONS OF CHAOTICS

This is really a book about optimism. It is about solutions, creation and understanding.

We feel it is needed more than ever today, because the pace of change is so aggressive: it fills our world with downright unpredictability and instability, a constant feeling of insecurity. When we consider any corner of the earth today the news is so similar: total economic collapse in Africa, ultranationalism in Russia, militarism in China, a shooting war in the former Yugoslavia, extreme violence in the Middle East, violations of human rights in many countries, the spread of AIDS, drug addiction and increasing organized crime—it forms a terrible list. We see the emergence of new power centres in the brushfires of Islamic fanaticism and the militarism of some developing nations. Eventually we all tend to ask

Does progress have a future?

Are the complexity and chaos we seem to be creating ourselves leading to our own destruction? After escaping the prison camp of Orwell's *Nineteen Eighty-four* over the last sixty years, are we only to enter the nightmare of Huxley's *Brave New World*? But all this gloom may not be justified. Our agenda in this book is to show a way forward for the future. We want to look at the world in a new light, and then to focus that understanding, to illuminate alternative solutions that will perhaps be more successful in social, economic and scientific terms than our current ones.

And all this is coming from a most unlikely source. Pointing the way are the theories of chaos and complexity, developed over the last 50 years by mathematicians and experimental scientists better to understand the messy pieces of nature intractable by classical methods and models.

1

A Routemap to the Concepts and to the Book

Chaos often breeds life, when order breeds habit
Henry Brooks Adams
Although this may seem a paradox, all exact science is dominated by the idea of approximation
Bertrand Russell

This book is about chaos. And complexity. Together they spell 'chaotics'.

We take their combination as a kind of entity, because together they seem to be driving our world. The foundations of chaotics (of chaos and complexity) touch on all aspects of the real world. Everything real is a chaotic environment, be it space flight, electronic circuits, deserts, the upper layers of the atmosphere, jungle ecologies or the economy of Britain or Bangladesh or one business. But we can go further, into conceptual frameworks, ways of thinking. The role of experiment, axioms, metaphors, number systems and the process of invention and discovery can all be redissected using this approach.

More obvious direct applications of chaotics concepts are in understanding biological complexity, society and self-organization. Less obvious ones lie in applying chaotics to viewing cultural drift, new sorts of computer system, space–time concepts in everyday life, environmental decay and economics. But there is also a need to make chaotics (as complexity plus chaos) tangible. We must attempt to visualize chaos meaningfully, to view the edge of chaos and the limits of complexity.

Such concepts are very appropriate for business: 'For the foreseeable future, there is no such thing as a solid, or even substantial, lead over one's competitors. There are two ways to respond to the end of the era of sustainable excellence. One is frenzy ... the second is paradoxical—meeting uncertainty by emphasizing a set of new basics: world-class quality and service, enhanced responsiveness through greatly increased flexibility, and continuous short-cycle innovation and improvement aimed at creating new markets for both new and apparently mature products and services,' wrote Tom Peters in *Thriving on Chaos*.[1]

Reality is where little is ordered

However, perhaps there is a third and better way, nearer to Peters's second alternative but going further, cutting through 'old-speak' remedies to zero in on a chaotic reality. Because, like it or loathe it, that is our reality—a business world where little is ordered and everything is up for grabs. But with chaotics, we tend to reverse certain classical economic theories. The approach here is not really so new, but centuries old, published ten years before Adam Smith's epoch-making *An Inquiry into the Nature and Causes of the Wealth of Nations* (1776). It is based on the work of Anne-Robert Turgot entitled *Réflexions sur la formation et la distribution des richesses* (1766), which in some ways overturns—anticipatively—much of what Adam Smith has brought to modern thought on economics, essentially by applying certain principles that we term 'chaotics'. Chaotics also illuminates some new views on product and technology forecasting—for instance why Sony's Betamax would lose the videocassette standards battle and JVC's VHS would win, or the critical conditions for the success of Microsoft and Intel in setting PC standards.

The 20th-century mess

But it is in political, environmental and social issues that chaotics spreads its wings. Our 20th century has witnessed two World Wars—one with atomic destruction—close to two hundred localized bloody conflicts, the rise and fall of Western colonialism in Asia and Africa, Nazism, Fascism, Francoism and most recently the fall of Marxist communism. Finally the break-up of the Soviet Union has led to a new balkanization inside Russia. Now we are rapidly endangering our atmosphere and destroying our forests, lands and seas.

The end of the 20th century is characterized by being ever messier, ever more confused and harder to understand. Baffled by the mix of complexity, uncontrollability and variety of choice, nobody (especially those in business or government) can navigate with confidence. We have less and less certainty about improving our living and cultural standards, personally or globally. We see the welfare state breaking down, the gap between rich and poor widening. Politically, far from being 'the end of history', the disappearance of the Soviet Union has only signalled the beginning of a different but more complicated chapter.

Multiplier effects, feedback and mad cows

And where we have apparent order, this can act as a conductor for catastrophe.

Multiplier effects with long-term incubation periods become enormously power-ful. These may be amplified as our world seeks order through uniform processing with ever higher volume. So very small changes can wreak havoc, perhaps a long time later. Predicting future events becomes a higher-risk game. For instance, in producing plenty we can produce devastation and disease—one apparently small change in the treatment process for beef offal (the temperature) in the UK in the early 1980s produced the Bovine Spongiform Encephalopathy (BSE) crisis in the UK 12 years later, leading to massive reductions in beef sales and partial destruction of the national herd, with the loss of thousands of jobs in the UK and beyond. An enormous incremental feedback cycle set in, whereby from feeding contaminated sheep offal to cows, the cows themselves were forced to eat con-taminated feed made from the offal of their own kind.

Whether it is geopolitics, production and consumption, welfare and ethics, or standards of living and the quality of life, the overall effect is very much the same—anything can happen, and usually does. Especially when we least anticipate it. Any appearance of stability in our world is a delusion. Beneath the surface are more upheavals.

Can science help, or is it the culprit?

Can science, and its step-child, technology, explain this increasingly disordered worldscape as we prepare to enter the 21st century? But remember that science and technology are hardly ever 'innocent parties', because the random use of science is ultimately responsible for many of these errors. With its unique philosophy of life that transcends the separate disciplines and categories, science tends to call the tune. So science and technology participate equally in the glories and the tragedies of 'progress'.

Not that technology has always led us into gloom this century. It has helped us cross to the sunny side of some streets. The threat of mass starvation by recur-ring famine is basically a thing of the past. For the first time in history the human race is in a position to produce more than plenty while using fewer resources. Health care is making some tremendous strides.

The role for chaotics

Perhaps the ideas behind chaotics could help us better understand all this. In particular, could chaotics help explain our global mistakes, the causes of which seem to be as mysterious as they are massive? For instance could the long-term impoverishment of the Third World be partly due to their apparent benefactors operating mistaken strategies? Chaotics thinking may perhaps show us the new 'how' in acting decisively on underdevelopment—the condition of half the world's population. Also can we learn to choose the right policies for the world's 800 million unemployed and underemployed? The recurring questions in examining all these catastrophes are:

- how could we have done better?
- and, specifically, how can we better predict a failure?

In turning to chaotics theory we seek new value systems that may provide a better understanding of the real consequences of our quest for 'sustainable development'. Any new value system has to encompass an approach to full employment, breaking the vicious circle of underdevelopment and clarifying why our actions have upset balances in ecologies, environmental protection and destruction.

Worldscapes, philosophies and scientific attitudes

Think of the Italian Renaissance and of Galileo, of Newton's 17th century, of the industrial revolution—every major historical period develops its own brand of comprehensive world outlook or worldscape (Goethe's *Weltanschauung*) based on its particular perception of the universe, as well as a social superstructure attuned to that vision. Invariably, the philosophical view is conditioned by the current scientific position. That perspective, the philosophical and scientific testament that the 20th century is about to hand down to its 21st century successor, is worth examining.

For the 20th century, a new worldview began to be formed with the first formulation of quantum mechanics by Max Planck in 1900 and the special theory of relativity of Albert Einstein in 1905. The third pillar of our contemporary philosophy is a few years older. It was in 1889 that the French mathematician Henri Poincaré described the behaviour of systems that were truly chaotic, but without actually using the word. However, it is only over the past 30 years that a growing number of scientists have come to abandon the idea of a clockwork universe. And today, the concept of an orderly, harmonious world (culminating with the mathematical physicists' deterministic formulae and social scientists' mechanistic models of human behaviour) appears to be a trap, an intellectual cul-de-sac.

However, the Quantum and Relativity theories seem only to concern the extremes—the extraordinarily small and the extraordinarily large ends of the scale. From the point of view of ordinary people, 'so what?' seems to be a justified reaction for everyday life. But we have begun to realize over the last 30 years that even everyday phenomena on the scale of human size are subject to uncertainties. Have these been underestimated by generations of scientists because science has been rooted in a deterministic tradition going back to Isaac Newton, Pierre Simon Laplace and René Descartes? Typical examples occur in something very everyday—weather forecasting—but also in biological equilibria and economic forecasting. Whenever modellers stray from linear mathematical functions, they are faced with surprises that, cumulatively, go beyond traditional beliefs and theories. And most systems of interest in the real (chaotic) world turn out to be non-linear.

The rationale of chaotics

What do we put in the stead of the conventional theories based on simpler, deterministic models? What can we say about this alternative worldview emerging from the work of certain researchers in mathematics and philosophy? What kind of 'New Deal' for a philosophy of the surrounding environment and its processes can the 21st century expect to see? Our aim is to attempt a brief formulation of this, a *synthèse*. So the main title, 'Chaotics', calls for a more detailed analysis, more than just a word we have forged as a short-hand expression to describe non-deterministic processes. Let us start with chaos.

In everyday parlance, 'chaos' has a fairly imprecise meaning. We can see this from its assorted synonyms, e.g. 'disturbance', 'turbulence', 'disorder', 'confusion', 'upheaval', 'catastrophe': you name it, you've got it—but never quite. Our first objective is to make the reader aware of the ubiquity of chaos as a dynamic phenomenon of major importance. Chaos permeates our physical and social environment; it affects nearly all systems, natural or synthetic. To explain such widespread erratic behaviour and to try to understand its cause and the circumstances, pioneer researchers from very different areas—principally nuclear physics, weather forecasting, communications theory and genetics—have put forward hypotheses and concepts on random events and series. Generically, these form the theory of chaos. The theory has proved its value in helping researchers in engineering and the social sciences, and even political leaders, cope with the complexities of real systems, including modern society. But we want to go beyond the theory of chaos, to integrate pioneering work from a disparate set of thinkers—Poincaré, John von Neumann (the originator of modern computer architecture) and Werner Heisenberg (discoverer of the uncertainty principle). Often their work was no more than experiment—findings and inconclusive questioning. We will attempt to fill in the gaps where the vision is incomplete. Global disorder cannot be understood without some help from a new range of concepts and examples. In other words, we need a new reference framework, one that is scientific and philosophical at the same time.

Chaotics includes complex systems behaviour. Chaotics applied to everyday problems mocks the fallacy of composition, or the possibility of complete solutions. Such fallacious axioms underlie some of our most cherished concepts, such as the Keynesian target of full employment or the relentless pursuit of optimal output by each and every firm, in whatever market circumstances. Chaotics questions the sacrosanct basis of social protection, and many other traditions or taboos that have their roots in deterministic thinking. It is one of the few systems of axioms that has something meaningful to say on issues such as massive unemployment or the nature of returns on investment in high-tech industries. It provides a framework within which to rethink causes and solutions for inadequate development, rural depopulation and the growing frustration of joblessness.

Looked at from a pragmatic, operational point of view, chaotics should provide a fundamental organizing principle. It should enable us to form a coherent picture from widely scattered evidence, based on random or unpredictable events, plus trends that seem more often to conflict than to converge.

Frozen wage structures, youth unemployment in France and strange attractors

Let us take a practical example. It will contrast reality with our immersion in deterministic thinking. The latter accepts a basic tenet of neoclassical economics, that wages or salary scales are primarily governed by differentials in skills and productivity. The real world is somewhat different.

For fairly evident reasons, the actual productivity curve over the working life of most people progresses as several phases. At first it rises with the acquisition of skills. Later on, it levels off. Finally it declines with age, or loss of interest. Yet the actual remuneration, based on seniority, tends to keep rising.

Clearly, other contributing factors are at work in determining wage scales. With the aid of chaotics, the root cause of the latent conflict (which becomes a conflict of generations) can perhaps be identified, because the relationship between the generally uniform rising curve of earnings and long-term individual productivity, which varies over the lifecycle, is analogous to the notion of a specific kind of behaviour of chaotic processes.

Just as the orbit of a planet (or the swing of a pendulum) attracts all other objects in nearby orbits, irrespective of whether the loops are periodic or non-repetitive, so most job classifications (which overlook both the new skills required and the rapidly evolving age pyramid) tend to freeze pre-existing wage structures. This creates excessive rigidities in the system of production and promotes social tension all round.

Small wonder that this widening mismatch generates frustration among young people on the career ladder, and far more frustration among the many who are jobless and cannot even get on the ladder. France, for instance, has suffered a persistent 12 per cent unemployment rate for the first half of the 1990s, with a continuing 25 per cent unemployment rate among those under 25 years old. It is now hit by youth discontent and a related unhappiness with the educational system. The effects on crime have been dramatic. This chaotic behaviour is due to a phenomenon called a 'strange attractor', explored further in Chapter 2.

The Layout of the book

The book is laid out in the form of a trilogy. Each Part deals with a small number of key problems that are likely to loom large early in the 21st century. We have grouped them under the following headings:

Part I: Foundations of Chaos

Part II: Business Chaotics: Perspectives on Wealth Creation—a positive approach

Part III: Social Chaotics: Principles for Designing and Building Society—a sea change in the philosophy of living

Inevitably, there is some overlap between the three 'galaxies of issues' involved, since the material world of production and its new organization impinge on the world of ideas, on social and political spheres, and vice versa.

Part I offers an overview of the key features of the theories of chaos and complexity. This should guide the reader through the application of chaotics to business and social/economic questions in the subsequent Parts. Chapter 2 begins with an overview of chaos theory and complexity. We outline the pioneering work in this area, principally in applied physics, astronomy, genetics, mechanics and weather forecasting. We then look in Chapter 3 at the attempts made to validate observations and theories, using analytic mathematics and elementary dynamics. Fractals and other geometrical phenomena, from Julia Sets to Cantor Dust, highlight the advances. Lately, attention has turned to biological systems as models of real-life complexity. Taken together, the resulting approaches amount to a gigantic cultural shift. We then go on, in Chapter 4, to search for a more comprehensive system of axioms to fit this culture shift.

In Part II, beginning in Chapter 5, we look at business applications of chaotics. Just as life teems with variables, all interacting, so the creation of new wealth involves a myriad parameters whose interaction creates change and disturbs old routines. The malaise in our economic traditions points out a need to rethink our basic understanding of the economy. It has grown complex beyond anything known in the past, and is reflected not only in the running of the global economy but also in the management of companies. More and more firms, especially in high-tech industries, now tend towards a new pattern of returns that is becoming the strategic mainstay of companies in software, especially networked software, and in products as diverse as aeroplanes and micro-processors. We examine just why such returns are analogous to positive feedback, a mechanism exploited for some time by physicists, engineers and researchers in medicine and biology.

Realizing that even a trifling change can have massive consequences, man-agements—simply to survive—must constantly be on the alert for any pointers to turbulence in key business parameters. In so doing, they shed any remains of 'scientific management'. These two trends may trigger off a managerial and information reappraisal, as examined in Chapter 6.

Next, in Chapter 7, technology forecasting is explored. We return to basics, reappraising the assumptions on technological evolution as a formal deductive model (which has even been presented as a set of equations). Moreover, can a glimpse of the future still rest on the consensus of a set of experts? In a world where anything is possible, although nothing can be taken for granted, we explore why managers, designers—indeed all of us—must resist the 'tyranny of the uniqueness theorem' (i.e. at most one solution).

By the end of Chapter 7 we hope to have laid out a basis for understanding the key directions for forecasting major technology-triggered upheavals (and consequently for charting policies) for a 21st century agenda. So in Chapter 8 we move to an analysis of the dynamics of techno-industrial breakthroughs. This is another building-block in rethinking the economics of production of services and goods.

The conceptual and scientific effects of chaotics (Part I), together with principles of a new economics (Part II), should be brought to bear on the greatest challenge of the next decades: how to extract ourselves from our current social decline and its stormy horizons—this is Part III. Three problems cry out for attention:

- massive unemployment and underemployment
- underdevelopment for two-thirds of the world's population
- the destruction of our environment, both global and local

We could add a fourth, our crisis of identity. This has many facets: self-interrogation about our station in life, generation gaps, our social mobility in both directions, membership of groups, outsider and minority syndromes, corporate loyalties, work location/relocation. We constantly want to set our existential fears against the purposes of modern technocratic civilization and its rapidly changing modus operandi. In the process, we will discover the changes required in our system of values.

What do these four problem areas have in common? The answer is two-fold. First, flawed analysis has so far delivered fairly unsuccessful remedies, while piecemeal application has only aggravated the ills. Second, in all four instances things have reached such a stage of decay that a shock therapy is called for.

We examine whether all four issues are amenable to more promising approaches based on the principles of chaotics. However, this demands, and is conditioned by, people's readiness to adapt to new working conditions, new ways of learning, unfamiliar places to live and untested social relationships. In short we need to rethink our philosophy of living.

To begin this rethinking, we examine a modern interpretation of space–time in Chapter 9 with a scaled-down, humanized vision of space–time. Earth has been shrinking since the Victorian era (when it took a minimum of 80 days to circumnavigate our planet): global communication has become instantaneous and intercontinental travel has become a matter of three hours for the rich and seven to twelve hours for the middle classes. Space–time trade-off is the key to all sorts of previously unthinkable changes, substitutions and permutations. It is the basic rationale behind new patterns of international trade, the relocation of work (with the migration of industries to low-wage countries), new divisions of labour and even staggered education patterns during our lifetimes. Everywhere, a new flexibility is being introduced to challenge existing lifestyle boundaries. The newer forms of organization increasingly dispute traditional, centrally controlled, territorial entities and business corporations.

In Chapter 10, we turn to the problem of joblessness. Quick non-fixes are all that the employment policies of most Western democracies have amount to—subsidized retraining schemes, early retirement, across-the-board work-sharing and so on. Wreckage could be the image that most accurately describes the failure to combat massive unemployment. Just what are the alternatives to end the waste of having over 800 million people forced into idleness? Is it possible to satisfy the right to decent living conditions, while providing employment? Bolder moves are called for. Going further, we examine whether the objective of full employment should be renounced and replaced by a new set of values on work and its 'ownership'?

Two-thirds of the world's population live below the poverty line. Chapter 11 explores some possible conditions for economic take-off, and for cumulative growth to take hold long-term. These are in striking contrast to the current practices and policies in most of the Third World. We examine technology transfer, the role of central planning, investment in human capital, the value of macro- versus microeconomics, and four states of development from chaotics.

Chapter 12 reviews the environmental question. Overall, our *ad hoc* measures so far have been insufficient. While radical solutions are not an end in themselves, there are situations where they are the only method of breaking through. We give serious thought to a radical solution and to the concepts of humanity's environment beyond the natural environment. We clearly need a far better protection against nuclear waste, crime and violence, AIDS and other horrendous woes. But this involves redefining priorities, changing our system of values.

Chapter 13 brings together our agenda for the 21st century, with a brief summary for thinking with chaotics: the seven pitfalls in thinking, seven pillars of business dynamics and seven therapies for social decay.

In the appendices, we consider several technical subjects in depth. Appendix 1 looks at applying the views of chaotics to computer science, specifically for preventing failure in computer systems, using biological systems approaches. Appendix 2 examines some of the mathematics of chaos in more detail.

NOTE

1 Tom Peters, *Thriving on Chaos* (New York: Pan Books, 1987).

2

An Overview of Chaos and Complexity

Does the flap of a butterfly's wings in Brazil set off a tornado in Texas?
Edward N. Lorenz, MIT

Can we ever really know reality? Even our own memories of our personal reality are just decayed, partial versions of what really happened. Those who specialize in past facts and memories, historians, can never really return—they can at best only touch fingertips with the past. And it is the same with chaotics—we can only approximately define a chaotic reality with its myriad processes; but we need a framework for further thought. So here we are taking chaotics to cover both chaos, as manifested by certain dynamic systems, and the more recently emerging subject of complexity (more properly the behaviour of complex systems). Until now these have been treated largely as separate but related branches of areas such as mathematics, physics, chemistry and biology.

Chaotics presents at least two peculiar problems of exposition. While many of the constituent parts are clearly interconnected, several other components seem to be floating in mid-air on their own. Yet unless the layperson can catch an overall vision of the chaotics 'galaxy', her or his understanding of each part is likely to be incomplete. Our experience shows that on first approaching the subject of chaos and its underlying theory, such notions as fractals, strange attractors, the edge of chaos and the like at first only evoke a hostile confusion of axioms with a hotchpotch of jargon. We hope our overview helps to overcome this barrier and aid understanding of the true nature and relationships, so that the various pieces of the puzzle fall into place, and chaotics can be comprehended as an integrated whole.

The language of chaotics consists mostly of common concepts and images, yet they often emphasize a special meaning or imply unfamiliar connotations. They include, in particular: pattern, randomness, bifurcation, clustering, non-linearity, unpredictability, order and disorder. In fact the list of chaotics-inspired metaphors comprises surprisingly few genuinely new terms. Perhaps new to most readers are: phase space, the horseshoe, the butterfly effect, artificial life and attractors. Furthermore, some complexity and chaos theorists refer frequently—almost lovingly—to: recurring processes and continued flows, feedback, scaling, the principle of self-similarity, self-organization, locked-in situations and so on.

Another difficulty is the absence so far of an agreed approach to evaluating and proving the phenomena and theory of chaotics. Different possible methodologies are viable:

(1) *Ad hoc* experimenting, predominantly in applied physics (e.g. mechanics, astronomy, weather forecasting, etc.)
(2) Validation by mathematics, using first simple, then increasingly sophisticated, equations
(3) Figurative demonstration and visual aids
(4) Using biological systems as microcosmic models of real-life complexity
(5) Assessing the cultural shift resulting from recognition of the limits of deterministic predictability

Each of these specific ways of tackling the dual problem of reconnoitring the reality of a disturbance and explaining its roots and nature yields a somewhat different vision of chaotics as a whole. In practice, things are less clear-cut than this five-way typology would suggest. For instance, field tests in applied physics and mathematical analysis can often be combined, with excellent results. Likewise, fractal geometry from the third approach may help in solving analytic mathematical conundrums from the second.

We often see conflict between the fields of chaos and complexity. For instance, some complexity theorists tend to overemphasize biological processes to the point of belittling the contributions of the first-generation students of chaos, who did not have at their disposal high-performance simulation techniques. We propose to show that the two standpoints can usefully be integrated. This attempt at an integrative synthesis marks the beginning of a more systematic search for a few universal rules of thumb or principles that are applicable or extendible to most scientific disciplines as well as to modelling social organization and group behaviour.

Hotchpotch experimenting

In the 1960s a score of pioneer researchers, active in different areas—from nuclear physics to weather forecasting and from fluid dynamics to the study of wildlife populations—became fascinated by rapidly mounting evidence of disorderly behaviour of systems that, they contended, could be traced back to minute events or fluctuations, or even to minor errors of measurement at an earlier stage. The starting assumption that a tiny prior, or even precursor, event can play havoc with the entire system has subsequently been refined into a theory of sensitivity to initial conditions. However, the crux of the matter lies at a deeper level. The *causa causae* of the ultimate turmoil is to be found in non-linear dynamics.

These findings have led, over the last 30 years, to a wealth of experimental studies, the formulation of various working hypotheses and the enunciation of some new concepts and embryonic theories, principally grouped under the banner of 'Chaos Theory'. Only now, in retrospect, has the full significance of these discoveries been revealed and their value for practising researchers and engineers recognized as pertinent in an ever greater variety of situations.

Chaotic versus non-chaotic

The world around us contains a great many non-chaotic systems and a very wide range of other systems that are at least potentially chaotic. The first question to be examined is: what differentiates the latter from the former? In a chaotic system any minuscule input error, or a tiny change, accumulates exponentially fast as the system evolves. By contrast, in a non-chaotic system the error—or difference between the subsequent states—grows by and large in proportion with time, or possibly a small power thereof, and does not run away to infinity. In fact such non-linear effects can be explored in pure spatial geometry without reference to time. This is illustrated symbolically by Figure 1, in which various points on the circle, denoted by P_i, are projected on to the line tangent to the circle at its lowest point, O, by the straight line joining them to the topmost point, N. Suppose the points on the circle represent the inputs to a system and their projections, Q_i, on to the straight line OX the corresponding outputs. The tight clustering of points near the top of the circle represents the initial inputs into a chaotic system, because an infinitesimal change from P_i to P_{i+1} will result in an enormous change in output from Q_i to Q_{i+1}. On the other hand the points on the circle close to O represent the inputs into a non-chaotic system, where a small change in input results in a comparable shift in output.

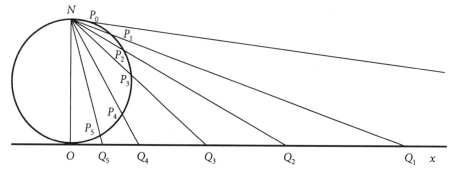

Figure 1. *A symbolic representation of linear and non-linear effects*

In Figure 1 the reader will have recognized a simplified (two-dimensional) version of stereographic projection, a mapping technique used to show the earth's lines of latitude and longitude projected on to a tangent plane by radials from the point on the surface of the sphere opposite the point of tangency. In other words, this is how to map the curved surface we inhabit on to a planar piece of paper in such a way as to maintain angles between lines and the shapes of small regions, more or less.

Of paramount interest is the way that small errors or differences in initial data evolve with time in a system that exhibits chaotic behaviour. Adjacent points near the bottom of the circle in Figure 1 stay near to each other when projected on to the tangential line *OX*, whereas points close to each other near the top of the circle become very distant from each other after projection and are thus analogous to the initial conditions of a chaotic process. Small uncertainty about position on the arc of the diagram is thus associated with enormous uncertainty about the corresponding point on the horizontal line. Before long, minor imprecision of input values renders all future calculations meaningless, and the predictive power is lost for all practical purposes.

Actually, the study of chaos theory began with weather forecasting, or more precisely, as a result of exploring John von Neumann's conception of weather control back in the late 1950s and early 1960s. Yet the role that von Neumann was to play in this connection is illustrative of a general maxim: any hypothesis, however incongruous, may be useful if it is so thought-provoking as to incite other workers in the field to conceive relationships in hitherto unexpected ways.

The Hungarian-born mathematician is famous for composing (with Morgenstern) the Theory of Games. In computing, the 'von Neumann architecture' is a basic tenet inasmuch as the principles he began to expound in 1946 still exert a strong, guiding influence on the design of most computers currently being built, from microprocessors to mainframes, and from the most powerful workstations to notebook PCs. Von Neumann believed that any problem can eventually be encapsulated in a set of mathematical equations, which, he convinced himself, can be solved to any desired accuracy through the application of discrete arithmetic in high-speed computers operating serially. Furthermore, in the Newtonian world in which he was immersed, it seemed perfectly valid to routinely extrapolate past and current trends into the future to provide guidance to decision-makers and planners. Essentially he saw a purely deterministic world. Supremely self-confident, von Neumann built his first computer at Princeton in the early 1950s with the specific aim of modelling and ultimately controlling the weather—a particularly risky gambit. Subsequently he repeatedly endeavoured to link, symbiotically as it were, computing with forecasting and computer architecture with predictive methodologies, all on a deterministic basis.

The 1950s and early 1960s witnessed a flurry of activities involving many meteorologists and other scientists inspired by von Neumann's ideas, gathering mountainous data, perfecting analytic tools, refining the parameters and imagining and testing new conjectures. Although von Neumann recognized that complex dynamic systems could have points or regions of instability, he thought that with the help of interlinked, ever more powerful radars and computers, the reported irregularities could be brought under control.

When 2 and 1 do not add up

And no wonder weather turned out to be more complicated than the most sophisticated sets of equations the weathermen could ever put together. The major challenge to von Neumann's approach came from MIT's Edward N. Lorenz, a mathematician-cum-meteorologist, who proceeded to selectively concentrate on a few key variables and reduce the number of parameters to a minimum. With the help of his simplified model and a primitive computer, Lorenz studied not only cyclical patterns, but also how the accompanying disturbances propagate in the medium to long term. Figure 2, which comes from Lorenz's computer records, shows how two nearly identical runs of weather first match almost perfectly yet soon begin diverging in a significant way. Eventually (i.e. after three or four runs), the time lag between the two patterns became unbridgeable. They were uncorrelated and chaos had set in.

Lorenz's experiments led to a startling discovery. Chaos was far from being a mere byproduct—a step-child as it were—of complexity, as many people including von Neumann believed. It could just as well be equated with the tendency

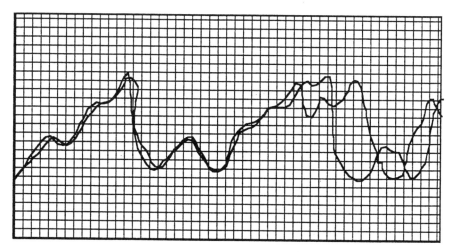

Figure 2. *Illustrating how seemingly repetitive weather patterns diverge over time, making unrealistic anything other than short-term projections*
Source: Based on Lorenz's 1961 printouts.

of the simplest non-linear system to spontaneously generate irregular gyrations when initially free from random fluctuations. To put it another way, 'complex behaviour need not have complex origins'.[1]

In order to dispel all ambiguity, Lorenz then imagined a system consisting of just three simple but non-linear equations. They were non-linear because they expressed relationships that were anything but proportional (see Chapter 3 and Part II for further discussion of what mathematicians really mean by linear). Unlike linear equations, which can generally be solved by algebraic manipulation, non-linear equations frequently cannot be resolved analytically. Lorenz showed that chaos and instability could arise at any point in his system and not just under very special circumstances, as von Neumann would have it.

However novel, Lorenz's formulation was not without precedent. It was reminiscent in many ways of the so-called three-body problem, which had been tackled, but not resolved, by the French mathematician Henri Poincaré at the turn of the century. (But be assured: this problem can be understood without going into technicalities of advanced mathematics.) According to Newton's law of universal gravitation, two massive bodies attract each other with a force directly proportional to the product of their masses and inversely proportional to the square of the distance between them. From this formula we can deduce the precise equation expressing the motion of one body relative to the other—e.g. a circle, an ellipse, a parabola or a hyperbola, depending on the initial relative motions.

But what is supposed to happen when the interaction involves, as in the solar system, more than two bodies? Despite a few early attempts at finding an answer to this intriguing question (notably by Laplace in the 18th century) the problem was practically ignored. Inasmuch as the sun's gravitational field dominates the motion of all the planets, it was indeed a fairly good approximation to consider that each planet moves in only the sun's field, with some mean field perturbation from the other planets giving the elliptic orbits. This problem became a key area for Poincaré in the late 1890s. Realizing the innate puzzle arising from the gravitational interaction of *n* bodies, Poincaré worked hard on the apparently simpler case of three bodies. In the end, all that he was able to achieve was a demonstration that the problem had no simple, general solution. And so it is unsolvable generally, however elemental it might look initially—just as Lorenz suspected for most dynamic relationships.

The study of chaos in recent years has revealed that our solar system, far from being fully deterministic and predictable, is itself chaotic. The orbits of the planets, including the earth's, are chaotic too. How do we know? In 1989 Jacques Laskar, of the Bureau des Longitudes in Paris, published a paper on the numerical integration of the equations of the solar system over 200 million years. In it he showed that an error of a mere 50 feet in measuring the position of the earth at a given time would make it impossible to foretell where in its orbit the earth would find itself 100 million years later. This example provides a telling illustration of the famous 'butterfly effect'. If, in accordance with the theory of extreme sensitivity to initial conditions, infinitesimal shifts in a parameter or a minuscule error of estimation are able to jeopardize the whole system, for instance to displace a planet in (or from) its orbit, then the rate of forecast divergence is of key significance. It can reach astonishing proportions and change the system by several orders of magnitude in a very short time.

'Does the flap of a butterfly's wings in Brazil set off a tornado in Texas?', Lorenz asked, half-jokingly, in a paper dealing with predictability. And this emblematic metaphor for chaos has stuck.

Domesticating the beast

Significantly, it was also Lorenz who, perhaps unintentionally, hinted that intimate understanding of chaotic behaviour can help the designer and the technologist to cope with irregular perturbations in mechanical devices. The very first chaotic system described by Lorenz in the 1960s was a simple waterwheel driven by water poured in at a steady rate. As long as the inflow is slow, some of the water is lost through leaks and the wheel never starts to turn. If the flow is accelerated the top bucket fills up and sets the wheel in motion. Eventually the waterwheel may settle into a rotation that goes on and on at a steady pace. But if the flow of water is further increased the spin can become chaotic, slowing down, then reversing. According to Lorenz, this recurs constantly but without ever settling down to a steady rate and without repeating itself in any predictable pattern.

Lorenz's waterwheel was meant to illustrate fluid motion, such as takes place under laboratory conditions in a convection cell. Imagine a carefully designed box with a perfectly flat base that can be heated and a perfectly level top equipped with a cooler. The convection flow inside the box is governed by the temperature difference between the (hot) base and the (cold) ceiling. By careful manipulation of heating and cooling devices, one can actually control the flow of the fluid, making it move for instance in a continuous circle between top and bottom. This type of system is useful in fluidized beds and chemical-processing plants. The process just described is of special interest for weather forecasting—it is highly analogous to nature's atmospheric convection flows. Desert floors become overheated by the burning sun, sending rising, rolling air currents to shape shadow-like patterns in the sand or, more often, in the clouds overhead, and thus influence weather change.

It is one thing to imply possible future developments of the phenomena of chaos. It is another thing to turn a discovery into practical innovation. Technologists took quite a long time—between 15 and 20 years—to come up with neat, efficient ways of counteracting chaos in electronic circuits. As is well known, miniaturized chips and other electronic components, being intrinsically imperfect, tend to behave unpredictably. Little by little, electronics engineers have learned how to use positively what seemed a nuisance at first sight. For instance, consider microwave oscillators and hi-fi amplifiers. In practice, all such devices suffer from two principal drawbacks. They not only generate 'extra' oscillations at various frequencies, but their output tends to fluctuate unexpectedly in either power, or frequency, or both. Viewed from the perspective of chaos theory, these apparently random characteristics of electronics are assumed to be the result of myriad non-linear interactions between the electrons and the atoms they move between, perhaps due to imperfections and to distortions in the silicon lattice. Here chaos theory brings understanding of the behaviour of less-than-perfect electronic systems and devices. Engineers are thus in a better position to produce improved, or in other words less chaotic, oscillators and amplifiers. As a next step they may be able to design entirely new systems that actually use chaos to good effect in the future.

Moreover, the inherent leverage available in chaotic systems, arising from their extreme sensitivity to tiny perturbations, can be put to good use in specific situations. For instance, a few years back, when NASA operators decided to send the spacecraft ISEE-3/ICE some 50 million miles across the solar system, they could use only limited amounts of the remaining hydrazine fuel to achieve what was to be the first scientific rendezvous with a comet. They needed a system that could magnify the very limited amounts of power available. The whole feat was made possible thanks to the butterfly effect, or more specifically, to the sensitivity of the three-body problem of celestial mechanics to tiny perturbations. The key point is that this could not have been done in a non-chaotic system. A non-chaotic system requires a large effect to go hand in hand with a large control system.[2]

This newly acquired know-how has many, often surprising, applications. Thus, radio signals in military communications can now be designed to hide in artificially created noise so as to mislead eavesdroppers and yet in actual fact be as noiseless as their classical counterparts. Chaotic oscillators do the job. The same technology—spread spectrum—will probably revolutionize mobile radio in the 21st century, enabling it to progressively replace wireline local communications, both inside and outside the office and home.

In chemistry, chaotic autocatalytic reactions have successfully brought wayward processes under control using newly designed mechanisms. So far these have been studied under laboratory conditions, pending their introduction into standard industrial processes. Yet another instance concerns physiologists preoccupied with patients' cardiological troubles. They are beginning to see glimmerings of a chaotic control system in heart problems, and are using chaos theory to understand cardiological signals. And there is no end in sight, for in a chaotic environment engineers are not restricted and tied down to a single, deterministic solution. They become free to choose from a whole range of new possibilities, as we shall discover in the course of what follows. In the next section we shall be considering the anatomy of non-linear dynamics in more detail, and movement between three states of behaviour. We shall see that for certain para-meter values (or operating conditions) a single, well-defined system will reach stable equilibrium and stay there, but that for other values even such a system will move between multiple stable states. For yet other values it can move in chaotic, or random, patterns.

NOTES

1 M. Mitchell Waldrop, *Complexity: The Emerging Science at the Edge of Order and Chaos* (New York: Simon & Schuster, 1992), p. 279.
2 Troy Shinbrot, Celso Grebogi, Edward Ott and James A. Yorke, 'Using small perturba-tions to control chaos', *Nature* 363 (3 June 1993), p. 411.

3

Insights from Numbers and Visualizing Chaos

Could it be that a pile of sand 'remembers' and thus is capable of learning?
Douglas R. Hofstadter

To think about unforeseen change, we may need new ways of thinking, especially when we have to consider the future tsunamis, or tidal waves, of change that may sweep over us in the early 21st century. The common meaning of the word chaos—to describe a situation of confusing complexity where nothing is clearly defined—is not our focus. We are interested in going further and establishing some useful, if surprising, insights that can be applied to economic and social issues where complexity and chaos apparently reign. Every major discipline has its own way of presenting and addressing its core concepts, one metaphor that transcends all others. Chaotics can be most easily stated in terms more palatable to mathematicians than anyone else, and most easily contrasted in mathematical terms with non-chaotic views. It is through mathematics in particular that we can explore chaos in detail, at least in the sense used here.

However, mathematical symbols and language tell only half the story, as we now realize. In a sense, ours is an image civilization in which visual representation and perception challenge both the spoken and the written word. Indeed, the biologists' image of chaotics supplements most usefully the mathematicians' vision of chaos and complexity. Thus, the plan before us is to dwell in turn upon the two perspectives, starting with that of the mathematicians.

Fast straights and puzzling chicanes

When the variables appearing in an equation are 'linearly related' then a whole body of well-established mathematics enables analytic solutions to 'what if?' questions to be obtained with certainty. When the variables are non-linearly related, this perfect predictability is lost. The system of equations becomes more difficult to solve. Analytic solutions obtained via simple algebra are rare. So we have to resort to computers.

What is meant by the expression 'linear equation'? It is a very precise mathematical concept. Simply put, it means that the variables appear only to the power of one in the equation. That is, there are no squares, cubes, fourth powers, etc. When these higher powers do occur, a first trick is to try and transform them away, e.g. by taking logarithms, but this does not always work, so we are left to grapple with a non-linear problem. Another, more physical, way of grasping the significance of linearity is to consider a system with inputs and outputs, such as an electrical circuit or a production process. Suppose that input A_1 to the system gives rise to output B_1, and input A_2 produces output B_2, then if the simultaneous input of $(A_1 + A_2)$ gives rise to output $(B_1 + B_2)$ the system is said to be additive. If, in addition, when the input is multiplied by a constant factor, c (to give cA_1), the output is increased or decreased (depending on whether c is greater or less than 1) by the same factor (to give cB_1) we say the system is homogeneous. If a system is both additive and homogeneous, then it is a linear one. All other systems that do not have these properties are called non-linear and are represented by other types of equation. Massive simulations using powerful computers and mathematical analysis tools for studying non-linear systems have enabled researchers to go beyond the usual approximations. With a fresh eye, we can begin to explore the incredible, multiform world in which we live—the world where chaos, innovation and change are the norm, and nothing stays the same.

It is clear now that, as far as everyday living is concerned, the non-linear bits are not only more interesting than the linear ones but also more productive in understanding our environment and our social conditions. In many of these endeavours, a handful of chaos theorists have played a leading role.[1] They first discovered the traces of certain key patterns and the breaking of underlying symmetries in the world around us. It was they who elaborated the major concept of bifurcation, who injected new meaning into the established notions of turning-point, focus, node and limit cycle, and who distilled a fascinating zoology of 'attractors', including the class of 'strange' ones.

Playing simple games with numbers

The chaotic behaviour we are interested in is essentially deterministic, and yet paradoxically, unpredictable. In order to get a feel for the way this strange situation can occur we can, as a preliminary exercise, look at simple games with numbers. This will give a first impression of the strange types of output a non-linear system can produce even when the input changes smoothly and by infinitesimally small amounts. Later we shall see applications to the real world. For those with a mathematical bent, Appendix 2 and Box 1 (on iterative systems and attractors) give more detailed examples of the games. To play the game in Appendix 1 you may need a pocket calculator.

Box 1. *The mathematics of iterative logistic functions and attractors*

We could just jump straight into some simple mathematics, but it will help if we start by relating to a physical process.

Suppose we have a system that changes with time. The instants of time t_0, t_1, $t_2 \ldots t_n$ are those when we are interested in the system, so we measure its state at all these times. Moreover, let us assume that the state at time t_{i+1} is entirely determined by its state at time t_i through an equation of the form:

$$x(t_{i+1}) = f_a[x(t_i)].$$

So, if the value of x is known at instant t_i then we can calculate its value at the following moment t_{i+1} via this functional relationship, and a is a parameter we can vary. Then, given the value of x at some initial time t_0, we can compute its value at t_1 and feed this value back into the equation to compute its value at t_2, and so on to compute the value of x at any subsequent time.

In this way an iterative mathematical procedure represents the dynamics (or evolution) of the system. A well known example coming from population dynamics is the logistic function where:

$$f_a = ax_t(1 - x_t).$$

You may recognize this functional form as that of the parabolas you studied in school, i.e. $y = px^2 + qx + r$, where $p = -a$, $q = a$ and $r = 0$. Thus the iterative procedure for studying population dynamics is:

$$x_{t+1} = ax_t(1 - x_t).$$

Without loss of generality we may consider x to lie between 0 and 1; if it did not we could simply apply a scale factor to ensure that it did. Now, we are ready to play a simple game with numbers that will give insight into the complex dynamics of what at first sight appears to be an extremely dull system.

Choose a value for x_0, say 0.4, and carry out the iteration for a value of a, say 2. Then:

$x_1 = 2 \times 0.4 \times (1 - 0.4) = 2 \times 0.24 = 0.48$
$x_2 = 2 \times 0.48 \times (1 - 0.48) = 2 \times 0.48 \times 0.52 = 0.4992$
$x_3 = 2 \times 0.4992 \times (1 - 0.4992) = 2 \times 0.4992 \times 0.5008 = 0.49999872$

and so on. In fact, if you continue the process for only two more iterations you find that x_5 becomes exactly 0.5 and stays there for all subsequent iterations. This is called a stable state for the physical system being modelled, or limit point to which the iteration converges, or a point attractor.

If one varies the starting point of the iteration by setting x_0 to values other than 0.4 in the range from 0 to 1, then the iteration always finishes up at 0.5, though the number of iterations to get there varies. Starting at $x_0 = 0.5$, the iteration never moves away from that point; the further one moves away from $x_0 = 0.5$ in either direction, i.e. towards 0 or towards 1, the more iterations it takes to reach the limit point. For example, if you start at $x_0 = 0.000001$ (quite close to 0) it takes 23 iterations, rather than the 5 in the example given above. Interestingly, if one starts at $x_0 = 0$ or 1, the value of x never moves away from 0! This is a different stable state or attractor and, what is more, it exists for all values of the parameter a.

What happens when the parameter a is varied? The short answer is very many remarkable and fascinating outcomes; for some ranges of a we see a rather boring, slow convergence to a single limit point. But for some specific values of a we have a rapid approach to a cycle of end-values, rather than to a single one. For example, when $a = 1$ the values of x converge very slowly towards the attractor at $x = 0$. If a lies between 0 and 1 ($0 \leq a \leq 1$) the attractor is always at $x = 0$, with faster convergence of the iteration the nearer a is to 0. For $1 < a < 3$ there is a single attractor at $(a-1)/a$, the convergence of the iteration slowing up as a approaches 3.

When $a = 3$ at iteration numbers the values of x continue for ever to cycle between two values: approximately 0.66237 and 0.67091. The convergence to this so-called 2-cycle is extremely slow. Even after 10,000 iterations these end-values are still wobbling about a bit!

These 2-cycles continue as a increases above 3 (albeit with different pairs of end-values for each value of a) with increasingly rapid convergence of the iteration until a reaches the value $1+\sqrt{5}$, when only 10 iterations are required to get to the clear-cut values 0.809017 and 0.5.

At a approximately equal to 3.449 we can see that a cycle of four end-point values has started for the iteration, and beyond $a = 3.544$ we see an 8-cycle. This doubling up continues at an ever increasing pace until, at about $a = 3.57$, chaos sets in. The iteration essentially generates pseudo-random numbers, although it is worth bearing in mind that we are dealing with a completely deterministic algorithm. And perhaps even more surprising, between $a = 3.57$ and 4, intermittent $2P$-cycles occur, where P runs over the positive integers.

What is amazing is the complexity of a stable solution to a non-linear equation, even for a seemingly innocuous equation. A system is stable if small initial disturbances do not cause its final state to wander off to infinity. Many physical and other systems exhibit asymmetrical behaviour, unstable equilibria and chaotic behaviour. In so doing, their static and dynamic states show qualitative differences. They are attracted to new and sometimes unexpected steady states. They can oscillate and fluctuate in unpredictable ways, even totally mysterious ways.

Attempts to visualize chaos

The interpretation of raw data presented as a list of numbers is not usually evident. We usually can 'bring the data alive' pictorially. The same data, presented in a flowchart, a trend curve, a sketch or a 3D landscape can tell a simpler, more complete and more easily understood story in which divergences and trends become obvious. Such pictorial graphics generally fall into two basic categories: supportive and self-contained. Examples of the former are the phase-space portrait and the bifurcation diagram, which are perhaps the two most important visual aids for the experiments and applications of interest to us. In contrast to these two supportive visual aids, fractal geometry is self-contained—an investigative method in its own right. Even though fractals and chaos theory have of late often moved along parallel tracks of thinking, in reality they each sprang from different roots and only occasionally do they converge.

Phase-space portraits: an underestimated representation

When drawing a street scene or sketching a group of buildings, we can represent on a two-dimensional plane the three-dimensional space relationships of natural objects as they appear to the eye, even though we may not consciously know about the laws of perspective or and when they were discovered. The use of two-dimensional diagrams to represent time-series statistics, implying some notion of coordinate geometry (as originally devised by Descartes in the 17th century), is common for most of us. In contrast, few people have been given the opportunity to familiarize themselves with phase space, one of the most potent representations of modern science. Three of the illustrations included in Figure 3 (*c, e* and *g*) show how phase-space technique turns dull statistical data into a telling picture, abstracting all the essential information from the moving parts and providing us with an easy-to-grasp overview of a system's behaviour over time.

The great advantage of thinking in terms of phase space is that it makes motion easier to watch, particularly when the system be defined by two variables, say its position and its velocity. (Strictly speaking, instead of velocity, it is usually momentum, velocity times mass, that is plotted. For systems of constant mass this does not change the picture much, only its vertical scale.). Using Cartesian coordinates, we may plot one variable on the horizontal axis, the other on the vertical. A point in the diagram provides the complete known state of movement and position of a dynamic system at each instant. As the position and velocity of a system change, so its representative point in phase space moves, to trace a path or orbit through phase space with the passage of time. The movement of one single particle moving in one dimension can be portrayed in such a two-dimensional phase space. But the same concept can be used to describe pictorially the complicated motions of any system of n particles in a $2n$-dimensional phase space. Spaces of four, five or more dimensions are not conceptually different from a two-dimensional representation, only more difficult to imagine.

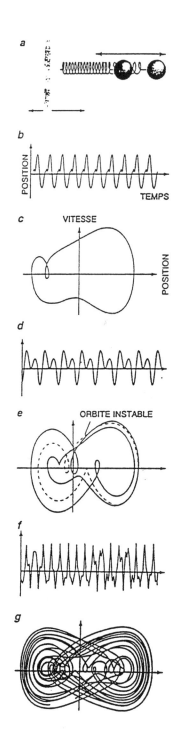

Figure 3. *Illustrating how phase space techniques turn dull statistical data into a telling picture, abstracting all the essential information from the moving parts*

Let us return to the three pairs of diagrams in Figure 3 (*b, c, d, e, f, g*), which relate to the board and ball illustrated in panel (*a*). In the first instance, the board at the left applies a weak to-and-fro force, and the ball attached to the spring follows a simple trajectory with each cycle of the board's motion. A clear picture of the ball's motion is given in panel (*c*), the phase-space representation. In the second instance (time-series (*d*) and phase space (*e*)), the force applied by the board has been increased, and the ball's motion shows a more complicated trajectory in phase space—it takes two cycles of the board's motion before the ball's trajectory in phase space repeats itself. Finally, when the force applied to the board is further increased and passes a certain threshold, the ball's motion does not repeat—it becomes chaotic, as illustrated in (*f*) and (*g*).

Let's take a breath here. We have in reality been toying with two kinds of 'attractor'—namely fixed points and limit cycles. They are simple and easy to understand in comparison with another kind, the so-called strange attractor, which taxes our imagination much more. But this too can be understood without the use of higher mathematics. 'Strange attractors' occur when dynamic systems behave chaotically. Instead of phase portraits that repeat themselves (such as limit cycles) or are even static (like fixed points), repetition never occurs. The system may return to the same position an infinite number of times but its velocity will be different each time. And it may have an identical velocity at an infinite number of different times but each time it will be in a different place. Phase portraits showing the dynamics of chaotic systems tend to look like scribbled elliptical orbits.

We have talked about position and velocity (momentum to be precise) but the concept of phase space can be generalized to other pairs of so-called canonical (or basic) variables. This is key, because economic and other systems, such as organic and social systems, can use the technique. As well as these attractors, there is a fascinating menagerie of geometrical forms—e.g. flip and pitchfork bifurcations, illustrated in Figure 4—and there are also turning-points, nodes, saddle points and foci.

All these states produce diverse equilibria and patterns of evolution in dynamic systems, governed by non-linear differential equations (or difference equations in computing). Some of these erudite terms can be a little misleading. For instance, bifurcation is a rather pedantic description for a simple concept—a division into two branches. It crops up all over the place in the study of the dynamics of systems where the variables are not related in a linear way. And bifurcations can lead to chaotic behaviour. The basic methods for solving all these equations and of classifying the steady states, periodic solutions and bifurcations were provided in the late 19th century, by Henri Poincaré. This fascinating world of extraordinary patterns can be explored on a desktop PC using numerical analysis software programs and interactive graphics packages. Poincaré's work has been applied in physics, chemistry and engineering over the last 50 years. Now it is the turn of the social and economic sciences.

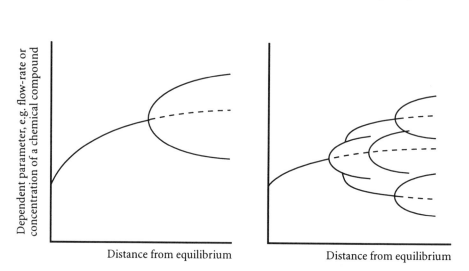

*Systems far from equilibrium
can split into two stable states . . .*

*. . . or the slightest disturbance
may trigger many splittings*

Dependent parameter, e.g. flow-rate or
concentration of a chemical compound

Distance from equilibrium

Distance from equilibrium

Figure 4. *A menagerie of geometrical forms—flip and pitchfork bifurcations*

Fractals play two distinct roles

In the range of graphic devices and visual aids that are of interest to us, fractal geometry occupies a special though ambiguous position. The term was coined in 1975 by Benoit Mandelbrot, a mathematical physicist. Several years later he wrote,

> Fractals are geometrical shapes that, contrary to those of Euclid, are not regular at all. First, they are irregular all over. Second, they have the same degree of regularity on all scales. A fractal object looks the same when examined from far away or nearby—it is self-similar on all scales.[2]

Fractal geometry began with the observation of all sorts of irregular shapes in nature and in the universe at large. On closer inspection, the shapes usually turned out to be repetitive or recurrent. Examples abound—broccoli and cauliflowers, coastlines and broken rock configurations, sediments of solidified lava flows, the shapes of hills and mountains, the distribution of galaxies in the cosmos. The natural list is endless. The geometry of fractals has revolutionized computer graphics, partly as a result of their contribution to data compression. Before fractals, there was no simple, efficacious way to create realistic landscapes on computer. Using fractals, computers (even PCs today) are able to generate scenery that looks amazingly real—almost like a photograph. The synergy between fractals and computers has contributed in no small way to the spectacular development of computer-generated (or synthetic) images and movies, increasingly sophisticated video games, virtual reality systems and more realistic and reliable flight simulators.

Besides being part of the geometry of nature, fractals play yet another crucial role. They are visual descriptive tools of great value, since they can vividly portray the behaviour of chaotic systems and describe the form of randomness. In fact fractal geometry is sometimes confused with chaos theory itself, rather than just seen as a descriptor.

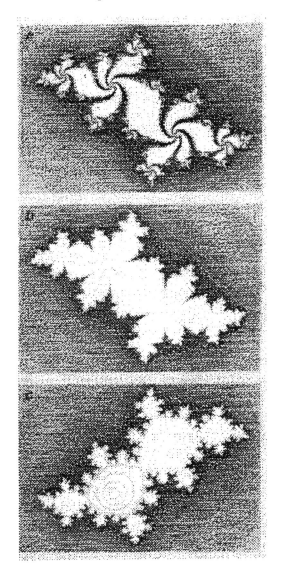

Figure 5. *Julia sets*

Note: Julia sets, composed of the boundaries of these three intricate shapes, are, in general, fractal. Points inside the boundary stay within it when the iterative function $f(z) = z^2 + c$ is applied, where z is a complex number computed on each iteration and c is a constant complex number parameter.

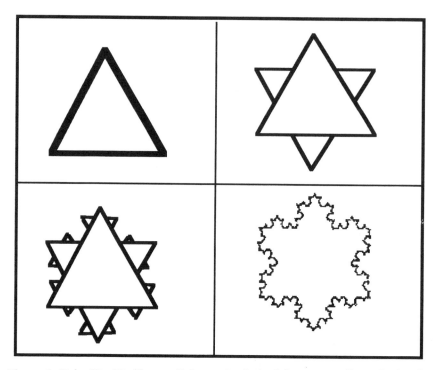

Figure 6. *Helge Von Koch's snowflake can be derived from an equilateral triangle*

The origins of fractals go back to the 19th century. In addition to Poincaré, two other French mathematicians, Pierre Fatou and Gaston Julia, started in 1918 to collect, describe and analyse shapes that were subsequently identified as fractals.[3] Examples of what have become known as 'Julia Sets' are given in Figure 5.

Before Julia, in 1904, the Swedish mathematician Helge Von Koch, the discoverer of the Koch curve or polygon, had demonstrated how an elaborate, beautiful and symmetric snowflake can be derived from an equilateral triangle, as illustrated in Figure 6.

After being left obscure for so long, fractal geometry has become fashionable. Fractal shapes and patterns have become the talk of the electronic community. Without a new technique of data compression based on fractals, digital high-definition television (HDTV) might have been kept in abeyance until the next decade. Physicists have found that the atoms in glass materials follow a fractal distribution. Photographic series first revealed the fractal dimension of vegetation patterns. And at the Los Alamos National Laboratory fractals are used to study the chaotic behaviour of turbulent fluid flows.

Some time after joining IBM's Thomas J. Watson Research Center, to which he was to dedicate the better part of his working life, Mandelbrot was called upon to help IBM engineers overcome the problem of noise in telephone lines used for

Figure 7. *Cantor sets, postulated by German-Russian mathematician Georg Cantor*

data communications. By increasing the power of the signal the researchers could reduce the effects of random noise on the line. But they were unable to eliminate spontaneous noise bursts, when pieces of the signal were lost in noise and the error rate became unacceptable. A solution came with Mandelbrot's remarkable discovery—the stuff of legend—that over any and every time scale, from hours to minutes to seconds, to nanoseconds, the ratio of actual errors to periods of noiseless transmission was a constant, exactly as postulated by the German–Russian mathematician Georg Cantor (1845–1918). Cantor had a highly inventive mind and made major contributions to set theory, the notion of transfinite numbers, the idea of the arithmetical continuum and many other areas. Constructing the Cantor set (see Figure 7) is disarmingly simple.

From a line, of whatever length, remove the middle third. Next, remove the middle third of the remaining segments, and continue to do this, using the same rule in every successive pass. In the end, what remains is an infinite dust of points that help us understand how intermittence works in real life. The exercise is far from academic. It teaches us how to control the occurrence of errors in transmission lines. Accepting that errors are inevitable and using a strategy of redundancy to spot and correct them proves to be more efficient than the earlier practice of increasing signal strength. Settling for a moderate signal, rather than trying to increase the signal strength, is a perfect illustration of the new wisdom, the new philosophy that more is less, and less is more in chaotics.

The biologist's image of complexity

We have now reached an important point in our analysis. Above we have laid out three different approaches to the study of the symptoms and patterns of chaotic phenomena:

- First we stressed their ubiquity, evident from experiments carried out over several disciplines (all loosely related to applied physics) such as weather forecasting.

- Second, we briefly glimpsed the anatomy of non-linear dynamics in mathematical terms and explained that an apparently stable equilibrium reached under specific operating conditions may yet give rise to chaotic or random fluctuations when certain parameters change, however slightly.
- Third, we have shown that visual aids—phase space and fractal geometry —can play an active role in waking us to the realities of chaotic behaviour, as pointers or as confirming evidence.

Stressing self-organization

A fourth approach—perhaps more pragmatic—is to use biological analogies. First, we shall focus on the concept of self-organization and the seemingly twin idea of self-organizing criticality. From there we shall venture into the twilight zone that complexity theorists call 'the edge of chaos'.

To nutshell it, the core idea of the contemporary evangelists of complexity is 'Darwinism in a modern disguise' plus the newly acclaimed principle of self-organization in nature. Humankind, like all other living things, is the final deliverable from perhaps four billion years of a production line of haphazard struggles for survival, uncontrollable calamities and random mutation. That, in essence, is the fundamental concept of evolution rooted in Charles Robert Darwin's theory (*c.*1859). It is still very much alive after being marginally amended by modern knowledge of mutation and somewhat more seriously revised by artificial genetics. Evolutionary metaphors and parallels have lately been popping up all over biology, spilling out into other sciences.

The other half, self-organization, is taken here to mean broadly 'matter's incessant attempts to organize itself into ever more complex structures'[4] despite the ever-present forces of decay and dissolution. Just why is there this search for increasingly more complex structures? Because the principle of self-organization is absolutely general, according to its exponents. It is inherent in the spontaneous configuration of snowflakes, the emergence of convection cells in a pot of boiling soup and above all in the creation and transformation of all living organisms. One more or less obvious manner in which self-organization could occur in evolution is via adaptation. Most—if not all—complex, self-organizing systems are adaptive, in as much as they are not content to respond passively to events, but rather try to turn happenstance to their advantage. And this adaptation, so goes the argument, inexorably results in a pyramid of ever higher levels of complexity. However, the argument can also be turned round the other way. Is not this upward cascading of level upon level just another form of self-organization? In its most developed form it is a theory of an underlying ingenuity that propels self-organization. Pioneered by leading think-tank the Santa Fe Institute of New Mexico, two dozen scientists—including Nobel Prize-winners with distinctly different backgrounds—share a vision of an underlying unity. They believe that they have come to 'understand the spontaneous, self-organizing dynamics of the world . . . with potential for immense impact on the conduct of economics, business and even politics'.[5]

In a recent book entitled *Neural Darwinism* (1990) Rockefeller University's Gerald Edelman cited a number of neuroscientists who are convinced that the human brain grows by Darwinian-type multiplication and selection. And when the prophets of neural networks talk about finding solutions to topical problems, stressing their networks' ability to learn, they mean proceeding by a similar successive selection among many different approaches—the Darwinian kernel.

So what then, really, sets biological systems apart? What in fact accounts for the almost infinite diversity of living systems in nature are the powers of self-assembly and self-replication, in addition to the powers of self-organization. These ideas were already implicit in some work on molecular engineering, for which Professors Donald Cram of the University of California at Los Angeles and Jean-Marie Lehn of the University of Strasbourg jointly received the Nobel Prize for chemistry in 1987. Since then, understanding how molecules assemble themselves and self-organize has become perhaps the number one goal of organic chemistry and inspired many competing techniques.[6]

Another recent contribution to the evolutionary theory was the discovery made by Yale University's Catherine L. Craig, a leading ecologist. She demonstrated that a spider's web, far from being a passive structure that catches insects flying blindly into it, as was long believed, is actually a wily device. It is intentionally designed to lure insects, by exploiting ever more effectively their irrepressible need for such food as freely floating flowers. This trend resulted in an exponential (37-fold, to be precise) diversification of web-weaving species. Professor Craig's work not only demonstrated convincingly the reality of the learning process in nature. It also threw fresh light on predator–prey interrelationships and the mechanism through which new species arise.

The critical level problem

We have next to see how self-organization works in nature. We also have to ask: to what extent can findings drawn from the biological sphere be stretched to encompass the inorganic, then economic and social worlds?

First the inorganic: in 1986 the ideas of self-organization and critical points were put together as a theory of self-organized criticality by a physicist, Danish-born Per Bak. The theory is best understood starting from the elementary observation that no matter how many grains one pours on to a pile of sand, the pile invariably retains the same shape. One may of course use sugar cubes or rice instead. Before one's eyes, at first the pile grows higher and higher until it cannot grow any more, triggering off an avalanche process. Old sand—or rice—begins cascading down the sides just as an extra trickle of sand is added. And if one starts off with a huge box of sand, removing the container makes the excess sand fall away until the 'critical' slope is restored, exactly as before. Bak and his colleagues, working at the Brookhaven National Laboratory in Long Island, also built a computer model of a sand pile, using uniform square 'grains' stacked on top of each other in columns of unequal heights placed randomly. Figurative grains were added one by one, again at random, on to the tops of columns. Eventually, the computer model simulated the successive avalanche movements when each of the different columns had risen beyond the critical height, confirming fully the results of many real-life experiments.

The idea of self-organizing criticality has quickly caught on in fields as diverse as the study of earthquakes, turbulent flows, city traffic jams and stock market fluctuations. Bak himself, with the help of his colleagues, soon began collecting piecemeal evidence pointing out the reality of thresholds and saturation levels in a wide range of areas. The hypothesis was all the more exciting because it suggested that a single framework exists for interpreting similar odd behaviour in many different areas—be they natural complex processes, such as the weather, or processes in our own realm, such as economics.

At best, however, the relation or parallel between the principle of self-organization and the suggestion of self-acting criticality is only a partial one. To be sure, both mechanisms operate spontaneously and appear to be self-induced. But the comparison between the two stops there. Bak's critical state did not seem to have anything to do with either learning in the sense of simple adaptation or retro-action. Moreover, whereas in biology the degree of complexity tends to vary, generally rising over time, Bak's critical threshold remains unchanged no matter what happens in the environmental conditions. This raises the question of whether inanimate substances can be treated on a par with living matter, particularly in the light of today's evolutionary thinking.

Perhaps surprisingly, Bak's theory has come under fire from his own peers at the Santa Fe Institute for failing to produce a general theory capable of specifying which systems will experience criticality and which will not. This is rather unfair as neither chaos nor complexity theory is able to predict a specific catastrophe, phase change or similar discontinuity or transition. In fact, surveys of actual earthquakes show that, whereas the multitude of small earthquakes fit the pattern of self-organized criticality, the largest earthquakes recorded in modern times lie entirely outside the critical level pattern. Despite these lingering doubts, the theory of self-criticality has not lost its appeal altogether. The question then comes to mind of whether it could be improved upon or supplemented by new facts or findings.

A research group at the IBM Laboratory at Yorktown Heights, New York, has investigated patterns of sand-pile flows in relation to avalanche size and conjectured that differences were attributable to the presence, or absence, of dirt.

Seizing on this finding, researchers at Cambridge and at Norwich in England hypothesized that layers of grain located near the surface are affected by friction between the grains and consequently act very much like a memory bank for the sand pile. The phenomenon is known as hysteresis. Could it be that a pile of sand, or a fraction thereof, effectively 'remembers' and is thus capable of 'learning', as much as the common spider? The assumption has yet to be verified.

Before leaving the subject, let us mention what looks like an uninvited contribution to a more sophisticated theory of self-criticality, grounded in mathematics. In 1981, two little-known Czech scientists, J. Schmidt and J. Novosad, began to measure the forces acting at the base of a pyramid of apples, using pressure sensors. They found that the pressure was not greatest at the central point of the pyramid's base, as they had expected, but was spread among a ring of apples some distance from the centre of the base. Their experiment brought to light other puzzling questions regarding unexplained variability between minimum and maximum stress as the size of the pile of apples increased. Professor K. Liffman of the University of Melbourne is presently trying to solve the problem with the help of a dynamic computer model, but so far has run into unexpected difficulties in his attempt to duplicate the precise pattern of forces.[7] The issue is of more than academic interest. While a pyramid of apples or oranges seems a trivial example, industry makes frequent use of piles of ore, fertilizers and other bulky materials for long-term storage. It is important to be able to evaluate properly the risks of caking, encrusting, fragmenting, etc. under the weight of stocked particles. The Australian researchers working on the conundrum now believe that the case is analogous to the n-body problem, which Poincaré was unable to solve even for such a low value of n as 3.

NOTES

1 E. N. Lorenz, 'Deterministic non-periodic flow', *J. Atmos. Sci.* 20 (1963): 130–41. See also A. N. Kolmogorov, 'Preservation of conditionally periodic movements with small change in the Hamiltonian function', reprinted in R. S. Mackay and J. D. Meiss (eds.), *Hamiltonian Dynamic Systems* (Bristol: Adam Hilger, 1987); D. Ruelle, 'Deterministic chaos: the science and the fiction', *Proceedings of the Royal Society of London A* 427 (1990): 241–8; J. A. Yorke and E. D. Yorke, 'Metastable chaos: the transition to sustained chaotic behaviour in the Lorenz model', *Journal of Statistical. Physics* 21(1979): 263 ff.
2 Benoit Mandelbrot, 'Fractals—a geometry of nature', *New Scientist*, 15 September 1990, pp. 384–3.
3 Caroline Series, 'Fractals, reflections and distortions', *New Scientist*, 22 September 1990, pp. 54–8; see also Michael Barnsley, *Fractals everywhere* (New York: Academic Press, 1988), ch. 7, pp. 248–96.
4 L. Mitchell Waldrop, *Complexity: The Emerging Science at the Edge of Order and Chaos* (New York: Simon & Schuster, 1992), p. 102.

5 Ibid. p. 13.
6 David Amabilino and Fraser Stoddart, 'Molecules that build themselves', *New Scientist*, 19 February 1994, pp. 25–9.
7 Andrew Watson, 'The perplexing puzzle posed by a pile of apples', *New Scientist*, 14 December 1991, p. 19.

4

Contrasts in Chaos Theory, Complex Systems Theory and the Search for Chaotic Axioms

He thought he saw a Rattlesnake that questioned him in Greek
He looked again and found it was the middle of next week
from 'Sylvie and Bruno' by Lewis Carroll

Conflict and harmony in the theories of chaos and complexity

In elaborating a doctrine as ambitious as the theory of complexity, to look to the social sciences for inspiration, as reported in the preceding chapter, is a perfectly legitimate way forward. Furthermore, to do so revives a tradition that can be traced back to Aristotle, whose biological works were encyclopaedic, consisting of his astonishingly accurate observations of natural life and his categorizations of it. However, the approach entails certain risks, of which two are serious.

The first risk arises from the fact that this 'bold edifice' of complexity theory and chaos theory is barely half finished and is constantly in danger of collapsing, because of its still shaky scaffolding of logic and insufficient supportive evidence. The second threat is a lack of clear definition and exaggeration. The inflated language used by some authors on the subject, and by their reviewers, does not help. At this point we might consider a question:

> To what extent is chaos theory compatible with, or in conflict with, the new science of complexity, which claims to be a unified way of thinking about the universe, life on earth and human social behaviour?

Things would be much easier—and the layman's understanding would be helped—if the overall label were changed, say, from 'complexity theory' to 'the theory of complex systems'. This is not a fine question of semantics, but one of integrity. Many leading researchers in the area have systematically shied away from study of the behaviour of the really simple structures. Their unconcern for the elementary systems is quite understandable, from their point of view. Self-organization, which is one of the cornerstones of the new wisdom, cannot operate solo, in a kind of vacuum. By definition self-organization works only in conjunction with the powers of self-assembly and self-replication. By contrast, chaos theory deals with both kinds of system and aims in particular at elucidating how simple systems evolve into complex ones. Some biologists, as we have seen, concentrate on studying the evolutionary processes through which structures that are already complex grow still more complex—but that is a somewhat different proposition.

The second, perhaps even more fundamental, difference between complexity and chaos theories lies in their respective conjectures as to the ultimate outcome of evolutionary change. Most complexity evangelists have persuaded themselves that, in spite of appearances to the contrary, the interactions of the components (and especially the like components of a complex system) result in the quasi-automatic emergence of a degree of order. The underlying assumption is that complex systems are governed by rules, which may be simple but are potent enough to generate spontaneous order. One prime aim of the new science of complexity is to identify a set of laws (based on experiment and data) that cannot possibly be deduced from the laws that govern the individual components. This is in contrast to chaos theory, which does not admit of granularity and scale,[1] of differences between components and groups. However, the questions 'Where does this spontaneous order really come from?' and 'how do we know it is valid?' are far from new.

Way back in 1776, Adam Smith, the godfather of modern political economy was already enthralled by the recognition of an all-pervasive order in the economic system. In *An Inquiry into the Nature and Causes of the Wealth of Nations*,[2] Smith expounded the principle of the 'invisible hand'. Each individual, by simply pursuing his own selfish good, as if led by an invisible hand, is in fact contributing to the attainment of what is best for all, instinctively pulling supply into balance with demand, at least under perfect competition. Thus, the 'modern' principle of self-organization (as spelled out by Ilya Prigogine, a Belgian of Russian extraction and 1977 Nobel Laureate)[3] is perhaps in essence an older theory presented in new clothing.

Moreover, some commentators, perhaps jumping ahead rather, have judged complexity to be in many ways the opposite of chaos. Some go as far as equating complexity with 'anti-chaos' and, by implication, have associated chaos with total disorder.[4] On closer inspection, it turns out that between chaos theory and the complexity vision there are several points of convergence and the similarities outweigh the contradictions, apparent or real. More specifically, we summarize the arguments in the Box 2.

To equate the edge of chaos with the balanced, poised state between two extremes is a matter of convention. Spokespeople for the Santa Fe Institute visualize

Box 2. *Convergence between the schools of chaos theory and complex systems*

• Complex systems are seen to exist in one of three main states: rigid order, order with a little flexibility, or chaos. But an extremely important fourth state exists, a poised state, marked by some kind of equilibrium, however precarious, between the second state and chaos. On the above definition, sooner or later, the balance in a complex system seems to tilt either towards a set pattern or else total disorder. Now these two alternatives inherent in the complexity viewpoint can be compared to the so-called 'bifurcation' of chaos theory. Chaos purists are unlikely to find much conflict here.

• Moreover, the ultimate outcome of 'rigid' order in a complex system is a concept that we can stretch, without undue ideological violence, to what chaos theorists would term 'steady state'. This results from the action of a periodic attractor, or a limit cycle[4] in chaos theory. Attractors of this kind have the similar property of stability. Furthermore, the steady state of chaos theory—or the self-organized stability of complex systems—comes about without visible outside interference. This is another point of agreement between the two schools.

• Both schools realize that the ultimate outcome between the 'forces' of order and those pulling in the opposite direction cannot be predicted on a case-by-case basis. Only via a more global explanation of patterns, features and functions can this be seen. Somewhat surprisingly, both expect that complex systems or chaos can to some extent be brought under control—or made more efficient—by tuning key parameters. If this is valid, the implications are of major importance for business management and in systems design, network management, etc., and far more so for economic and social systems.

• How serious are the remaining divergences between complexity and chaos theories? The most obvious ones are only preferences for specific metaphors. For example, chaos theorists emphasize that life exists at the edge of chaos. Why at the edge only of chaos? Why not at the edge between chaos and order? The two expressions could be used interchangeably.

the state of affairs rather as a phase transition, during which the components of the system never quite dissolve into turbulence, yet never quite lock into place.[5] A study sponsored jointly by both schools of thought ought to be on our 21st Century agenda, because the paths mapped out by each school should converge in the near future. That, however, presupposes that both get together and investigate relevant phenomena, variables and parameters in a concerted programme. The subject area most appropriate for study may be what the complexity school calls 'the inherent dynamics of complex systems' and the older school of chaos 'the inherent dynamics of non-linear systems'. These investigations might exploit massive computer simulations. But achieving the goals may demand an extension of the current state of the art, with radically new computing paradigms and a more powerful philosophy of logical analysis—more on that in Appendix 2 and Chapters 5 and 6.

Granted, the two approaches are not fully identical and areas of discrepancy remain to be settled, but any differences should not lead to a kind of schism between two chapels, because the profoundly original lessons they jointly teach us are all-pervasive. Both influence our perception of the world, specifically forcing us to rethink our social priorities. 'Chaotics', as used in the title of this book, was intended to provide a bridge between the two schools.

Cultural drift

One of the most exciting characteristics of chaotics is that it enables us to pass, with scarcely any transition, from an apparently trivial local disturbance to either major technology-cum-marketing breakthroughs or to a stock-exchange crash. Moreover, deciphering the mysteries of evolution through the concepts of chaotics may even provide a blueprint for reactivating economic growth, discovering new employment patterns and so stimulating new hope and lifestyles.

The transition between local and global events is made using methods that largely defy the long-accepted ways of working in science. We will start with the issue of methodology. Along the way we will pass the 'cumbrous corpses of reductionism' and Newtonian brands of determinism. This rotting heap is piled higher by defunct fragments of two related philosophies, self-similarity and gradualism. Among the refuse will be cast the debris of such family treasures as the concept of equilibrium, the innate belief in continuous social progress and the eminence assigned to a score of hallowed inventions, discoveries and inventors. We then want to reassess objectively a whole range of half-working 'toy' theories. Subsequently, our sentimental journey will lead us to the need for a new way of thinking with a new set of primary axioms, as new patterns push our current laws backstage:

- the ancient Greek concept of analogy is reassessed;
- new deduction/induction mixes gain in respectability;
- wider use of the metaphor becomes necessary;
- information accedes to the status of primary resource; and
- space–time invades our daily lives.

Holistic views prevail—an attack on reductionism

We first come across a hunting scene, where the hunters are fast growing into ugly hordes and the prey they seek to slaughter is reductionism. As the subject has been discussed *ad nauseam* in the contemporary literature, we restrict our review to a brief recollection of the essentials.

The reductionists asserted that 'a whole can be understood completely if you understand its parts, and the nature of their sum'.[6] The classical, time-honoured, scientific approach to any system—simple, intricate or complex in the sense referred to above—was to dissect the monstrous problem into the smallest and simplest pieces you could, then identify all the bits and try to figure out how they fitted together, and possibly interacted. Most 20th-century physicists, bio-logists, neurologists, economists *et al.* have followed the precept, breaking their universes down into the simplest elements.[7]

Reductionism is, of course, anathema to both the theorists of chaos and the upholders of complexity. 'Compound behaviour' is the name of their game. They are united in denouncing the futility of studying parts in isolation from the whole. Their agreement is by no means coincidental. All share the belief that 'the whole is greater than the sum of its parts'[8]—the essence of the philosophy of holism. Here lies the fundamental discriminant that demarcates non-linear sys-tems from linear. In the latter, the whole is just equal to the sum of its constituent parts. But in non-linear dynamics the whole really may be greater than the sum total of its parts.[9] Likewise, a macroeconomy is not a mere juxtaposition of *n* micro units. Nor is a collective (e.g. national) posture a large-scale replica of individual behaviour. To use a parallel (in keeping with the biological view in the preceding section) a system like the brain functions the way it does, not because of the nature of the pieces out of which it is made, but because of the way these elements are self-organized and interact. It is their collective behaviour that is important.

To follow on in the same spirit, two other scientific principles, self-similarity and gradualism, are in need of serious reassessment. The story of self-similarity comprises three phases. Firstly, before the discovery of relativity theory and quantum mechanics, it was believed that a grain of salt contained the whole world and vice versa. A whole teeming universe was seen to be embodied in a single drop of water. In a second phase, the myth in its initial rough version died hard as the perception was extended by the telescope, the microscope and just as importantly, the supercomputer. By the 1970s, the theory of self-similarity was highly chal-lenged. But in a third phase, fractal geometry, as discovered by Benoit Mandelbrot, seemed to give a shot in the arm to the principle of similarity across scale by emphasizing a fairly comparable concept in natural patterns. But the Mandelbrot set, the very emblem of chaos, eventually led to a different con-clusion. For instance, the fractal dimension of say a coast-line, real or computer-generated, is 'constant' so that the meanders look repetitive as the image is enlarged to two or three times its initial size. That is not the end of the story. When blown up, the collection of points making up the set looks similar enough as long as the magnification proceeds stepwise. But a markedly greater magnification shows that the enlarged pictures (of points, or of molecules, etc.) fail to match the preceding, smaller-size, photographs or computer printouts. The scale effect has set in, upsetting the Mandelbrot apple-cart altogether. It is as if self-similarity is pregnant with a 'built-in threshold', or 'self-criticality' to use expressions popularized by physicists and the new-wave biologists.

Usually left out of these sophisticated discussions among specialists is a fundamental issue. What makes the difference between a stepwise process and a break in continuity, or a rupture? This raises the key but often overlooked question of gradualism—in science, politics and everyday life. Time and again we come across the problem. How far can incremental increases (be they in GNP, medical expenses, wage levels or standards of living) go before hitting some limit—causing saturation, bringing about a turnaround or entering a new behaviour pattern? Effectively, just where does the threshold of non-linear behaviour take over? Here, the metaphor of the Tower of Babel comes to mind, as does the art of strategy, especially military strategy. Every general wants to push the build-up of the forces under his command as far as possible. Yet only a truly great captain will understand when overkill becomes self-defeating. The issue is perhaps even more topical nowadays with 'small wars everywhere'. For instance in the Gulf War, General Colin Powell spent a long time in building up massive superiority before attacking Iraq—what determined the threshold at which he stopped? And why did the US intervention in Somalia largely fail?

The same is true in business—incremental or gradual strategies may not be apt. Those industries whose environment and competition is changing quickly will go through abrupt change. For instance, in telecommunications a gradualist approach will leave the old school of Bell operating companies and European PTTs out of the new markets. That is why many telecommunications operators are seeking alliances, mergers and new areas for convergence so quickly. In politics the same rules apply. 'Enough of the same', seem to say the Europeans, in election after election, to the leftist parties in Britain, France and Italy that long flourished on pursuing a policy of increasing social welfare by gradual stages. Political change in Central and Eastern Europe is abrupt, and the gradualists are in full retreat, being perceived as insufficiently radical in a world in rapid transition.

Having rejected reductionism and argued the need for a radical reappraisal of the value of gradualism, self-replication and self-similarity, the major tenet standing behind them can no longer be avoided. What about determinism, both as a fundamental scientific methodology and as a philosophy of life? And what about the power of prediction based on determinism?

On the one hand, we cannot bury determinism altogether. But neither can we continue as usual. We must realize that the early simplistic proposition of determinacy everywhere is no longer tenable. Followers of Newtonian determinism (as perfected by the mathematician Laplace and the philosopher Descartes) have claimed an ability to predict orbits, individual shapes, even specific events with absolute accuracy. And all on the basis of a few fundamental laws of physics.[10] By extension, determinism has also been applied to foretell human attitudes and behaviour. As a minimum, an attempt ought to be made to broaden the concept of determinism to accommodate the holistic vision referred to above.

One useful clue as to how to proceed with this extension and to the implications is illustrated by the well-known argument about technological development. How do scientific discoveries and inventions occur? There are at least two possible answers. According to some, breakthroughs and inventions are essentially exogenous events. However, pointing out a number of specific examples, it is equally plausible to contend that inventions come when society—or a significant segment of it—actually needs them and is able to make widespread use of them. For instance, the advent of the automobile came with better roads, the jet engine gave a new generation of flight, television extended the radio world, satellites extended communication and TV technologies, and so on. The pressure of life-dependent necessity, especially during wartime, has acted as a major catalyst of technological advance, where technology has been the determining factor—the atomic bomb is the key example. The 'inevitability' of invention is further substantiated by the appearance of prior or precursor event(s) and the fact that some highly significant discoveries, e.g. the transistor, were made simultaneously by two or more inventors or competing research groups. A fuller discussion of the twin-track approach to technological forecasting is continued in Chapter 7, which poses a much broader question: to what extent are breakthroughs system-induced? But we continue with more fundamental issues first.

In search of a system of axioms

Does chaotics, as previously defined, imply—perhaps even require—a new axiomatic platform? This is the really controversial subject area. Although we cannot deal with the matter in great detail, we do suggest a framework for thinking.

A first axiom: patterns are substitutes for laws

Are laws out of tune with the spirit of a 21st-century world? The notion of a law has been basic in our traditional culture. But the so-called 'exact sciences' have relatively recently seen their hitherto immutable principles downgraded to nothing more than general propositions or statements of tendencies, more or less certain, more or less definite.[11] This state was—and still is—considered the norm and practice of the so-called 'soft sciences' of sociology and psychology and cognition. The implication is an emerging unification of science with social preoccupations, economics and psychology after a long separation.

Now much of science is about finding patterns in observed data, patterns that give insight and meaning. This started with astronomy. The ancients noted the special nature of the sun and moon. They looked for patterns in the night sky.

Qualitatively, they soon identified the need to distinguish bright objects that changed their positions rather rapidly from fainter light sources that formed a relatively stable backcloth to the celestial scene. Early astronomers realized that to understand more, quantitative data had to be painstakingly collected—and this was done for some 2,000 years. Up until the middle of the 20th century, most patterns in data identified by scientists had been simple, and as far as possible based on linear relationships between measurable quantities. Even when these relationships were not linear, tricks such as taking logarithms would render them almost, if not exactly, linear. We could continue to regard the universe through 'linear' spectacles, more or less satisfactorily. But the introduction of massive computer simulations plus mathematical analysis tools for studying non-linear systems has enabled scientists to go beyond approximations. Researchers are beginning to explore our incredibly multiform world with a fresh, non-linear eye. Science in general is moving from linear to non-linear—a key axiom.

Axioms from unscrambling a Greek omelette: deduction, induction, metaphors and analogies

All the ingredients in our philosophical bowl come from Greece, but the mix can be made to your liking. Let us examine them and see just what we will leave out, or add, for the 21st century.

Deductive reasoning from general or self-evident premises was invented by ancient Greeks. So was reasoning from a part to a whole, from particular to general, and from the individual to the universal. In short, induction had arrived, with Aristotle as its first evangelist. And our current prefixes *para-* (as in parabola and parable) and *meta-* (as in metaphor) were also derived from the ancient Greek. Metaphor is usually defined as a figure of speech in which a word or a phrase denoting one kind of object or process is used in place of another to provide a model or vehicle for thinking. It also suggests a likeness or analogy between the processes or objects. The operative word is the verb—'suggests'.

Analogy was originally a Greek concept also. The initial meaning has become blurred over time. Strictly speaking, analogy was a proportion, or ratios, as in a statement of the form $(a \times b) = (c \times d)$, where knowing three of the four values permits us to calculate the fourth. Loose usage has eventually given rise to two almost contradictory interpretations. To some, analogy has become 'an inference that if two or more things agree with one another in one or more respects, they will probably agree in yet other respects'.[12] According to the same reference others see in analogy nothing more than 'a resemblance in some particulars between things otherwise unlike'. This may be familiar ground. But when we pass on to ask ourselves how these various notions and methods interlock, we soon discover that each period and each school of thought saw the matter in a different light. 'Science works mainly by metaphors', said the economist Brian Arthur, a member of the Santa Fe think-tank, whereas 'non-scientists tend to think that science works by deduction'.[13] And in the introductory pages we have already used a number of allegorical figures of speech, sometimes in a very direct manner—the invisible hand, artificial life, the edge of chaos, artificial intelligence. So contemporary theories of chaos, and especially of complexity, can be traced to metaphors, akin to the growth of a plant from a small seed. Thus the use of metaphors becomes a generally accepted principle in chaotics theory, an axiom, since patterns must substitute for formal laws.

To drive their point home, chaos and complexity theorists began stressing that most of their predecessors have used very much the same technique—the elliptic, regular motion of the planets provided the basis for the Newtonian metaphor of clockwork predictability. Douglas R. Hofstadter's monumental work on a triple parallel, *Gödel, Escher, Bach,* explicitly carried the second title *A metaphorical fugue on minds and machines in the spirit of Lewis Carroll.* The vogue that metaphors seem to be enjoying may also be due to the rise to pre-eminence of the search for patterns, as substitutes for formal laws. Let us take the example of the terrible twins weather and the climate. So many different factors influence atmospheric conditions that certainty of any weather forecast, even for a very short period (hours), is impossible. On the other hand, it is possible to talk of climates and climatic changes in much clearer terms. In truly complex systems, the patterns never repeat themselves exactly, yet there are modules, intermediate or overriding, that are identifiable. For North Americans, Europeans, and some other peoples, for instance, talking of the four seasons makes sense. In the same vein, in the area of social history, the concept of a revolution is akin to a metaphor standing for all the kinds of social upheaval, even though they occur under very different circumstances and may follow a distinct phasing and development.

For scientific thought to progress, both axioms of induction and deduction are needed. The Ancient Greeks, with the exception of Aristotle, attached more importance to deduction as a source of knowledge. Modern philosophers and scientists tend to stress the role of induction, even though it yields only a probability, not a certainty. The number-crunching power of the computer has enabled researchers to use deduction and induction iteratively on a massive scale. Pioneers in chaos and complexity have used this key tool as an opportunity to explore further. It has induced the brightest of them to test radical, hitherto unthinkable hypotheses with far bolder assumptions.

But now this tool must overcome a problem that has arisen over last decades. The task of almost any business, technology or science is painstakingly to collect facts and arrange and interpret them on the basis of tentative hypotheses, to arrive at patterns of relationships binding those facts together. However our powers of investigation, though vastly extended through computing, can also be seriously curtailed by that vast extension, in two ways. The first is the sheer mass of data accumulable in such enormous databases and the second is the range and intricacy of the combinatorial logic possible. The size and detail of marketing databases in a leading consumer products company or the extent of inventory databases and their links into the supply and retail chains would amaze many people. What we can learn from them by data-mining would also astound many, in terms of buying patterns, demographic preferences and the spread of new tastes in consumption, and the operational research processes for replenishment of stocks.

As an illustration, take only a simple game problem—a microcosm of a real-world business problem—the number of combinations on a chess-board. It is such that it exceeds the possibility of analytic treatment within an economically justified time. Chess matches between supercomputers and grand masters do not pay the computer company back, even in marketing (and especially since the supercomputers tend to fail in creative play). This is why there is a constant search for new lines of computational attack, e.g. inventing new, more powerful algorithms, developing data-mining, neural networks and rule-based (or expert) systems of artificial intelligence with higher-level reasoning skills. To navigate between incomprehensibility and irrelevance in these enormous data stores, business, sociology and technology need a superior intuition, rather than resorting to induction and deduction based on computer simulation with mathematical analysis.[14] This raises an intriguing question—is intuition innate or can it be taught? Can it be learned? And can it be improved upon by repeated exercise? In replying affirmatively to these questions, Mandelbrot carried with him the mainstream philosophers of chaos theory.

Space–time invades everyday life

Before we leave the subject of the cultural drift brought about by chaos theory and the vision of a universe growing in complexity, let us single out a key axiomatic issue that both chaos theorists and proponents of complexity have ducked.

'[S]ince Einstein, distance is between *events* and not between *things*, and distance involves time as well as space', wrote Bertrand Russell.[15] Although they seldom miss paying lip service to it—the theory of relativity—neither chaos nor complexity theorists have yet thought through the full implications of space–time. Both camps accept it in an abstract sense. Yet they do not understand the advent of global information networks so that electronic collaboration tends to compete with or even replace purely local relations and partnerships. As everyone—whether it is insurers, newspeople, market makers, design teams or whole firms—and everything becomes more interconnected on a worldwide scale and less dependent on a particular location, profound changes are inevitable in the style of work, patterns of employment and professional hierarchies—and consequently also in systems of education and training. Thus, the new metaphor the 'virtual office' is now common practice, but its connotation as a traditional 'office' has been modified. But how soon will this metaphor become general for the production of all goods and services? We take these ideas up in subsequent chapters.

NOTES

1 Giorgio Parisi, 'Statistical physics and biology', *Physics World*, September 1993: 42–3.
2 For more on the subject, see Chapter 5 below.
3 Ilya Prigogine, 'The laws of chaos', *Annales des Mines*, December 1993: 61–2.
4 Ian Stewart, 'Nature's semantics' (Book review), *Nature* 361 (11 February 1993).
5 M. Mitchell Waldrop, *Complexity: The Emerging Science at the Edge of Order and Chaos* (New York: Simon & Schuster, 1992), p. 293.
6 Douglas R. Hofstadter, *Gödel, Escher, Bach: An Eternal Golden Braid* (London: Penguin, 1979), p. 312.
7 James Gleick, *Chaos: Making a New Science* (London: Sphere Books, Penguin Group, 1988), p. 14.
8 Hofstadter, *Gödel, Escher, Bach*, p. 312.
9 Waldrop, *Complexity*, p. 64.
10 Bertrand Russell, *History of Western Philosophy*, new edn. (London: George Allen & Unwin, 1961), p. 551.
11 The second half of the sentence follows closely a passage extracted from Alfred Marshall's *Principles of Economics* (New York: Macmillan, 1952, 8th end., p. 33), a great classic, which has withstood the test of time.
12 Webster's *Third New International Dictionary* (see under 'analogy').
13 W. Brian Arthur, 'Positive feedbacks in the economy', *Scientific American*, February 1990: 80–5.
14 'By intuition', wrote Henri Bergson, the leading French philosopher of the first half of the 20th century, 'I mean instinct that has become disinterested, self-conscious, capable of reflecting upon its object and of enlarging it indefinitely.' The definition could have been written by either a chaos proponent or a complexity theorist. (Quoted from Russell, *History of Western Philosophy*, p. 758). It was also Bergson who, several decades before the founding of the Santa Fe Institute, maintained that '*evolution* is truly *creative*, akin to the work of an artist' (our italics).
15 Russell, *History of Western Philosophy*, p. 88 (italics are Russell's own).

PART II

BUSINESS CHAOTICS: Perspectives on wealth creation— a positive approach

One need not be a confirmed evangelist of dialectical materialism to acknowledge that economic well-being conditions most of our activities, including our intellectual endeavours. Moreover, economic well-being measures our actual progress.

Following the post-Second World War boom, which lasted some 30 years, nourished on sustained economic growth, *en masse* innovation and an information and population explosion, the world has been through nearly two decades of slowdown, stagnation, even regression here and there, amid widespread frustration and scaled-down expectations. The big issue is how to regain the lost momentum, how to get mankind moving forward again and, by the same token, ensure more equitable worldwide sharing of the fruits of expansion and social progress.

For things to improve all round, significantly and durably, it is not too difficult to point out a few prerequisites for success in material terms. Clearly, a first imperative is to produce more, and better-quality, goods while using fewer resources, by recasting some production processes and organization.

The second basic condition is to increase the efficiency of management at both the macro- and microeconomic level, possibly inventing a new managerial culture. Inasmuch as science and technology are changing more rapidly than ever, there is a pressing need to improve the tools and methods of technology forecasting to avoid costly failures. Lastly, there is a long list of unfulfilled promises that have been spelled out over the last three of four decades, e.g. close to a 100 per cent literacy, uniform health standards, artificial intelligence, household robots, knowledge processing, the electronic office and so on. It is high time that these long-promised breakthroughs were delivered, but 'the how' is just not evident.

By a kind of paradox, chaotics opens new, more optimistic perspectives on wealth creation. In particular it offers alternatives on the distribution of wealth, which has always been the sore point of economic evolution. It also goes some way towards fulfilling the preconditions of economic and social advance referred to above. Embracing chaotics is somewhat comparable in its effects to the benefit derived from cheap energy being made available to everyone in our age or the invention of the printing press four centuries ago.

Not that chaotics should ever be taken as some management gospel of the minute. When focusing on the need to overhaul management theory and practice, we do not take to pieces the style and manner of so-called scientific management. Instead, we deliberately concentrate on relevant tools and aids to management, and assess their pertinence with suggestions for key adjustments. Our first chapter in Part II deals with increasing-returns production, now almost a classic in the eyes of chaos and complexity theorists, yet looked upon, at best, as a temporary freak by the upholders of unmitigated determinism.

5

Production for Increasing Returns

All the business of life is to endeavour to find out what you don't know by what you do

Arthur Wellesley, Duke of Wellington (1759–1852)

Modern, high-tech firms are a far cry from the old-style traditional companies of the past. Yet, technology apart, you would be hard put to tell in what ways they differ in pure economic terms. Chaotics, and so far only chaotics, has much that is worthwhile to say on the subject. And what it says stands some classical economics on its head. The heart of the matter is the dichotomy between positive and negative feedback, a phenomenon well understood by physicists, yet virtually ignored by economists. To nutshell it, negative feedback is analogous to diminishing returns; positive feedback to increasing returns.

This simple formula, although coming more recently from chaos theory, has historical precedents at least 200 years old. In the capital-rich England of the 18th century, entrepreneurs competing with each other were naturally compelled to operate under conditions of diminishing returns. In the capital-poor France of that time, setting up a new industrial adventure involved gambling on long-term profits to recoup relatively huge initial costs. So while Ricardo emphasized the inevitability of diminishing rewards, France's Turgot spoke hopefully of ultimately increasing returns on industrial investment. Yet today, the imbalance between fixed and variable costs borne by most high-tech firms is greater than ever, especially in relative terms, creating a situation more like that prevailing in Turgot's France under King Louis XVI than that found in most economics text books. The implications are highly important.

Under diminishing returns, there is only one equilibrium position, at which all players' gains are maximized. This applies to individual firms, as well as the economy as a whole system. On the other hand, under increasing returns, the outcome is uncertain, as there may be several equilibrium points; the good news is that there is therefore choice, offering rich rewards to astute managements. Conventional wisdom has it that only in the last stages of the end-game can you tell for sure in whose favour the balance will finally tilt. Chaotics suggests otherwise. The feedback approach provides an analytic tool to forecast the potential outcome of neck-and-neck competition at an early stage, for instance between high-tech products that are functionally similar.

Closely related to this are the twin concepts of lock-in and leverage, which will be illustrated below by reference to Microsoft and Intel Corp. While any lock-in situation tends to solidify the leading contender's earlier advantage, the clever and timely application of a lever can boost an upstart company (or economy) in spectacular fashion against its entrenched rivals. Finally, there is a question: given the movement among farsighted industrial firms from the commercial philosophy of diminishing returns to that of increasing returns, how long before the pendulum eventually swings back, and under what circumstances? Might it be possible to discern some anticipatory signs indicating the tentative beginnings of this turnaround in time to take advantage of it?

Clarity in a confused argument

But first it is necessary to draw a distinction between the two kinds of 'laws of return'. The first relates to increasing and diminishing returns resulting from changes in the proportions in which factors of production are combined; the second to increasing and decreasing returns due to changes in the scale of production. In order to clarify this, for our purpose, we may first dispose of the second law. It is less important to our discussion. Historically, it has been the scale effect that made possible the Industrial Revolution of the 19th century. The scale effect was driven by a massive substitution of mechanized processes for human and animal-driven ones. It brought a new type of organization that overwhelmed the traditional, small-size, personalized workshops that had survived from the beginnings of commerce through the Middle Ages into the 18th century. As the demand for industrial products grew, individual firms were able to expand to a size at which they enjoyed economies of scale, so that their average costs fell, opening the way for an iterative fall in prices under the impact of competition.

In popular imagery and economic theory, expansion of the scale of production was thus naturally associated with increasing returns, even though, on second thoughts, there are evidently some instances of constant returns, and even diminishing returns with scale. For example, when a fall in demand hits phonographs or mainframe computers or other products becoming obsolete, it eventually neutralizes previous economies of scale. Thus, in the eyes of many contemporary economists the idea of economy of scale has lost much of its earlier glamour. In reality the present trend is often towards smaller-sized production units, some of which may easily outperform the larger plants due to their ability to react quickly and flexibly to a changing environment. The mini-mills in the steel industry are one example of trend reversal.

Another, even greater source of confusion concerns the first 'law of variable

Table 1. *Effects of varying the factors on average and marginal production*

Labour (no. of workers)	Fixed land, capital and technology (index numbers)	Total output (units)	Average product per worker (units)	Marginal product per worker (units)
4	100	1,000	250	
				200
5	100	1,200	240	
				120
6	100	1,320	220	
				80
7	100	1,400	200	
				60
8	100	1,460	180	

proportions', which is often (perhaps misleadingly) called the law of diminishing returns. The law states that as equal increases of a variable factor, e.g. labour, are added to a constant quantity of other, supposedly fixed, factors (land, technological skills, organizational talent, etc.) the successive increases in output will after a while decline. This is illustrated in Table 1, which shows that, under the conditions specified, hiring extra workers beyond the initial workforce of four tends to lower the average productivity of each and every worker, from 250 units of output per head, to 240, to 220, etc., down to 180 when the workforce has been doubled. In other words, whereas going from four to five workers yields an additional output of 200 units, the hiring of yet another worker would increase total productivity by only 120 units.

This outcome was believed to reflect an important, often-observed technical and economic regularity, and hence furnished a baseline for prediction. Most traditional industries, and of course agriculture and mining, were reputed to operate under the law of diminishing returns. The law admitted very few exceptions—though these included manufactures in their infancy, military arsenals and some government-shielded industries.

But by challenging the universal validity of the principle of diminishing returns, chaotics strikes at the very heart of such classical economic tenets as marginal analysis, the theory of equilibrium of the firm, the assumption of basic stability of the economic system under competition and the vision of a self-perpetuating drive towards general equilibrium. The argument has reached a crux here. An appraisal of the pros and cons is therefore in order.

The chips may fall either way

According to classical economic theory, a firm is 'in equilibrium' when its net revenue is as great as it can be, i.e. when the difference between its total revenue and its total costs is maximized. This is assumed to be its most profitable output, one that is attained through a particular and unique combination of inputs. The corollary is that, at least under perfect competition, there is one equilibrium and one equilibrium point only. In that situation, the firm's management has no rational inducement either to vary the quantities of input or to attempt to change the level of output, because any move away from that enviable, exclusive equilibrium position would not only yield a smaller overall profit, but more importantly it would result in the loss of stability.[1]

Orthodox economists stuck to this position basically for reasons of intellectual comfort. As Professor W. Brian Arthur has pointed out, incorporating increasing returns and thus allowing for the possibility of more than one outcome would have destroyed their familiar world of a general, unique equilibrium (see Box 3 on page 58).[2] It would also destroy the axiom that the market's choice ensured an optimal distribution of resources, factors of production and end-products by itself.

But stubbornness cannot prevail against stark reality. The one-sided interpretation of the law of variable proportions became untenable in the light of the rise of high-tech industries following the Second World War. Today, the evidence points the other way. Computers, software, stealth aircraft, optical fibres and all telecommunications gear, sophisticated radars, medical electronics, pharmaceuticals and a myriad of information-related products are more often than not subject to increasing returns. This is because they necessitate, from the outset, huge outlays on research, development, designing/redesigning, prototyping, tooling and automated plants. Every time Boeing develops a new aeroplane, it invests a sum in excess of half the company's net worth. However, once the products start rolling off the production line, the cost of making additional units drops very sharply in relation to the initial investment.

This is illustrated by the cost schedules in Table 2, which refer to some hypothetical development by a telecommunications switch supplier of the software for an advanced digital matrix system, the nerve centre of a modern computerized telephone switch, capable of handling many tens of thousands of simultaneous calls.

The manufacturer's total revenue (column 3) is obtained by multiplying the number of units sold by the unit price, which is assumed to be constant. The total cost (column 4) comprises the total fixed cost (column 5), which in our illustration amounts to US$1 billion, and of course the total variable cost (column 6).

Columns 7, 8 and 9 are derived from the previous data. Thus, the average total cost is found by dividing the total cost by the number of units sold, and likewise with the average variable cost. The marginal cost (column 9) is obtained by dividing the increase in the total cost by the corresponding increase in sales. Although, for the economist, 'total cost normally includes *normal* profit' (roughly equivalent to the prevailing rate of interest), this is omitted in Table 2 for the sake of simplicity. Either way the break-even point is not attained easily. In our case the manufacturer operates at a loss as long as the volume of sales is below 20 units. At

Table 2. *Cost schedules* (in US$ '000s)

Units sold	Unit price	Total revenue	Total cost	Total fixed cost	Total variable cost	Average total cost	Average variable cost	Marginal cost
(1)	(2)	(3)	(4)	(5)	(6)	(7)	(8)	(9)
5	100	500	1,320	1,000	320	264.00	64	
								86
10	100	1,000	1,750	1,000	750	175.00	75	
								30
15	100	1,500	1,900	1,000	900	126.67	60	
								20
20	100	2,000	2,000	1,000	1,000	100.00	50	
								0
25	100	2,500	2,000	1,000	1,000	80.00	40	
								40
30	100	3,000	2,200	1,000	1,200	73.33	40	
								40
35	100	3,500	2,400	1,000	1,400	68.57	40	
								40
40	100	4,000	2,600	1,000	1,600	65.00	40	

Note: The marginal cost is equal to the average marginal total cost when the average total cost is a minimum.

double that volume his rate of profit jumps to 50% of his total cost. The situation just referred to, of increasing returns, is not unusual in those parts of the economy that are information-based. What we see is an increasing part of the economy governed by multiple points of equilibrium.

A telling analogy and a precedent

But what we are really after is a way of reconciling the conflicting principles, the assumption of diminishing returns with the newer trend towards apparent increasing returns. Effectively we are looking for a method of squaring the age-old model of classical industrial operations with the dominant (reverse) pattern of present-day business operations. A conceptual breakthrough came in the late 1980s. A few unorthodox economists, and primarily Professor W. Brian Arthur (see Box 3), realized that the issue of whether the graph of returns slopes upwards or downwards is basically equivalent to the difference between negative and positive feedback. They state that this inspiration is clearly traceable to a study of chaotic systems and subsequent investigations of complexity, especially the Santa Fe Institute's conceptual framework. Their theory, which has strong parallels with modern non-linear physics, may one day be considered an important milestone of the new economics as we enter the 21st century.

Self-reinforcing mechanisms, which are the cornerstone of positive feedback

Box 3. *The concept of economic feedback from Professor W. Brian Arthur*

Increasing returns and the possibility of more than one outcome come from the theories of Arthur, destroying the familiar idea of a unique equilibrium. Analogies can be made between feedback in physics and increasing versus decreasing returns in business economics. The business model is especially clear in the action of the new electronic markets, such as the Internet.

In physics, by feedback we mean the returning to the input of a machine, system, or process, of a part of the output, usually small. An electronic amplifier furnishes a simple illustration of how the mechanism works. The fractional return of the output to the input circuit is used either to obtain amplification of voltage, current or power (positive feedback) or, on the contrary, to restrict the amplification, improve linearity and reduce distortion (negative feedback). The device is usually so designed as to provide a continuous stream of information on discrepancies between intended and actual operation, leading to self-correcting action.

Most oscillating systems (e.g. the beating heart, populations of animals, etc.) possess an element of feedback that apparently results from the system's reaction to outside influences that pull in many directions. Feedback thus generates complex dynamics even in the simplest systems. Ferromagnetic substances, solid-state lasers and other non-linear systems consist of mutually reinforcing elements that may lead to many possible solutions or equilibria. Minute chance events at a critical moment affect the actual outcome. In other words, the introduction of non-linearities into the analysis demonstrates the possibility of multiple equilibria, inherently unstable.

The concept of feedback has found innumerable applications; first in technology and engineering, but also in biology, medicine, population studies and other social sciences. Business economics though stood aloof from this trend until quite recently. W. Brian Arthur of Stanford University, also working with the Santa Fe Institute, has become the moving spirit behind the recent reassessment of the crucial role of positive feedback in the economy, analogous to the self-reinforcing mechanisms to be found in the physical world of the harder sciences. This is most evident in the phenomenon of increasing returns in business, where positive feedback drives up sales once a threshold in investment has been reached (to provide the minimum output—the product) and the market has been driven to a threshold level of education and promotion. The mechanism has stronger effect when connectivity to consumers is multiplied, cheapened and accelerated, as with the Internet, so that products like browsers and Java applets can have greater and faster impact.

economics, come in different configurations and disguises. Take for instance Arthur's idea of a positive feedback loop. As more people adopt a specific technology, the more it improves and the more attractive it looks to the designers/adopters and to would-be manufacturers and sellers. Particular technologies thus tend to be frozen into technological conventions and standards. This leads to locked-in situations—for better, or perhaps for far worse, because this kind of rigidity may delay and even preclude the advent of a superior technology. However, Arthur sounds less convincing when he attributes the well-known geographical clustering of high-tech firms, e.g. in Silicon Valley, to the feedback theory, rather than to the older concept of external economies.

Central to the law of variable proportions and the way the balance eventually tilts is a 'sea change' in the relative importance of fixed and variable costs (see Table 2). In addition to the well-known spiralling of R&D spending, other factors are at work that pull heavily in the same direction—the rapid attrition of each successive technology; dual trends towards product differentiation and ever narrower specialization; the ongoing globalization of markets, which demands local, and thus different, product and market strategies. All these mutations add up to an apparently irresistible inflation of unavoidable fixed costs. By comparison, the variable outlays (chiefly inexpensive raw materials, component parts procured cheaply through outsourcing, and low-priced off-the-shelf tools) become dwarfed.

The radical changes that business accountancy has undergone over the last couple of decades, in particular in the handling of amortization, provides corroborative evidence that a new pattern of the split between fixed and variable costs has finally prevailed in many industrial sectors. The key problem for high-tech firms is how to accumulate the capital and recoup the huge costs they must nowadays sink into the business simply to stay in the running. This issue is directly related to increasing returns. In 1996 a world-class microprocessor facility as used by a corporation such as Intel cost around US$1 billion to build. In 1998 it will cost US$3 billion.

A little-known historical precedent is worth recalling. Although economic analysis sometimes claims to be a science (based on universal principles and observation), its most eminent proponents, from Ricardo to Malthus and from Alfred Marshall to Paul Samuelson, have somehow forgotten the teachings of the 18th-century French economist and statesman Turgot. It was Turgot who originally drew attention to the fact that the addition of more of a variable factor to a fixed factor often results in increasing output. In this, as in several other areas, Turgot was truly a precursor. His *Réflexions sur la formation et la distribution des richesses*, his major work, appeared in 1766, a full ten years ahead of Adam Smith's *An Inquiry into the Nature and Causes of the Wealth of Nations* (1776). A free-trader, Turgot advocated complete freedom, including freedom from taxation for commerce and industry. When appointed Controller General, a cabinet post under King Louis XVI in 1774, Turgot encapsulated his programme in a 'Reaganomics-sounding' motto: 'No bankruptcy, no increase in taxation, no borrowing—but economy'. With such credentials, Turgot's premonitory formulation of the law of increasing returns ought to have found its place in the history of economic thought. But by a strange coincidence, it may come to be recognized at long last, for its prophetic value in connection with . . . chaotics and complexity.

Sniffing out business opportunities

Chaos and complexity may lead us to a deeper understanding of the laws of chance governing markets and products. For instance, consider the problem of picking the likely winner between two functionally similar products, or guessing the outcome of a close contest between competing technologies. Let us take the case of the videocassette recorder (VCR). The advent and ultimate triumph of the standardized VCR, the hot technology of the early 1980s, lends itself to two distinct interpretations. A traditional rendering of the story goes like this:

In terms of speed, Sony was first in the market with its flagship product Betamax, beating by a short head its main rival JVC, a small Japanese firm that had developed its own VHS format. At that stage, the two technologies were generally considered neck and neck, with Sony's perhaps slightly out in front. Now to play in the same league as Sony, the little JVC company offered to sell its product and the related patents to its giant parent company, Mitsubishi. Furthermore, JVC then produced a two-hour recording format, making it possible to tape a feature film, as against Betamax's one-hour only facility. By the time Sony succeeded in stretching Betamax to two-hour recording, VHS had taken off.

Fine and good. What the classical analysis fails to explain, however, was how VHS could become a de facto world standard in a relatively short time and take virtually the entire VCR market, instead of just splitting the market with its more powerful rival. Chaos theorists tackled the case by emphasizing the similarities. Not only did the videocassette market start with two competing systems, unveiled at about the same time, and with comparable market prospects, but the two recorders sold at about the same price. Additionally, each format could, at least in theory, benefit from increasing returns as its prospective market share grew. Increased sales would, no doubt, encourage video shops to offer an even wider selection of prerecorded tapes in the corresponding format, and so enhance the value of owning the appropriate VCR and give a further push to the emerging market leader.

This line of reasoning led straight to the key conclusion that the winning technology must have benefited from small, emergent-phase, chance events that presumably tilted the competition towards VHS. In this way, increased returns on early VHS gains began building up exponentially, by positive feedback, argued W. Brian Arthur.[2] So the winning company's production costs fell rapidly as its market share increased, enabling it, as the leading vendor, to slash prices fastest.

The Microsoft and Intel positions

The story repeats itself, on a vastly increased scale, with the meteoric rise to pre-eminence of Microsoft. Way back around 1980, IBM bought the first version of the Microsoft MS-DOS operating system for its first personal computer, launched in late 1981. Two weeks after it had signed the deal with IBM, Microsoft in turn acquired the rights to the 16-bit operating system in a fortuitous deal with Seattle Computer Products for $50,000 (at the time it was called 86-QDOS, for 'quick and dirty operating system').[3] Microsoft's partnership with IBM continued through the early 1980s, and helped Big Blue rapidly to become the biggest PC maker, while catapulting Microsoft from nowhere to number three among the leading software publishers, behind Lotus, publisher of the 1-2-3 spreadsheet, and Ashton Tate, creator of the dBase relational database product. The contract ensured Microsoft royalties on every personal computer sold by IBM. In practice, MS-DOS soon became a de facto standard for the industry.

In other words, an astute initial deal with IBM, coupled with well-managed positive feedback, rather than clear-cut technical superiority, has resulted in Microsoft's sky-rocketing profits. This is a textbook example of increasing returns. Despite an enormous—some seven years—lead-time to produce a new product generation that approaches the rival Apple MacOS operating system (but at this date does not yet match it), complete market dominance, very early on, has protected Microsoft from any assault by others.

Moreover, it also allowed Microsoft to move into applications, by leveraging its knowledge of operating systems. This has been used to excellent effect with Apple, since being the lead supplier of spreadsheets and wordprocessors clearly exerts major pressure on rival operating system providers who still need those key applications, because customers buy applications, not computers. What was to follow, however, owed little to chance. The phenomenal success of Windows was due essentially to major marketing campaigns developed by Microsoft and through its control of distribution channels. Microsoft's contracts with PC suppliers were brilliantly successful in persuading them to supply MS-DOS in preference to rival operating systems.

Microsoft reported sales of some 25 million copies of Windows, in its different versions, in less than three years. The new software giant's gross margins, i.e. aggregate revenues minus production costs, jumped to a figure in excess of 80 per cent, a level unheard of before. The message is crystal-clear. Software, once written, beta-tested and debugged, costs peanuts to duplicate *ad libitum, ad nauseam*—until the designers/vendors on their own initiative decide that the time has come to enhance the product.

There have been six successive versions of DOS, and the current version of Windows is dubbed Microsoft Windows 95, with Windows 97 appearing as this book was being written. Furthermore, the last major version of MS-DOS (DOS 6) and Windows 3.1 were brought closer to each other, enabling them to operate as a team. Each of these versions has generated enormous new application sales because users are often forced to upgrade. So the operating system is used to leverage increasing returns on applications. The applications themselves also leverage enormous upgrade sales—in other applications that interwork with them (or do so no longer), new operating systems to host the new applications and especially new hardware, because the new applications may take two to ten times the disk and RAM memory of their previous versions and may demand much higher processor power. Forward compatibility, e.g. reading a version 6 document from a version 5 wordprocessor, is rarely accommodated.

Up to a point, the early development of Intel, founded in 1968 and now the biggest microchip-maker in the world, paralleled the initial take-off of Microsoft. In 1980, when IBM was looking for a microprocessor to drive its PC, still on the drawing board, it picked the slower 16-bit version of Intel's new 8086 chip, the 8088. For Intel, as for Microsoft, the association with IBM was to prove heaven-sent.

Under the umbrella of the Intel–Microsoft duopoly, and with the blessing of Big Blue, Intel was able to exercise full control—and indeed, leverage, over the timing and introduction of successive generations of chips throughout the period 1981–91. PC buyers were for all practical purposes locked into software usable solely on Intel-made processors, and its licensed second sourcers, such as AMD. This privileged situation allowed Intel to attain a profit margin of between 25 and 30 per cent and to become one of the world's richest corporations—thanks again to an astute use of increasing-return principles. From just high market dominance it was able to generate increasing returns and create ever increasing market dominance. For instance, as Intel has gained momentum and confidence its second-sourcing licensing deals for the later products have not renewed. This has provided increased market control.

Is competition thrown overboard in a world of increasing returns?

Intel's hegemony, however, was not to be unchallenged. It was broken briefly in 1991 when a handful of upstart firms, including some of its former second sourcers and subcontractors, succeeded in producing functionally equivalent processors, launching a price war. But Intel always has the key card up its sleeve—the next version. And the rights to that, the P6 (Pro-Pentium) and P7, up to P9 and beyond, will take Intel into the 21st century.

This turn in the tide of the strategy and possibly the fortunes of Microsoft and Intel raises the key question: to what extent are increasing returns compatible/incompatible with free competition if the company has market dominance?

Is this like the game of Go—the more you win, the easier it is to encircle your foe? While a few chaos theorists were busying themselves with looking for analogies between feedback in physics and increasing versus decreasing returns in business economics, another group of independently minded economists[4] took a somewhat different tack—via a challenge to the (by then largely) discredited neoclassical theory of growth. Their leader was Paul Romer, now a professor at Berkeley in California. He made his name with his 1983 doctoral thesis from the University of Chicago, which was entitled 'Dynamic competitive equilibria with externalities, increasing returns and unbounded growth'.

Instead of assuming that the output (of a firm, of an economy, etc.) depends on the amount of capital and labour employed, which was the cornerstone of neoclassical economics, Romer added another factor of production, namely knowledge. Eventually he extended his analysis, taking into account four factors: capital (in the traditional sense), unskilled labour, 'human' capital (using years of education as a measure) and ideas (perhaps measured by patents issued). Recall that in the neoclassical environment by doubling the input of both capital and labour, you would obtain twice as much output—which is equivalent to constant returns to scale. With multiple factors, argued Romer, this rule no longer holds water. We have a situation of a non-linear system, with apparently chaotic multiple inputs and complex feedback loops, some of them positive. If you take all the factors together the production function shows increasing returns. Thus if you double all the factors, output more than doubles. In this model, firms are able to make bigger profits by simultaneously raising their output, lowering costs and reducing prices as a means of fostering the sales. The neoclassical assumption of perfect competition is thus thrown overboard—at best competition is imperfect.[5]

The fact that increasing returns, combined with a chance event at an early stage, can lead to a position of dominance is exemplified by the Microsoft and Intel cases. Whereas in 1980 the PC business amounted to little more than pipe dreams, 15 years later there were close to 200 million personal computers in operation in the world—with 90 per cent of them built around Intel's processors. Never before has one high-tech firm enjoyed such undisputed pre-eminence—not even IBM, the once mighty computer giant. Both Microsoft and Internet exert enormous leverage for their size, and consequently high profits.

In conclusion, granted that more and more high-tech companies must work under increasing returns, and considering that this modus operandi leads to a situation of de facto monopoly, the question must be asked: how far can this trend go? Could it possibly engulf some, or perhaps the majority, of the more traditional industries? Or is it restricted to the 'knowledge-based' industries, and will have no effect on coal-mining or freight distribution, for instance? The persistence of the present trend, fuelled by the growing burden of fixed investment, would no doubt gradually undermine the very fabric of the competitive economies of the Western world.

But as the theory of chaos strongly implies, the pendulum may very well swing back before too long by a feedback reversal effect or by some form of intervention. There are many ways in which this intervention could happen, but it is too early to say which. Three possible methods are: through public regulation; through deliberate downscaling of specific operations; or again via devolution of some functions (of production, investment, marketing and the like) from giant corporations to freely negotiated industrial partnerships.

NOTES

1 The assertion is a special case of a more general proposition linking 'average' and 'marginal' quantities, such as the pairs average total cost and marginal cost, or again, average productivity (of labour, of capital, etc.) and the corresponding marginal productivity. According to Kenneth E. Boulding (*Economic Analysis*, rev edn. New York: Harper & Row, 1948; fn., pp. 167–8):

> The 'average marginal relationship' can easily be proved by algebra. Let a be the average total cost of x units, and a_1 the average total cost of $x + 1$ units. Then the total cost of x units is ax and of $x + 1$ units is $a_1(x + 1)$. The marginal cost of the $(x + 1)$st unit is $a_1(x + 1) - ax$, or $(a_1 - a)x + a_1$. If the average cost is constant as output changes, $a_1 = a$, and the marginal is equal to the average cost, a_1. If the average cost is increasing as output increases, $a_1 > a$, $(a_1 - a)x$ is positive, and the marginal cost is therefore greater than the average cost. If the average cost is decreasing as output increases, $a_1 < a$, $(a_1 - a)x$ is negative, and the marginal cost is less than the average cost.

In the situation described above, the typical firm endeavours at all times to target its output at that level at which its average total cost is a minimum and its marginal cost is equal to that average cost. The proposition holds when restated in terms of average and marginal productivity (e.g. of labour), which are just reciprocals of average and marginal costs. The firm under discussion is said to be in equilibrium when its marginal productivity is equal to its average productivity, which is then at its maximum.

2 W. Brian Arthur, 'Positive feedbacks in the economy', *Scientific American* (February 1990).

3 James Wallace and Jim Erickson, *Hard Drive* (New York: HarperBusiness, 1992).

4 'Economic growth: explaining the mystery', *Economist*, 4 January 1992. The article refers specifically to Paul Romer, 'Increasing returns and long-run growth', *Journal of Political Economy* (1986).

5 Simon Forge, 'Business models for the computer industry for the next decade: when will the fastest eat the largest', *Futures* 25(9) (1993).

6

Economics, Intelligence and Turbulence

We live in a postmodern world where nearly everything is possible and nothing is certain

Pavel Havel

In 1992, during one of its recurring fits of soul-searching, the normally sedate *Harvard Business Review* allowed itself to run the headline 'Is Management Still a Science?', to which it promptly answered itself, 'The old scientific management was about ensuring control. The new will be about making sense out of chaos'.

As in *haute couture*, fashions in management style come and go, whether they have value in some situations, a lot, or none. Business process reengineering (colloquially termed 'BPR') is one of the latest, stealing the show from management by objectives, by profit centres, just-in-time management and total-quality management. Often these attempts at introducing science to management have subsequently been derided as little more than gimmicks. This is somewhat unfair. On the other hand, few of them have proved capable of durably enhancing the prospects for business growth. Only business reengineering, the far greater plan behind BPR, has been shown to be truly effective, and only when it questions truly poor management, and only in the right expert hands, when sociology and industrial psychology are carefully used to effect change.

Can we analyse just why there is a progressive process of debasement of the managerial reputation? Is the process of short-sighted, mechanically applied 'MBA rationality' gradually destroying the once legendary efficacy and punch in the top echelons of all business sectors, government and international bodies? With few exceptions, corporate business deciders and policy-makers in the public sector have demonstrated little or no ability to adjust to our chaos-prone environment. Few of them have been bold enough to formulate and implement new strategies using non-linear effects on a truly global scale, such as those based on increasing (rather than decreasing) returns, as discussed in the previous chapter. Small wonder that many of the vaunted managers of the largest American corporations of the 1980s have lost their aura of invincibility. And the prestigious US business schools, once the envy of the world, seem less relevant as we prepare to enter the 21st century. Their deterministic approach clashes with policies arguing that a precise future cannot be taught.

To go in a new direction we need to know if the hallmarks of scientific management (see Box 4) and its new-look extensions, principles, practices and analytic tools, turn out on closer examination to be inappropriate in a 'global village' environment. This environment is characterized by rapid transformation of economies through new forms of competition and new power structures, in which centralized government power is usually diminishing. Along with it comes pervasive social upheaval—a struggle between the inertia of the traditional social structures and the momentum of new business power structures and invading cultures.

Conventional economic rationality

As a consequence of Taylorism, for the better part of a century business acumen has been viewed as resting on three pillars—an unshakeable belief in continuity and order, the idea of superior scientific methods, in particular scientific management, and reliance on quantitative data and our ability to analyse the 'hard' facts.

These are just the basic tenets with which chaos and complexity theorists tend to clash. Until quite recently, however, criticism of traditional approaches in business and government has been muted. But today we are faced with a new situation. A wholesale reassessment of these basic tenets is due in view of the changes sweeping business and society. Clearly, the turbulence that prevails in the world economy and the global markets will never go away. In this situation the key question is how to cope efficiently.

A vivid illustration of the inadequacy of the present approach is frequent recourse to extrapolation. In an orderly world, the assumption of continuation of the past or present trends is plausible—the self-fulfilling prophecy. Under rapidly changing conditions, it is a mere hypothesis, and must be tested. It is rather like driving by looking in a rear-view mirror—trying to judge the road ahead by what has gone before. In a stable market you could do it—just. In an unstable turbulent market you crash. And if scientific methods are to be truly applied, interpolation requires painstaking collection of all pertinent data, including evidence to the contrary, through observation and possibly experiment. Only then can we draw valid conclusions—and possibly recommend a course of action. This is very rarely done in business. But without such precautions the interpolation exercise is not worth the effort. Interpolation results are often misleading, even absurd. For instance, should the cost of social security keep rising at the present rate, it would absorb the entire GNP of America and Europe within two decades. Also, had cars grown more efficient at the same rate as computers did, they would now be able

Box 4. *Scientific management: an obsession with efficiency, mechanistic plans and mathematical models*

The catch-phrase 'Scientific Management' was invented by Frederick W. Taylor when he published *The Principles of Scientific Management* in 1911. Two years earlier, the evangelist of mass production, Henry Ford, had produced the Model T. By slashing the costs of production through control of raw materials and of distribution, and with the aid of the production-line on a conveyor belt, Ford was able to offer a robust, standardized car at a discount. His high-wage policy and unique profit-sharing scheme were also key factors for productivity. Iron ore entered at one end of his River Rouge plant; Model Ts came out the other. Scientific management was applied to a strong verticalization. This contrasts with today's motor industry, where the world leaders add less than 35 per cent of the total car's value within the assembly plant; the rest is in component suppliers. Specialization with the advance in technological complexity has forced a fragmentation of the supply chain into separate companies. Thus the concept of 'just-in-time' is a tool that adds an element of control in a more complex manufacturing world.

Obsessed with the need for maximum efficiency, as applied to industrial organizations, Taylor quite naturally came to see the manager as the embodiment of science. Thus he pioneered such 'scientific' techniques as time-and-motion studies, standardization of equipment, processes and tools, and the use of a planning and forecasting department. His overall concept was reinforced by the Taylor system, a piece-rate method of wage payment offering greater incentives to the individual worker, rather than collective bargaining agreements, which do not have the same granularity of control. In Taylor's view, no matter how complex the industrial process, it could always be sliced into manageable tasks, each tightly controlled by highly centralized management. This set of business axioms was consistent with what was the mainstream philosophy of science at that time, still deeply immersed in the deterministic and predictable world of Newton.

Over the past 30 years, however, the notion of scientific management has undergone several mutations, especially with the spread of business computing. One of the milestones was the concept of strategic planning (*c.*1960s–1970s) propounded by the Harvard Business School, which stressed the need to integrate standard business functions (i.e. production, financing, accounting, marketing, etc.) with a systematic approach to a company's overall strategy.

Two successive oil shocks, however, demonstrated the futility of highly mechanistic plans and mathematical forecasts. Operational research tried to build mathematical models of whole industries and economies in the mid-1970s, with little success, although Stafford Beer had some interesting ideas.

A little later, system dynamics became part of the deterministic tool-set. Its roots are in the theories of control engineering and information feedback concepts (developed at MIT by Jay Forester and others). This tool was used in combination with Harvard's decision analysis, which allows different cost criteria to be used simultaneously, to aggregate the perceived value of, say, apples, roads and holidays, as adjudged by individual outside observers. Both are risky exercises, since the first rests on assumptions about businesses as fairly simple, non-changing systems and the second often depends on subjective value judgements.

to go around the world on a single gallon of petrol. Thus rampant, extravagant extrapolation tends to ruin managerial thinking.

Overreliance on quantitative data and methods (as drilled in by business schools) can discredit the best. Sophisticated accounting, techniques of modern statistics and econometrics supplemented by sampling, operations research and business games have come to permeate the business philosophy and practices of private and public administrations, and to an extent unimaginable even a decade ago. That tendency goes a long way towards explaining the poor decisions—through a loss of perspective. Effectively managers may suffer from a lack of feeling for their job. They have less and less useful understanding of the market, or public sector in which they work, but see more of the internal rules and processes that govern corporate life. They only keep a close watch over internals—the daily, monthly, quarterly sales and earnings and the cash flow—analysing and re-analysing the various cost elements, scrutinizing financial and operating ratios galore, with an obsession for low unit costs, quick profits, high dividends and big size. More generally, the short term takes all, to the detriment of the knowledge of market directions, quality of product, competence of staff, business foresight and so eventually to long-term investment. Unable to escape the grip of this myopic rationality, the professional manager faced with an unforeseen difficulty tends to overreact. Typically, managers may plunge into a high-flying remedy in a display of assertive authority, or worse, a panicky search for scapegoats.

Gathering economic intelligence for management, with chaotics

Let us take a step back and view the fundamentals of the business management process. The true managerial process can be viewed as a system of facilitation, interactive support and command functions. Command functions are less important today than in the deterministic model of yesteryear. Our overall future management process should include at least six key items: creation of a culture; definition of the aim and objectives; formulation and periodic review of overall strategy; long-term policy and planning; shorter-term tactics and decision-making; coordination; and supervision. The list could include leadership, responsibilities, incentives and so on. Note that definition of the aim and objectives is secondary, while the looser concept of culture is primary—Hewlett-Packard (especially in its start-up years), Wal-Mart, and IBM in its good years teach us this, as do the many business failures. Because how these tasks are discharged is as important as the brief.

To do their job properly, managers at any level and in all sectors need two things: an array of information (which may be vast) and a set of managerial tools. The tools should enable managers to make sense of the implicit trends and causal relationships that underscore the raw data. That means an unimpeded access to 'codified and verified knowledge of knowable factors'.[1] The decades after the Second World War witnessed an extraordinary expansion and refinement of what may be called instruments of economic intelligence. In today's jargon, we would call these supports a 'management database', which, together with a management information system, at its most advanced corresponds to a 'data warehouse' topped by an Executive Information System (EIS).

We can only nutshell the range of quantitative aids to management that generations of statisticians, econometricians and other analysts have nurtured with loving care and keep refining. The real question is: are these tools relevant to a global marketplace, instead of a single town or country? Are they applicable— directly or with modification—to economies in rapid transformation, punctuated by frequent turmoil? A brief look at some of the traditional analytic forecasting techniques provides a clue to discovering some really useful techniques.

Two somewhat similar growth curves have been used extensively in economic analysis and forecasting. They have often been found to fit historical data quite well, partly because of their versatility and ease-of-use. They are the S-shaped Pearl curve, also called 'the logistic', and the skewed Gompertz curve (see Figure 8). The curves track and can even predict rising standards of living in a country, the spread of telephony, the continuous fall in unit computing costs and a great many other phenomena.

Correlation is another widely used analytic tool. But the job of economic analysis becomes more difficult when additional variables that simultaneously fluctuate exist. The first problem of course is to make sure that the observed covariation between inputs and outputs is not purely accidental, that it corresponds to a causal relationship between the variables under review, in particular the 'dependent' variable and the driving one. Thus as family income rises, spending on health or on leisure keeps rising in proportion. The result is generally summarized by a single figure, the regression coefficient, which tells us the strength of the relationship, but nothing more.

Curve-fitting and correlation as tools work reasonably well, as long as the phenomena under review do not fluctuate too violently or too erratically. However their practical usefulness from management's point of view can be seriously impaired when the problem at hand partakes of that common intoxifier, non-linear dynamics. Neither technique explains a sudden reversal or turnabout, nor provides the slightest clue to what might have 'caused' it, or again to whether the change might endure. So we need to understand if certain current aids to management can be revamped to take into account phenomena such as turn-arounds, competitive leapfrogs, sudden unsuspected leverage and other manifestations of underlying business turbulence.

Let us briefly examine one case-history and look at how these simple analytic tools can be applied in a more imaginative way. We shall use them to throw some

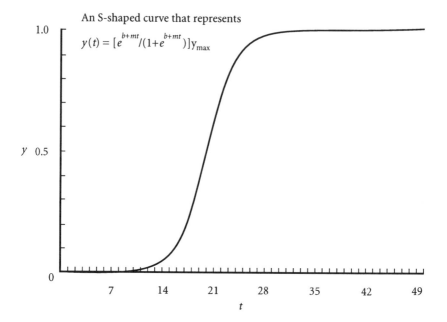

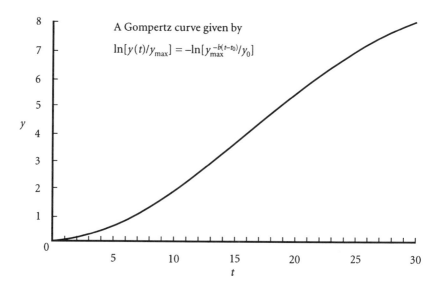

Figure 8. *The S-shaped Pearl curve, also called 'the logistic', and the skewed Gompertz curve*

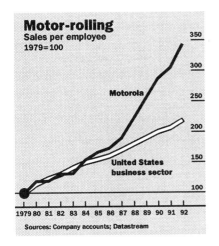

Motor-rolling
Sales per employee
1979=100

Motorola

United States
business sector

1979 80 81 82 83 84 85 86 87 88 89 90 91 92
Sources: Company accounts; Datastream

Figure 9. *Motorola's performance 1979–1992, measured by sales per employee, is compared graphically with that of the entire US business sector* Source: Copyright © *The Economist*, London, 28 August 1993. Used with permission.

light on the truly spectacular comeback of an American firm that had previously suffered. Motorola, Inc. is perhaps best known for inventing the car radio (soon after its foundation in 1928), but also, just as significantly, for its repeated lack of success in turning a number of brilliant ideas into marketable products at the right time. The tide turned with Motorola's heavier involvement in the early 1980s in wireless communications: cellular telephones and networks, personal digital assistants and all kinds of 'pagers'. Motorola has established itself as a market leader in mobile phones and equipment, which accounts for some 60 per cent of the company's current revenues. Motorola's impressive rebound is a vivid demonstration of the strength of non-linear leverage, the idea that relatively small, well-focused and well-timed decisions are capable of producing a self-multiplying, durable improvement. In Figure 9, Motorola's performance from 1979 to 1992, measured by sales per employee, is compared graphically with that of the entire US business sector, using a basic index with figures at constant prices.

It turns out that a very different trend line can be fitted respectively to the aggregate business record of American corporations and to Motorola's solo performance: the former is a gently-sloping linear expansion, whereas the latter is a curve that is more or less exponential.

What is particularly striking is the kinship of the graph in Figure 9, based on actual data, to the theoretical Figure 10, which shows the effect of non-linear dynamics in contrast to deterministic, linear growth. Setting up Motorola's exponential growth against the less exciting result for the average American firm adds a new dimension to both, a reading of the past form of evolution and the glimpse of the future. Motorola's story illustrates how an apparently small event at a specific point in time—greater commitment to two-way wireless communication —provided an ailing electronics firm with more than a shot in the arm. It has made up for lost opportunities. Figure 9 emphasizes that the crucial

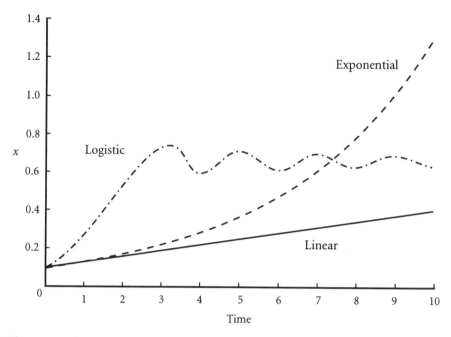

Figure 10. *Linear, exponential and logistic growth curves—the essence of non-linear versus linear*

turning-point occurred in or around 1983, when the non-linear effects began to take hold.

As we see, most economic and econometric models in current use are of the linear type. As such they are theory and are divorced from most of reality. The question is: can they be made more realistic and thus more useful by the inclusion of some dynamic non-linear elements? In some instances, it seems to work. For instance, the principle of self-similarity—borrowed from the theory of chaos and from fractal geometry—can be built into the simple device of an envelope curve. It can be used to explain and even predict the doubling, quadrupling, etc. of the ever-greater density of silicon chips and the inverse trend towards the decline of unit costs.

Nowadays, we are just beginning to introduce ideas of business turbulence, often because we have cheap high-power computing. The desktop PC can play a significant role in prediction by enabling us to forecast the outcomes of altern-ative courses of action, planning while learning at the same time. This can get quite sophisticated. The more so when prediction moves strongly away from determinism with techniques such as neural networks 'learning' the movement behaviour of markets. Mathematical models of the entropy and disorder of markets, with numerical processing based on quantification techniques (devised by mathematicians called 'quants') is de rigeur in the financial-market forecasting boutiques. Other refinements include making a map of creative thinking ('cognitive mapping') and analysing decisions into hierarchical sets of goals and alternatives, and the creation of 'micro-worlds'. In this exercise a simplified model of the company is formed, allowing the players to simulate alternative evolutions. Scenarios and alternative views of the future have added 'soft complexity', which one major oil company has used successfully, predicting—with hindsight—the oil crises of the late 1970s and early 1980s.

With these moves into assimilating complexity and chaos, we see that scientific management methods are on the wane. But finally, we need to search for radically new ways of tackling the recurring problem of how to guide managers to the correct choice with a higher probability of success than today's methods.

Are analytic models perfectible?

The discussion of the need for an overhaul of economic intelligence methods has been encapsulated by Czech statesman and philosopher Pavel Havel: 'We live in the post-modern world where nearly everything is possible and almost nothing is certain'. [2]

The special place that model-building occupies for economists is due, it seems, to their inability to conduct controlled experiments, as is common practice in the hard sciences. Economic models are theoretical constructs. They are deemed to reproduce the interplay between selected variables and their relationships. The aim is to understand the working of an economy or a specific business sector.

Economic models come in all shapes and sizes. Some incorporate individual economic units—e.g. households, firms, decision centres and the like. Often these are grouped into specific markets and industries, as well as the flows corresponding to multidirectional relationships between components. Microeconomic models throw some light on such issues as the determination of quantities produced and cleared through the market, or the formation of prices of individual commodities and services. National income accounts have provided the basis for developing highly sophisticated macroeconomic models, some comprising thousands of variables and parameters. Here, the aim is to explain and predict the performance of the economy of a country or industry, focusing on fluctuations in broad aggregates, such as GNP, the level of employment or unemployment, total consumption and the rate of price inflation. For his part in this, Professor Wassily Leontief earned the Nobel Prize for devising input–output models that combine both micro- and macroeconomic features. These showed how certain coefficients predetermine flows of commodities between different production sectors and groupings. British economists at Cambridge have constructed a particularly ambitious 'social accounting matrix' (SAM). The model is aimed at demonstrating the essential processes of growth, with a mixture of input–output analysis and regression techniques. In such models, tracing all the chains of actions and reactions between numerous variables and parameters is a tedious job. A mathematical device called a 'cross-impact matrix' provides a comprehensive framework for examining these interactions in a systematic way. It is considered especially suitable when sets of estimates of different origin and uneven reliability are to be harmonized or integrated. Although cross-impact matrices can stand on their own, they are often used just as one input in the construction of large-scale economic models.

At the other end of the spectrum, the microeconomic level, managers of individual firms or factories can use a variety of mathematical techniques traditionally grouped under the heading 'operations research'. Operations research grew up in the Second World War and was successfully used for a wide variety of applications, from logistics decisions to bombing-target choice to accuracy of airborne anti-submarine weapons. Of special interest to managers are various stock-control models, queuing theories, lifecycle modelling, travelling-salesperson algorithms, Markov chains and elementary stochastic processes and the well-known linear programming, the true embodiment of this branch of applied mathematics. Just after the Second World War, a number of operations research specialists on both sides of the Atlantic proposed going beyond linear programming by developing quadratic and dynamic programming. But management practitioners so far have chosen to largely ignore these ideas.

Relationships between economic data sets can be tersely expressed and pictorially visualized using models with mathematical equations and geometrical figures. We may thus establish hypotheses about comparative economic performance to test conjectures and validate theories. That, roughly, was the conventional view about modelling that prevailed until recently. But models may be deceptive. Take for instance the UK Treasury's practice of relying on its quarter-century old, though periodically enhanced, macroeconomic model. It uses the model to construct the annual budget and to evaluate the likely impact on the country's economy. But since the early 1970s, the Treasury's predictions of future growth have been wrong in any given year by a factor of more that a third.[3] The Bank of England's own model has performed just as badly. So have the highly elaborate ones created in a number of universities and research centres in Europe, the USA and Japan. Operational research workers in the 1970s built a complete model of the shipbuilding industry. But it was so complex and required so much processing power that its predictions only kept up with, rather than passed, the real industry.

Building a macroeconomic model implies steering the way between oversimplification and overabundance of parameters and variables. The UK Treasury model at one time comprised 1,275 variables, 700 of which were considered possibly unnecessary, before it was pruned down to about half that size. Among several possible equations the analyst obviously chooses those that he considers to be the most-likely determinants of a system, which runs the risk of being inherently slanted to driving or 'explaining' trends and outcomes; that is, predicting only a desired outcome. Examples of such outcomes are how to boost a growth rate or speed up the increase of the country's currency reserves or increase exports of a class of commodities.

Of course earlier explanations and predictions of economic performance have often been found wanting. What is new today is not only that people challenge the accuracy of results and models. More importantly, they have begun of late to question the appropriateness of an analytic approach at all. Modelling methods are strongly suspected of not being accurate metaphors for the real world. And so forecasting methods and assumptions behind the models are under equal attack. At base lies a growing suspicion that no economic process may be encapsulated meaningfully as a sort of deterministic waterworks or a giant mathematical automaton. Such structures endlessly execute a predetermined sequence of motions, with no adaptive behaviour, feedback or active comprehension, and so little possibility of 'learning' from past mistakes.

But is it premature to jump to negative conclusions? Should the analytic tools in current use be thrown overboard? Or should a serious attempt be made to stretch them beyond their present basic linearity? Some of the traditional instruments of economic intelligence can be made more realistic and hence more pertinent. For instance, a dose of non-linear dynamics may be injected, by varying some key, hitherto passive-looking parameters, or again, by putting the whole exercise into a new perspective. Here is a case in point.

Figure 11 represents the envelope curve used for identifying and explaining the development of a rapidly evolving technology and possibly for forecasting its future pattern. The specific example used in this curve refers to the long-term evolution of unit costs of electronic memory chips. The general method is based on the observation that a given technological capacity is replaced by a superior one whenever the former begins to display diminishing returns. The data for each successive phase are plotted against time, giving a family of similarly shaped, partly overlapping curves, to which an envelope curve has been fitted.

Initially, this graph-plotting seems to have nothing to do with fractals or with chaotics at all. On reflection, however, we may realize that the concept of an envelope curve implicitly embodies the principle of self-similarity across scale, which lies at the heart of fractal geometry. The concept is widely applicable, for example to the spiral-like curve of hyperinflation when a certain threshold of price inflation has been passed. Or take the continual growth of unemployment throughout Europe over the past several years, or consider the deeper and deeper sinking into indebtedness of the entire African continent. In every instance of this kind, the successive phases of acceleration can be fitted with reasonable accuracy to a similar envelope curve.

But however useful grafting dynamic features (e.g. chaotic elements) on to the traditional tools of analysis may be, the endeavour soon meets an inherent barrier—the incompatibility between the linear and the non-linear approaches. A

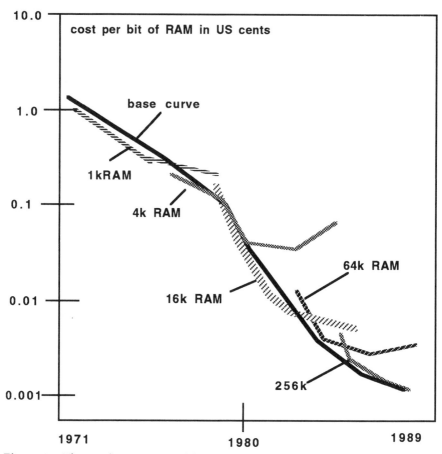

Figure 11. *The envelope curve used for identifying and explaining the development of a rapidly evolving technology*

Note: drawn from electronic memory prices, estimates 1971–84 and forecasts 1985–9 (in US cents/bits).

Source: adapted from Georges Anderla and Anthony Dunning, *Computer Strategies 1990–9* (Chichester and New York: John Wiley & Sons, 1987), p. 20.

change of tack appears the only way forward. We shall take an example to illustrate this. Let us assume that the market for a relatively new product, e.g. the cellphone, is expected to grow in the next few years, as suggested by curve A in Figure 12. Dotted-line curves B (lying above A) and C (below) have been added to indicate the likely range of error of estimation. Usually the exercise stops there. The decisions-makers are often quite impressed by the ingenuity of the model and the elegance of designs. But by building on the mathematics outlined in Chapters

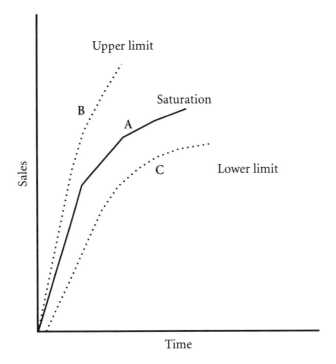

Figure 12. *Market for a new product, e.g. cell phones*

2 and 3, on attractors and bifurcations, it is possible to push the exploration of the alternative outcomes further.

First, notice that all the three curves A, B and C are parabolas, or more specifically distinct portions thereof. Their respective shapes could also easily be confused with a significant portion of the familiar Gompertz curve, during the phase of deceleration (see Figure 8). What differentiates each of A, B and C from the other two is the value of the crucial parameter, namely the assumed average rate of growth, r. For values of r below 3.0, the pattern of growth is generally smooth. However, once the rate of growth has passed a certain threshold there follows a succession of ups and downs, oscillating between some number of values that is a multiple of 2, i.e. 2, 4, 8, 16, etc. (see Figure 13). Our example refers to a family of parabolas. A key threshold exists beyond which chaos prevails—the critical value of $r = 3.57$.

How are we to interpret these erratic movements, as they alternate with lengthier periods of relative market-price stability? The simplified model we have used above is better known as the 'logistic map', initially proposed in the context of population dynamics. Lately, it has been used to explain and predict the financial bubbles and crashes that occur in commodities and financial markets.

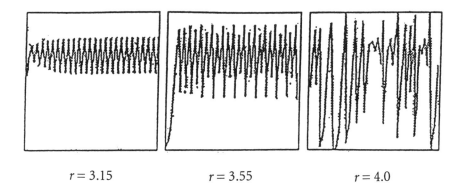

$r = 3.15$ $r = 3.55$ $r = 4.0$

Figure 13. *Showing passage from see-saw growth to chaotic growth (fitting a family of parabolas)*

Source: from 'Chaos on the trading floor', Robert Savit, *New Scientist*, 11 August 1990. Copyright © 1990 by New Science Publications. Used with permission.

These too, are characterized by their underlying structure of non-linear dynamics. Originally applied to the gold market, the logistic map is equally applicable to currency markets, e.g. the price of the yen in terms of the dollar. The common feature of all financial markets is the presence of limited self-regulatory mechanisms and, in particular, the working of feedback. For example, a steep increase in the price of an item causes demand for it to contract, bringing the price down (negative feedback), and vice versa (positive feedback). The parameter r (the rate of growth) quantifies the strength of the feedback, in other words, the amount by which the feedback is correcting, upwards or downwards, the anticipated output or volume of sales. Accumulated evidence suggests that for money and gold markets the adjustment process is non-linear as a rule.

Recently, Santa Fe Institute researchers developed a piece of software to simulate the stock exchange. As on the trading floor, there are (fictitious) buyers and sellers whose actions determine the price of the stock. Initially, their 'decisions' may have been programmed to buy and sell randomly. After a while, however, having learned from experience, the 'traders' begin to be guided by the respective dividend yield in relation to the going rate of interest—almost exactly as postulated by the classical economists. Still later, having analysed the stock's past performance, they 'discover' how to make money—i.e. to increase their holdings, by bidding a stock above and below its real and/or actual value. But so far, the Santa Fe Institute has not come up with a testable computer version able to simulate the behaviour of the whole economy or even a major economic sector. Macromodellers should take note that successful modelling is not yet within our grasp, even using chaotics.

NOTES

1 Quoted from Webster's *Third New International Dictionary* (see under 'scientific management').
2 Quoted from an address made at Independence Hall by the President of the Czech Republic on 4 July 1994, after being awarded the Philadelphia Liberty Medal (*International Herald Tribune*, 11 July 1994).
3 Robert Chote, 'Why the Chancellor is always wrong', *New Scientist*, 31 October 1992.

7

Technology Forecasting, with a Safety Net

You cannot fight against the future—time is on our side
from a speech by William Gladstone in 1866

Forecasting myths bite the dust

Two decades ago a leading specialist lamented, 'the current state of the art of technological forecasting models is quite primitive'.[1] Today it is no different. Technological forecasting is a key subject, and every year its importance grows, because the need to predict the creation, take-up and effects of new services and products has become far more critical as we have become so dependent on technology. For instance, a 1971 technology forecast became the blueprint for South Korea's economic take-off.[2] We should like to be able to understand technology directions across all sectors of industry. We need methods that help the professional manager (and the political leader) to form a more realistic, multifaceted vision of what the future is likely to hold for the core business, as well as to bring some understanding to the ordinary person in the street. For there is a growing realization that our contemporary world is becoming less and less certain in its technology assimilation. As possibilities expand, so it becomes less tenable to predict future development of technology by simply extrapolating current functionality. Not only has technological change gathered momentum of late, it has begun to zigzag in step with the turbulence of our economies and markets.

In this situation, many of the myths around technological forecasting are biting the dust. Fitting a trend to a set of historical data (e.g. the increase in the speed of aircraft over the years) and projecting this trend into the future to make inferences and generalizations has never been an exact scientific methodology. It takes a very brave researcher to use only such a mathematical model to predict directions, time-scales and the extent of a technological change. Quantitative forecasting, and in particular linear mathematical models initially designed for purposes of economic intelligence under stable conditions, are unable to relate to forecasting the birth and effects of the latest technological developments. This is especially true when the general outlook is one of perplexity, and so they are not included on our 'agenda' for the 21st century. Nor shall we devote much time to the other traditional methods—usually a choice between 'exploratory' forecasting (what-if or try-it-and-see scenarios) and 'normative' (or goal-setting) forecasting. The dividing line between the two is increasingly blurred and the normative approach may imply the introduction of quantitative measurements and methods, the value of which is doubtful.

And if we turn for alternatives to the qualitative methods, essentially based on intuitive assessments, there is little helpful or new. Nothing is fundamentally wrong with the flagship method of intuitive forecasting, the Delphi technique. The Delphi technique consists of interviewing a panel of experts ('oracles') on their views on a given subject (such as a future technology) and forming a summary document from the views, which is then critiqued by the group to produce a final version.

Pluses and minuses of Delphi

Developed in the mid-1960s at the Rand Corporation in Santa Monica, California, the Delphi technique is a family of methods that aim at insuring group participation in the preparation of forecasts. Before Delphi, predicting what the future might hold for technology or industry or social evolution was left mostly to fiction writers or at best to knowledgeable individuals—here an expert, there a famous guru. What is challengeable about Delphi is perhaps the pure form of its application. Inevitably it tends to leads to consensus forecasts, which may be inherently biased.

But these techniques can be boosted. The key thing in really useful futures forecasting is never to throw out from the oracles any early ideas that are novel and give new avenues for thought. For instance, supplementing the Delphi reductive approach with a parallel economic development analysis and barrier analysis research (looking for social and psychological barriers to technology take-up) can be a better route forward. We also look at two other techniques below—brainstorming and 'morphological' research.

In the past three decades, there have been literally hundreds of Delphi surveys made by or on behalf of a variety of public organizations, research institutes and private firms on every conceivable subject. Perhaps the largest Delphi study was carried out in Japan[3] with the participation of some 4,000 scientists and other specialists who were asked questions about more than 600 technological events. The above-mentioned Delphi-based research report sponsored prior to 1971 by South Korea's Ministry of Science and Technology became the blueprint for the tiger's spectacular development—holding economists spellbound for 20 years. The modern history of Delphi has had its ups and downs: witness a subsequent survey report issued by Rand Corporation, the original initiators of the method, according to which 'conventional Delphi is basically an unreliable and unscientific technique'.[4]

More recently, however, there has been a marked revival of interest in Delphi. Thus, in 1993, an official UK White Paper entitled 'Technology Foresight Programme' provided large-scale crystal ball gazing to identify techniques and technologies most likely to shape the global economy during the next 10 to 20 years.[5] The emphasis was to be on the 'feasibility' and the 'attractiveness' of future generic technologies, with applications across many different fields and industries.

In retrospect, on balance these endeavours offer a strangely contrasted picture. A great many technological forecasts have proved to be reasonably accurate, both as regards substance and the date of occurrence. This includes such technology events and phenomena as computer developments, growth of the use of databases, computerization of offices and factories, digitalization of telecommunications and landmark achievements in medicine, space research, biotechnology plus a host of military applications.

On the other hand, practically all Delphi surveys have erred in their predictions in some key areas. For instance they have mistakenly predicted reliable early-warning systems for natural disasters—major earthquakes, typhoons, etc. Likewise, we are far from the long-predicted technique of simultaneous translation of the spoken word into other languages, and accurate text entry from voice recognition software at low cost. Also, we have far to go before we can understand and cure mental diseases, understand the mechanism of ageing or simply learn how to design hardware-cum-software systems for direct processing of knowledge. All are things that groups of experts had forecast collectively as being 'just around the corner'. In view of the mixed-bag nature of the results, three aspects of the Delphi procedure are particularly open to challenge:

- the limited relevance of the basic methodology to forecasting technology;
- the conditioning of the experts; and
- the problem of focusing on significant events.

The popularity of the Delphi technique has generally been attributed to its distinctive features:

- equality of views via anonymity—no dominant view in group interaction;
- a built-in iteration to filter out 'noise' from the responses; and
- quantifiable responses if required.

These alleged advantages are more often than not a mixed blessing. While the confidential character of the panellists' responses is supposed to guarantee their sincerity some experts (often the most qualified) may choose to stay aloof.

Inviting the participants to comment at least twice—i.e. on the statistical results obtained during the first round and subsequently those of the second round—ensures an effective, substantial reduction of initial divergences of opinion. The danger, of course, is excessive conformity. Unconventional views, and especially unorthodox visionary thinking, get discarded, or at best are buried under the heap of safe-average estimates. The chaotics element has been removed. So forecasts tend to a norm and may be banal, just the expected and perhaps a long way from reality.

The ineptitude of the expertise of experts in futures prediction

Even the very involvement of experts in technology forecasting is controversial. After interviewing a range of experts from universities, government and industry, science and technology reporters from the *New York Times* came up with a rather impressive list of revolutionary and/or vastly enhanced technologies expected to play a crucial role before the year 2000. Witness the headline: 'In the '90s: Floating Trains, Mini Motors, Supercrops'.[6] The report was more accurate in citing enormously powerful computers that will understand speech and design new drugs, but perhaps less so on edge-of-space planes that fly at many times the speed of sound, non-conventional metals, abundant and clean energy. In reality, scientists as experts on the future are often completely off track. A month later, *The Economist* commented, 'it is notable how bad inventors are at predicting the success of their inventions, or even the uses to which they will be put'.[7] For instance, Edison was convinced that the phonograph would be an office device. He disliked the distraction of musical recording for the home. Ironically enough, the personal computer was initially thought to be most suitable for the home, yet it was the office that proved to be its natural environment.

The cloud overhanging so-called informed opinion cannot be easily dispersed, especially in connection with Delphi surveys. Yet, in quite a number of areas and processes, from invention to innovation, from prototyping to marketing the real product, there seems to be hardly any alternative but to seek the views of the researchers involved beforehand, the designers and engineers and other workers in the field. For instance, virtually all the Delphi surveys carried out in the last few years have confirmed an overwhelming consensus among leading computer designers that the medium-term future was to belong to massively parallel processing involving thousands of interlinked processors. And this was a technology considered by all concerned to be an underdog just four years earlier. Summing up, using experts and Delphi may lead to a kind of tunnel vision in spotlighting the average opinion of 51 per cent of the panellists. The pure form of the technique looks away from whatever does not fit the central image.

Sniffing out promising ideas

Another tricky problem in forecasting is picking out auspicious ideas and translating them into technologically significant events, advances or new discoveries. How to proceed generally can be influenced by the scope of the survey—be it assessing ongoing broad trends or pinpointing specific foreseeable innovations. The purpose of the exercise is also crucial, e.g. whether the sponsor organization aims at defining a new development strategy or has a more limited goal, such as redesigning readily marketable products. Here, Delphi cannot be dismissed so lightly. It does highlight avenues that would never be dreamed of, if the results of the first round are used.

Moreover, two approaches could enhance Delphi surveys if properly used. We concentrate below on these two—brainstorming and 'morphological' research. In the present state of economies, markets and technologies these can offer potential advances. Another useful way of looking at the future world, multiple scenarios (or 'multiplets'), can be superior to a single-vision exercise, and a further technique is to build detailed parallel analogies to a particular situation. Both may be combined with brainstorming and both are well fitted to focusing on gaps in technology and providing inputs into research planning.

For a Delphi analysis, it is possible to start off with a blank sheet of paper and ask the panellists themselves to compile a checklist of what they regard as relevant events to be taken into consideration. When the panel members are drawn from researchers and technical people, they may be provided with a 'context' statement, specifying the political, economic and environmental conditions and constraints. Overzealousness can lead to giving a tentative scenario that restricts the freedom of vision of experts. A better approach in some cases is to begin with a list of events, generated independently of the panel. The panel is then asked to give their opinions as to the likelihood of each event and the probable date of fulfilment. This is where the brainstorming ought to come in. It should decisively inject just the required dose of haphazard, non-linear effects into any sclerotic views of what comes next in a technological development or what the market is likely to choose.

Using Brainstorming to introduce chaotics: self-organized consistency in brainstorming

Brainstorming is essentially an exercise in creative thinking through live interactions. It is mostly used to elicit as many solutions to a specific problem as possible and more generally to generate potentially rewarding suggestions. Ideally, the outcome is a wide range of choices for the decision-maker to act upon, with options and alternatives reminiscent of bifurcations in chaos theory. Some of its basic rules might include the following. Freewheeling must be unimpeded and uninhibited. The most paradoxical of solutions are welcome. The 'crazier' the idea, the better. (Italian poet and philosopher Dante noted that science is never fostered by restatement of previous findings and hearsay evidence.) Criticism, however well-meant, is banned. But piggybacking on the ideas of others is fair game, since it encourages synergy within the panel of experts. Brainstorming, after all, is intended to act as a stimulus to creativity, and this is often best achieved by stealing other people's bright ideas and extending them (as all academics must know well to succeed).

But not every brainstorming session succeeds in producing innovative solutions. Inconclusive exercises are as numerous as dismal failures. Much depends on the panellists' expertise, real depth of understanding of the particular problem and the goals. Their reactivity to coparticipants and, of course, the special abilities of the group moderator are key factors. However, when the fit is good and the interplay of ideas and associations operates properly, the results have sometimes been very useful. The end-product may not take the form of a blueprint for decision-making and implementation. But it clearly amounts to significantly more than a listing of random suggestions—a compilation of disconnected predictions. Such a group can somehow manage to come up with 'findings' and 'prescriptions' that are by and large mutually compatible or complementary with each other and crystallize around a few distinctive themes. Such group-induced consistency arises spontaneously in very much the same way as matter self-organizes into ever more complex structures, according to theory of complex systems. This harmonization of individual views cannot possibly be ascribed to a specific recipe, but rather to the group's internal chemistry. Perhaps what we are seeing is the organizational effect of chaotics at a mental level—cognitive chaotics.

Morphological mapping

Most Delphi tabulations are presented in terms of the median and the two middle quartiles leaving out altogether the two outer quartiles, i.e. 49 per cent of the opinions collected (see Figure 14).

To make good some of these drastic shortcomings, it has been suggested that, perhaps, a 'minority report' should supplement the unduly curtailed, time-compressed views of the majority of experts. However there is rarely a single homogeneous minority viewpoint, but at least two opposites. If you need unconventional, possibly outrageous estimates of the future in a given area, the minority views should become the initial raw material for another distinct Delphi survey, with a fresh set of uncommitted experts.

		Time of Realization
		1975 1980 1985 1990 1995 2000

Advances in diagnosis and therapeutics

Complete surgical treatment

16. The problems of immunization, rejection reactions and organ donors in transplants will be solved and human heart transplants will become common

17. The problem of immunization and rejection reactions in transplants will be solved and social, ethical and religious problems will also be solved. Heart transplants from animal to man will be performed without emotional resistance.

18. The implantation of man-made hearts will become a common therapeutic method. (complete substitution of an artificial heart for a living heart.)

19. Development of a method to permit the removal of affected organs from the body and return thereof after complete treatment.

Obtaining and preservation of blood, tissues and organs

20. Development of artificial blood which is able to carry oxygen.

21. A blood transfusion between different blood types will become possible

22. Development of a method for low temperature preservation of organs for transplants without damage to the tissues

23. To provide sufficient operation time for first-aid treatment in the case of accidents, a method will be developed for hibernation of the patient temporarily at low temperature.

Figure 14. *Extract from a Delphi survey*

Source: Science and Technology Developments up to A.D. 2000, published by Japan Techno-Economics Society, Tokyo, 1972. Used with permission.

This is where 'morphological research' comes in. In the words of its inventor, the astrophysicist Fritz Zwickey, the method is intended 'to identify, index, count and parameterize the collection of all possible devices to achieve a specified functional capability'. The purpose is to ensure that all feasible solutions are considered before a choice is made. Zwickey is known for his contribution to the development of the jet- engine and it was in this area that he made his original analysis.[8]

The systematic approach embodied in morphological research presupposes that the problem to be solved can be defined with great precision. Characteristic parameters must be identified, and each parameter must be broken down into component elements. Finally, all possible combinations must be listed and mapped and their relative performance estimated. In one such study of the options available in rocket construction, 11 parameters were identified, which gave a total of some 25,000 possible combinations.[9]

This fairly heavyweight—even rather cumbersome—procedure has been applied not only in aviation and defence research but also in ocean transport, automatic transmissions for cars, agricultural fertilizers, functional fluids, retail sales data capture and many other areas—with varied success. After going through a period of oblivion, the essentials of morphological research are once again coming into their own. They are recognized as a valuable stepping-stone to improving our comprehension of an open-ended evolution of a technology, so characteristic of today's world.

The technique employs the same condition that a master chess-player (or a Japanese master Go-player) uses—concentrate on the essentials by eliminating or suppressing whole classes of irrelevant parameters and combinations. There is no one way to implement this and several approaches have been used. For example faced with the overwhelming task of dealing with several hundred, or several thousand, combinations, some researchers resign themselves to employ a simple rule of thumb. Take one 'plausible' configuration at a time and vary just one parameter to see what improvements can be obtained. This has been dubbed the 'small perturbation' approach. Other researchers have banked on pruning down the number of combinations to a more manageable size. They eliminate those configurations that are logically conflicting, physically unfeasible, or manifestly inferior to some alternative solution. But this can entail the risk of missing truly innovative, hitherto untested configurations. A more sophisticated approach is aimed at developing a morphological matrix. It delineates all combinations that have previously been tried and concentrates on the periphery, where *terra cognita* meets with *terra incognita*. This is where known configurations may be altered—albeit marginally—by the addition of novel, untested features.

This concept, despite being attractive, fell victim in the 1970s to the prevailing craze for quantified deductive reasoning. Robert U. Ayres, the godfather

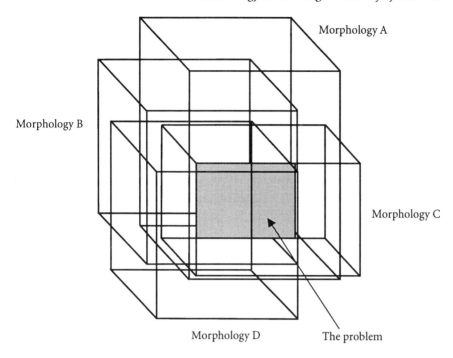

Figure 15. *Morphological mapping*
Cutting through the maze of overlapping morphologies A, B, C and D with a view to locating the central technological problem to be solved

of technological forecasting has developed the somewhat pedantic-sounding 'breakthrough opportunity index for differing densities of occupied territory on morphological space', complete with an intricate set of postulated parameters and weights.[10] Unfortunately, however ingenious it appears at first sight, most attempts at formalized reasoning of the logical-deduction type (whether supported or not by numerical weights) flounder when confronted with engineering constraints. A current practice is to use the morphological map to identify existing bottlenecks and to assign priorities to their removal. What is really at issue is how to scoop up hundreds of variables into one technique, together with specifications for the enabling technologies to be developed first, and the additional prior research that might be required.

Figure 15 suggests a short-cut approach to this conundrum. It is based on the idea that, whatever the number of basic parameters used, the resulting virtual technologies are partly overlapping. The most effective (and also the most time-efficient) method is to avoid treating them sequentially. Instead concentrate on the 'problem focus' represented by the shaded area in the diagram, a parallel, overlapping approach.

What-if and if-not scenarios

A further key question remains to be considered in laying down the lines of a dynamic approach to technological forecasting, because it should be consistent with the accelerated change of technology, as is embodied in chaotics. Besides brainstorming and in addition to morphological mapping, are there some other significant ways to form creative inputs to working out whole sets of alternative predictions?

Anticipations, futures, vignettes and scenarios are loose, partly interchangeable terms that come immediately to mind. On the other hand, scenario-writing is a specific technique that attempts to set up a logical sequence of events either leading to a stated outcome or specifying the way of achieving a desirable objective. In either case, a single, one-track chain of events is envisaged. There is practically no room for iterative tinkering. This is future determinism in its extreme form. For instance, the 1967 Kahn–Wiener scenario for the postindustrial society asserted that income per head would reach 50 times its preindustrial level, that business firms would cease to be the major source of invention and that 'efficiency' would no longer be a motivating force.[11]

To appreciate the frailty of the single scenario technique, try to put yourself into the shoes of a seasoned businessperson or a government official whose responsibilities include monitoring the ups and downs of post-Soviet Russia's conversion to a market economy. If you were on the board of a sizeable corporation with established connections in Russia, would you be prepared to recommend investing in the creation of a manufacturing unit there in order to gain a solid foothold in this potentially vast market—and in what branch or speciality? Assuming you were the boss of a small high-tech outfit in America or Western Europe, would you rush to Moscow to forge a link with a Russian partner whose products are hopelessly obsolete? And if you were a Western banker, would you anticipate more turmoil in that market, or stable conditions sooner rather than later?

Some tentative answers to some of these highly topical questions are to be found in an article that appeared in the *International Herald Tribune*[12] (see Box 5). Although written shortly after Prime Minister Viktor S. Chernomyrdin, a conservative industrialist, had set up a new Russian government, back in January 1994, the analysis retains much of its value. Under the heading 'Where the Kremlin Goes from Here', the author, Fred Hiatt, identified four sharply contrasted scenarios, ranging from moderately optimistic to frankly apocalyptic.

In many ways, Hiatt's report is a remarkable piece. It has the perspective, the large sweep and the alternative formulation of hypotheses that benefit the difficult exercise of forecasting in a truly chaotic situation. Although the author is alien to chaos theory, he deliberately uses the technique of bifurcation, which lies at the heart of chaotics, in constructing his sequence. This is especially noticeable

Box 5. *Four scenarios for Russia's future follow the concepts of chaotics*

Scenario No. 1, 'Things Get Better', assumed that the Prime Minister and his like-minded colleagues will be able to 'develop a rational industrial policy, giving the state a substantial role for years to come', allowing firms elbow-room for initiative, protecting them from excessive foreign competition and altogether preserving Russia's scientific and technological position.

Scenario No. 2: Should, however, moderate reformers fail, 'Ukrainization of the Russian Economy' could become a more likely alternative. 'Ukrainization' stood for massive, wasteful featherbedding of unproductive, overstaffed, government-owned enterprises, leading directly to hyperinflation, scary government deficits and a general impoverishment of the population.

Scenario No. 3 'A Strong Hand': 'The industrialists lead Russia down Ukraine's path, as in the second scenario. Crime, corruption and cynicism grow. The regional fragmentation of the nation . . . accelerates. Voices increasingly call for a strong hand, for order, for national-patriotic or fascist solutions. "There could be a social explosion", said Gleb Yakunin, a reformist lawmaker. "The situation may destabilize, the army may step in and other forces, too. The situation is dangerous." '

Scenario No. 4 is significantly entitled 'The Muddle Continues'. It goes like this: 'The conservatives have the upper hand, but Mr. Yeltsin insists that he still backs the free market. The government zigs one way, zags another . . . Cushioned by vast oil and gas reserves, Russia, unlike Ukraine, can slide along this way for a long time, with a declining standard of living. Brave foreign firms, betting on the long term, continue cautiously to invest. Meanwhile, private business fitfully grows, increasing the constituency for reform. But the gap between rich and poor grows, too, increasing the appeal of the nationalists.

'Of course, in a country as contradictory as Russia, where the nation's age can be counted as more than 1,000 years or barely 2 . . . and where so much still turns on Mr. Yeltsin—any predictions are almost certain to be proved wrong.'

---

when passing from scenario 2 to scenario 3. And by quoting a score of Russian economists of all shades, he creates the sense of acting as a mouthpiece for them all.

For all the 'advances' in forecasting techniques and more powerful computers, the new 'crystal balls' still seem rather clouded, in particular the consensus forecasts such as Delphi. Generally, keeping the options open for as long as possible, especially in the field of technology, is the critical success factor for management in times of transition and turmoil. This somewhat reinforces the arguments in favour of a flexible approach to technological forecasting. The lesson of all this is: never end up stuck with one solution to a problem (what mathematicians refer to as uniqueness theorems). Techniques to avoid this danger include multitrack forecasting, parallel or multiple scenarios, morphological mapping and brainstorming with built-in consistency. And keep in mind that competitive (even duplicative) research and forecasting can sometimes provide more motivation and even be more innovative than cooperative ventures (especially when financed jointly by firms whose raison d'être is to share the market). Multioption forecasts highlight the forgotten turns and alternatives.

The philosophy of chaotics supports a pluralism of views and so generates more democracy in the various disciplines of technology and science, because the barriers of belief can be more easily overturned. Disputing and dissenting ideas are more forthcoming yet treated with more respect—and so are explored to their logical end. In some ways a chaotic world is a more democratic one.

NOTES

1 Joseph P. Martino, *Technological Forecasting for Decision-Making* (New York: Elsevier, 1972), p. 205.
2 *Korea in the Year 2000* (Seoul, South Korea: Korean Institute of Science and Technology, on behalf of the Ministry of Science and Technology, 1971).
3 *Science and Technology Developments up to AD. 2000* (Tokyo: published by the Japan Techno-Economics Society, January 1972).
4 Rand Report R1283, April 1974; quoted in Wayland Kennet (ed.), *The Futures of Europe* (Cambridge: Cambridge University Press, 1976), p. 28.
5 Robert Chote, 'Why the Chancellor is always wrong', *New Scientist*, 31 October 1992, pp. 26–31.
6 'In the '90s, floating trains, mini motors, supercrops', *International Herald Tribune*, 3 January 1991.
7 'How electronics learnt to stop worrying and love the quantum', *The Economist*, 16 February 1991, pp. 75–6; see also 'The edge of ignorance: a survey of science', *The Economist*, 14 February 1991, pp. 1–18.
8 Fritz Zwicky, *Morphological Astronomy* (Berlin: Springer Verlag, 1957); Fritz Zwicky, *Discovery, Invention, Research* (New York: Macmillan, 1969); see also Gordon Wills *et al.*, *Technological Forecasting* (London: Penguin, 1972).
9 Kennet, *The Futures of Europe*, p. 28.
10 Robert U. Ayres, *Technological Forecasting and Long-Range Planning* (New York: McGraw-Hill, 1969).
11 H. Kahn and A. Wiener, *The Year 2000* (New York: Macmillan, 1967).
12 Fred Hiatt, 'Where the Kremlin goes from here', *International Herald Tribune*, 22–23 January 1994.

8

Breakthrough and Soft Landing

The intelligence for a breakthrough requires a conversion to a radically higher and broader conception

Walter Lippmann

In Chapter 5 we showed the business model of increasing rather than decreasing, returns. In Chapters 5 to 7 the groundwork was laid for an understanding of the directions of change and consequently for charting policies and actions to be put on our agenda for the 21st century. The present chapter is another building-block in this series, in which we focus on the dynamics of techno-industrial breakthroughs. Just what is the process of arriving at a 'breakthrough'?

Chaos and complexity theories can offer credible alternatives to the deterministic vision of the universe and of life on earth. But we need a critical review of the whole idea of 'breakthrough' and the controversy it has stirred. The how and why of beneficial breakthroughs should become the primary concern of decision-makers. The breakthroughs we are especially concerned with often result from a concurrence of multiple forces and processes, by accidental or deliberate means. This is an event upon which the theories of chaos and complexity throw a refreshingly new light. It becomes rapidly apparent that to identify possible breakthroughs it is not enough to scrutinize the technological horizon and monitor early symptoms of forthcoming inventions. We cannot rely on the idea that breakthroughs can occur in a premeditated fashion, somehow induced by some kind of system. But chaos and complexity principles are insufficient by themselves to capture the intricate reality, the timing and events of the activities and actions that come together to precipitate a breakthrough. So the better part of this chapter focuses on the chemistry of breakthrough, specifically in the techno-industrial sphere.

The need for refocusing

The Economist proclaimed, half-jokingly, 'A breakthrough is neither a tadpole nor a statistical series'. What, then, is the thing we are talking about? Could, for example, breakthrough be in essence 'a conversion to a radically higher and broader conception', as the columnist Walter Lippmann once suggested?[1]

The more classic definitions are generally unhelpful. It is all very well to use superlatives such as 'sensational advance' or 'superseding the previous technology'. But they just muddy the waters of a clear definition by ambivalence between the terms 'breakthrough' and 'invention'. Is breakthrough simply a borderline case of invention, of innovation? Such academic debates are of little interest. Fortunately, we can fall back on more solid criteria developed recently by the 1993 Nobel Prize-winner for economics, Professor Robert Fogel.[2] He asserted that breakthrough implies a clean break with the past, sparking off a wave of transformation throughout the techno-industrial system and, presumably, in the basic patterns of distribution and consumption as well. The second half of the preceding sentence is our own, yet it is very much in keeping with Fogel's thesis.

According to this view, even when inventions are numerous and replace a previous technology—for instance, the transition from steam to electricity or the conversion to nuclear power—they do not by themselves amount to a breakthrough. By this, we imply modifications in underlying technical and socio-economic conditions. 'When this is the case', said Fogel, 'a new-age techno-industrial system is born.'[2] Or, a large enough quantitative change becomes a qualitative change. Clearly, the concept of a breakthrough for a whole industrial domain encompassing private and public consumption is considerably broader than that for a science or technology area alone. Furthermore, breakthrough in this sense fits in with the scheme expounded here.

What is astonishing in approaching the issue of breakthrough is the lack of a neat conceptual framework. There are basically two opposing views—with variants—but neither of them tells the whole story. Neither school is capable of elucidating convincingly the process involved in breakthroughs under different conditions and dissimilar circumstances. They overconcentrate on technology and are relatively unconcerned by such important areas as military research and warfare, globalization of markets, organization of work, or changing social systems. Let us look at these two schools of thought.

According to the first, major innovations and breakthroughs have their roots in outside events; that is, they originate from causes external to the system or field of application. They are usually ascribed to a lone inventor or small team of disinterested researchers, in principle unconnected with the would-be manufacturers, sellers or end-users. The opposing camp claims that significant inventions and breakthroughs occur when society needs them. And so they have to come on some kind of schedule. This is said to have been the case for the car, pharmaceuticals, rocket launchers and TV, among other things. It seems to be particularly true in times of war. For instance, the ancient Greek war galleys needed to be more manoeuvrable in the battle to defeat Xerxes of Persia in 480BC, and the sliding seat for rowing gave them the power and manoeuvrability (this invention was then forgotten until the 19th century). British radar was perfected in the 1930s in time for the Battle of Britain. The multiple rocket launcher was brought to perfection at the end of the Second World War to drive back German armoured divisions on the Russian front. Much of the expansion in Israeli high-tech industries has been fuelled by the military effort—for example, frequency-hopping radio, which is now used for mobile radio systems for businesses in the USA, was developed for the Israeli army.

The theory of the inevitability of inventions has many supporters, but the reasoning is frequently open to challenge. For example, the *Encyclopaedia Britannica* lends support to the argument that (more or less) identical, multiple instances of a discovery or invention are proof that the occurrence is 'in keeping with the natural order of things'. Under the entry for 'inventions and discoveries', one finds the following: 'Given a technical heritage and the right social environment, invention is inevitable'.[3] For instance, Israel is experiencing a wealth of high-tech expansion due to three factors: the impetus of military technology, the influx of over 600,000 highly qualified immigrants from the Soviet Union and the creation of a major venture-capital industry through the government's 'incubator programme'.[4] Three such relevant breakthrough case histories are summarized in Box 6 on page 96.

Just what are the early symptoms of a breakthrough?

The theory of the inevitability of invention can be thought of as a kind of baseline of technological foreknowledge. Behind this idea lies the desire to capitalize on prerecognition. In order to improve predictive powers and credibility further, various other warning indicators have been proposed. Below we briefly review three of perhaps the most popular notions: precursor events, equivalent inventions and technological fusion. The pros and cons of each are roughly comparable in weight. In principle each signal contains a piece of valuable information. It is the interpretation of the myriad bits of data without the help of a series of landmarks that poses problems.

Precursor events

Considering that any specific technology goes through a certain lifecycle, many people stress the importance of precursor events capable of providing the forecaster with advanced indications as to what is standing in the wings. In the example cited in Box 6, the invention by Kilby and Noyce of the integrated circuit (and eventually the advent of the microprocessor) could have been inferred from the invention of the transistor some ten years earlier. The link between the two events was straightforward, and the causal chain a simple direct one. However,

Box 6. *Three breakthroughs from reading the cards correctly*

The story of the steamboat has often been used to demonstrate the occurrence of repeat inventions and innovations. American-born clock-maker and brass merchant John Fitch began work on the invention of the steam engine and steamboat in 1785. Two years later, his first boat was launched, and it began operating on the Delaware river the same year. While Fitch was not alone in developing the steam engine and steamboat, there is good evidence that he was the first to invent the American steamboat, beating by a short head William Symington, a Scottish engineer, who built a marine engine in 1788. Robbed of the opportunity to commercialize his invention, John Fitch eventually committed suicide in 1798. Other men in America and in England had developed steamboats in the closing years of the 18th century, yet it was Robert Fulton's *Clermont*, launched with considerable fanfare in 1807, that is marked as an event in American maritime history. Besides enjoying a lucrative monopoly over the steamboat navigation on the Hudson River, Fulton won the image of the inventor of the steamboat that has stuck in the minds of most Americans.

Closer to today, the integrated circuit had two (interchangeable) fathers. In 1958, Jack Kilby of Texas Instruments and Robert Noyce over at Fairchild Semiconductor were making a strong push towards the monolithic circuit, in which the resistors, capacitors and transistors and their interconnections are fabricated in one piece of semiconducting material. In those days it was germanium or silicon. Thus the first all solid-state circuit, subsequently called the integrated circuit, was produced.

Their second brainchild was also destined to occupy a key niche in the history of modern computing. In 1968, a decade later, Kilby and Noyce separately succeeded in achieving another key goal, producing the first microprocessor—an entire central-processing unit of a computer, including registers and essential memory as well as input/output channels—on a single chip. By 1971, 4-bit microprocessors were in quantity production, first the Intel 4004, and soon afterwards the Intel 4040.

In each instance—the steamship, integrated circuit and the microprocessor—the techno-industrial breakthroughs seemed more spectacular because they had been prompted by keen, highly visible competition between rival projects.

foreseeing the transistor would have been a different matter altogether. There are those who believe that no forecaster, say back in 1939 looking 30 years ahead, could have anticipated the transistor, or therefore visualized the phenomenal development of consumer electronics. Others claim that by 1939, 'it could have been possible for someone to predict the transistor, on the basis of existing theory and from advanced warnings obtained from patents'.[5] But nobody felt confident enough to make that prophecy.

Are we any wiser today, possibly having learned from past failures? Recent business experience does not suggest an optimistic outlook. In the 1960s and early 1970s, mainframe manufacturers, including IBM, largely stood aloof from mini-computers, although their development occurred at the same time as the IBM System/360. Belatedly converted to the minis, leading computer vendors of those days again failed to capitalize on personal computers—until 1981, when IBM reversed its previous policy and suddenly launched its own PC, hastily put together with help from subcontractors. Unfortunately for IBM, it was too late to stop the trend, and IBM did not seem to forecast its true destiny in a 'legitimized' PC market. It was not the challenge from a competing vendor, perhaps the Japanese mainframe suppliers, but from a competing technology (the PC) that led to the unstoppable decline of IBM's core mainframe sales in relation to Big Blue's other businesses.

Technology and product differentiation

Necessity is said to be the mother of invention—perhaps even more so of innovation. History show that both materialize when the necessity arises. However, different inventors may come up with technically different solutions to the same problem. Interested businessmen may of course pick up the respective proto-types, or designs, and wrap them up in discrete packages, stressing the differences. A good illustration is provided by the three competing high-speed train technologies—Japanese bullet train, French TGV and German ICE. While monitoring for prior, or precursor, events can furnish advanced warning that a breakthrough is on its way, it is much trickier to anticipatively interpret parallel, yet distinct, technological developments, such as these rival high-speed train technologies.

Technological fusion

The well-known System/360, IBM's flagship computer, although now over 30 years old, still stands as an accomplished example of a major multidisciplinary endeavour—a technological fusion of disciplines. The System /360 effort led to simultaneous revolutionary breakthroughs in the philosophy of computing, the design of software and integrated hardware/software systems. It was rewarded by an unequalled commercial success—breakthrough in commercial computing. In a different field, chip-making, the Japanese dominance can be traced to the blending of skills in a concerted effort from 1978 onwards. Before, the Japanese had produced discrete devices, not microcircuits. This cooperation led to a specific infusion of know-how from Japanese solid-state scientists, who produced the pure crystals needed for the larger silicon wafers and the ideas for tighter packing of devices. This was combined with superior microcircuit-printing technology, perfected by Fuji, Canon, Ricoh and other camera makers. The cooperation was further consolidated by unique quality control, dust-free environments and similar technological infusions. All was orchestrated quite deliberately by MITI, the ministry that has pushed several waves of Japanese technical advance through the coordination of competing players. And MITI is the heritage of a military tradition, growing out of the procurement executive of war-time Japan. Thus, monitoring breakthroughs implies understanding events, variables, trends, a maze of figures and other indicators to build an overall tableau. But we need a comprehensive, realistic framework. And that is where chaotics comes into its own.

Two major types of breakthrough rule

We have now reached the point to bring together our various arguments. The fundamental question is: how can we conjecture with a reasonable degree of confidence that a techno-industrial breakthrough is in the offing.

This query may now be refined, by asking ourselves: how sweeping is the coming change likely to be? And furthermore: how can we minimize the risk of being caught in the wrong place at the wrong time? Such a haphazard approach to the monitoring of forewarning signals may not even offer a 50 per cent chance. What has been most frustrating and prejudicial on our trek into future supposi-tions has been the sad absence of some form of compass. Can chaos and com-plexity theories between them provide the guiding light and stepping-stones to an understanding of the dynamics of breakthroughs? Could they also identify any prerequisites and even assess the likely consequences (however roughly)? Let us start with a couple of well-known examples.

The discovery of penicillin and its rapid universal uptake is a clear case of a breakthrough. It underscores the close similarity between a random event in medical research (Fleming's route to first discovery was somewhat accidental) and the basic tenet of chaos theory. The latter claims that major upheavals or re-bounds, whether in science, industry or social organization, may be traced back to a trifling, often local occurrence, considered unimportant at the time. Let us call this a breakthrough of the first type. During most of the Industrial Revolution, independent solitary discoveries and inventions must have provided the better part of the 'innovation fuel' that powered economic and industrial progress, for want of other types of organized research. Breakthroughs of the first type dominated this period.

Now consider another breakthrough, perhaps the first landing on the moon, and its many spin-offs, such as Teflon non-stick coatings for pots and pans. This breakthrough was achieved through the culmination of a ten-year research effort pursued through trial and error, and in many ways it defied the odds. This type epitomizes complexity theory and its key axiomatic proposition, the principle of permanent self-organization/reorganization. We will call this a breakthrough of the second type. This type is symptomatic of advances nowadays, which are often achieved on a much larger scale, through wider multidisciplinary research with costly prototyping and comprehensive testing. Integrating the dynamic concept of increasing returns with the philosophy of large-scale multidisciplinary research—the holistic approach—produces 'creeping breakthroughs'. We are implying that techno-industrial breakthrough is a progressive affair. This type is beyond the resources of the limited-size specialized laboratory or individual researcher (with a few exceptions).

Essentially, by using two rather loose analogies we are trying to sketch out a new unified approach to the problem of analysing breakthrough and its forecasting. We are assuming that there is a kind of equivalence between (i) a potent, yet one-shot (chancy) discovery taking place outside the 'mainstream' or 'establishment' (which might eventually pick it up, amplify and exploit it) and (ii) the butterfly effect of chaos theory, capable of provoking a tornado elsewhere, which we look to for the creeping breakthrough. Additionally, the theory of complex systems seems to provide the clue to the 'invisible' coordination that eventually results in a focused attack on a baffling major obstacle. Then when the essential problem has been cracked, the effects of complex systems ensure spontaneous take-up and spin-offs. Some of the component actions of this forecasting may look ordinary. It is the make-up, and even more so, the making-up that counts. Perhaps our analysis needs to go deeper.

Analysing today's breakthroughs

We can look at the basis of nearly all major modern techno-industrial breakthroughs as an intricate catalytic process. But unless we can catch an overall vision of the breakthrough in the making (and its aftermath) it is hard to gauge the effect of each component on the outcome. The catalytic process of a successful breakthrough must ensure a close coordination of three business activities: not just technology research but also production and sales (all propelled by an appropriate culture and management). This triad must then galvanize other parts of the business into a kind of fury of related activities: services and support, production engineering, complementary research, feasibility studies, laboratory testing and market surveys. Cost–benefit analysis, financial studies and restructuring the organization for a new focus tend to follow on from this. This is a lot going on simultaneously. And it is hard to estimate the composite gain, because the total benefit from a breakthrough far exceeds the sum of earnings obtainable in its absence (by the previously separate activities or units). At this point, it may be useful to look for an example to guide us on the conditions for a breakthrough: the high-tech industries. Six core characteristics have been exhibited by such major high-tech industries as electronics, computers, biotechnology, chemicals and telecommunications. For the past two or three decades they have:

- had a far higher rate of technical breakthroughs than average;
- suffered cut-throat global competition—equivalent business conditions to all out war;
- swallowed enormous amounts of fixed investment, out of proportion to their variable costs;
- enjoyed prolonged periods of sky-high net earnings;
- operated under increasing returns; and
- outshone all other industrial sectors in terms of general inventiveness (numbers of patents, advances and new generations of product).

This gives us a feeling for the kind of prerequisites for a breakthrough.

Classifying technologies: is this the great breakthrough ... or not?

And there is a lesson to be drawn from these points, beyond the criteria for a breakthrough. They allow us to classify and relate technologies, ranking the technological components as a breakthrough, or as part of one, or as less than a breakthrough. We can also position new technologies that transcend conventional boundaries, between science and technology, or between different disciplines in their own class. We can designate an 'anchor' technology as one that has the potential for galvanizing around it a set of complementary techniques and inventions. It has the power to change the scale of operation or to provide an alternative modus operandi in any application. Additionally, it is capable of seriously curtailing the usage of an older technology. History furnishes us with quite a few illustrations of anchor technologies—e.g. printing, the steam engine, the assembly line and the small synchronous AC electric motor, which revolutionized appliances and made industry far more flexible. Within information technology, the transistor then the microprocessor, magnetic and optical storage, local area networks, digital processing of signals and messages, and industrial processors (built into anything from washing machines to industrial robots to cars) qualify as anchor technologies. In contrast, the minicomputer, parallel processing, the solid-state videoconferencing camera and the router would not qualify as candidates. Thus, before taking any implementation decision, management should be able to figure out what kind of Pandora's box is about to be opened with a new technology. But seldom does a particular technique or process stand on its own, in a sort of vacuum. Conventionally we would separately classify: competing technologies, equivalent (or parallel duplicative) technologies, supporting technologies and complementary technologies.

Even more crucial are the criteria of enablement. The complete implementation of almost any new invention or idea depends on the current state of the art and perhaps coinventions—really how fast and efficiently the missing links can be inserted. For instance, take the long-range jet bomber, suggested as a counter to Soviet rearmament in 1947. Due to its massive fuel demand, until the problem of its safe air-refuelling was solved the weapon was viewed as not being viable by the Pentagon. More recently, the development of multimedia communication and digital high-definition television awaited giant strides in data-compression techniques (based on fractal geometry). Although in many cases different technologies, disciplines or specific techniques advance more or less in parallel, even in sympathy as it were, there are also many instances of considerable delay between the discovery and the implementation. Conversely, many a contemporary breakthrough has its roots in an event that took place decades earlier. For instance fax took off in the 1980s. It was invented over 100 years earlier. But its real take-off awaited standards, a new technology for a much lower price-point and business and office conditions that demanded reuse of the ubiquitous voice telephone line for document images. Even ten years before, in the 1970s, many market studies predicted that fax would never be widely since it was inconvenient (you had to stand over it and feed in pages) and gave relatively poor-quality documents that had no legal standing.

Concepts of flight go far back into history. The detailed observations in the notebooks of Leonardo da Vinci (1452–1519) marked the beginning of the scientific study of flight. But implementation took another 400 years. If Alan Turing was the father of modern computing, Charles Babbage (1792–1871), designer of the 'analytical engine', is often recognized as its godfather. But the final Babbage engine was never built in his time.

What it takes to recognize a breakthrough: complex systems analysis following critical paths and climbing relevance trees

And it is not just an enabling technology that may be missing. The intellectual inability to see the electronic writing on the wall can be equivalent to the absence of an enabling technology for the implementation of a breakthrough. An instance: when Chuck Geschke and John Warnock left Xerox PARC to form Adobe and the PostScript success, had top management at Xerox been familiar with breakthrough recognition and perhaps chaos theory, they might have theorized that the early bird often sets the standard (with positive feedback market effects) and can then call the tune for some time, so a major investment in Adobe would have been wise. And similarly, Xerox's Alan Kay is said to have dreamed up the notebook computer in 1968, when huge, shared mainframes were reigning supreme. When, in 1974, Kay and his small team created a prototype PC, complete with icons, menus and screen windows, the project was not then recognized by management as suitable technology for a mass-market product.

To help decision-makers reduce the risks of missing such key opportunities, a systematic way to increase the likelihood of identifying breakthroughs is needed. The obvious question in such a game of chance is: can complex systems or chaos theory help? Perhaps. Walter Lippmann was not far off the mark when he asserted that the intelligence for a breakthrough requires a conversion to a radically higher and far broader conception. Such intelligence includes the ability to recognize that a breakthrough is neither a tadpole nor a statistical series. Traditionally the approach has been to:

- assess the relative importance of the different elements of a possible break-through and identify any enablers still outstanding; and
- recognize the potency of novel ideas, then synthesize the new usage scenarios and concepts, perhaps by combining old concepts in new ways.

The new approach is really to:

- ponder the relevance of chaos theory, complexity and chaotics to understand ambiguous or discordant messages and advice.

To turn this into a tangible technique, we may go back to systems analysis, an event-driven approach invented during the Second World War. In its traditional form it has become standard practice whenever a major project involves technology or engineering, because breakthrough may be viewed as a system, albeit a highly dynamic one. Systems analysis in its most rigorous project-planning form is found in the programme evaluation and research technique (PERT), which has even become a verb (as one British admiral is supposed to have declared when considering a project-management method for building the first nuclear submarine in the UK, 'we're gonna PERT this fucker'). Systems analysis brings together the required performance, constraints, resources and bottlenecks. The entire process is an iterative one. Such exercises do not perform miracles. But often, systems analysis can help decision-makers identify a preferred course of action from possible alternatives (provided all possible solutions and paths leading to them have been fully thrashed out). But could systems analysis be extended using complex systems theory? Approach techniques such as relevance trees and critical-path analysis may help. But for success, management must be clear and precise about the mission objectives. Many tries may be necessary before the true objectives become clear.

Critical-path analysis can be used in two ways, macro and micro. First it can be used in a macro sense to understand the power and impact of an invention or discovery. The new innovation is positioned on the critical path of a situation or a process, and its external influences assessed. For instance, ultra-low-cost radio communications could change the economics of telecommunications and in consequence the development rate of the Third World (since development and telecommunications are closely linked). In that sense, a breakthrough could be achieved. Critical-path analysis can be used in its conventional micro sense to track blockages in the path of the breakthrough itself—for instance, taking the same example, an essential ingredient of low-cost telecommunications would be a very cheap battery for the terminal, one that is auto-recharging. Fortunately, this problem also has a forecast solution. Recently, ten-year studies on distributed energy have looked beyond the current Lithium-ion technologies to Lithium-polycarbonate batteries, microgenerators (semiconductor batteries) and new recharger technologies.

In the macro sense, critical-path analysis must take us beyond current needs into imaginary domains. And here complexity theory can synthesize new forms of behaviour. Take two now classic examples of failure to imagine new behaviour patterns: first Western Union, which was offered the Bell patents for telephony in the 1880s, and second IBM, which was offered the Xerox patents in the late 1950s. In each case management looked at the technology in the context of traditional behaviour and turned it down—long-distance telephony seemed an unproven and undemanded, and so weak, challenger to the entrenched position of the telegraph network. Xerox copies were not replacing the typed carbon copy but creating a whole new market, based on a latent demand for cheap copies of any form of document. What is needed is to imagine and construct a new behaviour pattern. Critical-path analysis with complexity theory to drive out new situations can give this, because it questions rigidity in thinking, viewing rigidity as unstable.

Relevance trees can be used to understand the secondary or knock-on effects of an innovation and so assess whether it is really a breakthrough or not, and to further trace new behaviour patterns. Here we are trying to map the causal chain of complex systems interactions. For instance, an advance in teleshopping to an on-line international virtual supermarket that made mundane supermarket shopping easier and cheaper than conventional shopping, yet near-instant, would be widely used whenever people are short of time. The primary effects would be on numbers of conventional physical supermarkets, their construction and operation, and on passenger-vehicle miles spent in travelling to shop. A secondary effect would be on roads, road accidents, carparks and fuel consumption. Further on would be the tertiary effects on sand and gravel demands, refining capacity for fuels, road congestion and pollution, etc. However, there is a complicating interaction—delivery to the door demands a vehicle, with more fuels and vehicle miles, etc.

Using such approaches, effects of different innovation types can be compared. Substitutes for travelling to shop can be compared with, for instance, the new battery technologies that might replace the ubiquitous sealed lead-acid and nickel-cadmium types. By mapping the relevance trees, a comparison of impacts can be assessed socially and economically. Moreover, use of non-linear dynamics in combination with a supercomputer has considerably revived systems thinking and practice recently. Both are directly relevant to the study of breakthrough.

To sum up, chaotics can provide a new basis on which to understand business, by multiplying chances and choices. The current disillusionment with traditional scientific management makes economic intelligence based on turbulence far more attractive. Laws of diminishing returns yield to positive feedback principles of increasing returns. Similarly, technological forecasting arrived at through consensus gives way to a multiview, more confrontational approach using multiple scenarios and as many ideas as possible. And today's techno-industrial breakthroughs come from corporate research machines with a complex holistic approach, replacing the one-shot 'lucky breaks' of the solo inventor.

NOTES

1 Quoted in *Webster's Third New International Dictionary*, see under 'breakthrough'.
2 *I&T Magazine* (European Union), July 1994, p. 15.
3 In this connection, it may be recalled that a number of distinguished economists, among them Joseph Schumpeter and Harvard's Alvin Hansen, propounded the so-called innovation theory, which attributed the business cycle to the clustering of important innovations, such as the railways, or the piston engine, etc.
4 Richard Gourlay, 'Peace potential: the development of a venture capital industry lies behind the economic success of a new breed of high-tech Israeli company', *Financial Times*, 13 May 1996, p. 10.
5 R. R. Nelson, 'The link between science and invention: the case of the transistor', in *The Rate and Direction of Inventive Activity*, National Bureau of Economic Research (Princeton: Princeton University Press, 1962).

PART III

SOCIAL CHAOTICS: Principles for designing and building society—a sea change in the philosophy of living

Can we apply the principles of chaotics to more than business? Part III provides a counterpoint to Part II in many ways. In Part II, we centred on the new perspectives for the creation of material wealth—a departure into new future opportunities really. Taken together, such trends point to a very much more open-ended destiny for humanity than the scientific deterministic approach might compute.

But how do we deal with our current problems? Against the backdrop of such an uncertain and apparently purposeless world, four global societal problems loom large in the telescopes or microscopes of internationally minded observers. And we need bold initiatives to combat them. The three global problem areas that we (re)examine here are: unemployment, under-development and ecological disaster. These major concerns have several things in common. In each case, flawed analysis has so far delivered sterile remedies, and even aggravated some situations. But there is no need for overwhelming fatalism. Most issues under review are amenable to a more promising reassessment based on chaotics. This could foreshadow a brighter future, despite the advanced state of decay. If we do not shrink from shock therapies in certain areas, recovery might even be in sight.

There is a fourth issue. At a personal level a widespread identity crisis is growing. We constantly indulge in introspective interrogation about our role and purpose, our need for group and community affiliations, for meaningful relationships to counter isolation and other existential stresses. These stresses include our unease about the generation gap, the role of work in our lives, our vacillating corporate loyalties and our minority syndromes. For instance, in one computer company with a very rigid hierarchy, the average number of monthly pension cheques sent out to people who had retired at 65 was 13. People (largely men at that time) only lived for their job. Once it ended, they did too. Each chapter will touch on this crisis from a different perspective.

In Chapter 9 we concentrate on the philosophy of space–time trade-off when scaled down to human-sized preoccupations. The trade-off provides a new rationale for a wide range of lifestyle and economic processes. On the social side we gather insights into staggered or lifelong education, clues about today's general feelings of insecurity and also about the social state we are heading towards collectively. On the economic side are included insights into relocation of factories, migration of industry, a new division of labour and unconventional patterns of trade. What is new is treating relationships between space and time as trade-offs, in which one is a potential substitute for the other. The second advance is exploiting the principle of similarity across scale, borrowed from fractal geometry and from chaotics. The mixture of the two is interesting. But the key question is how to harness them together.

In Chapter 10 we move deeper into social issues. Overturning many of our prejudices becomes crucial, especially when we visit the graveyard of failed employment policies. As an example of a bold initiative, can there be a comprehensive scheme for the homeless? Such a policy might be feasible and realistic provided it is part of an overhaul of social convention. To get such innovative policies accepted the creation of thousands of new jobs must be linked into increased social welfare for the needy. Will it take a cultural revolution to destroy the twin chimera of full employment and fixity of tenure?

Next, in Chapter 11, the quintessence of the theories of chaos and complexity is focused on underdevelopment. Only recently, with chaotics, have three essential pieces of the puzzle fallen into place. We now realize that the trigger mechanism that sets an economic take-off in motion may be a trivial, unobtrusive event if certain simple laws are allowed to operate freely. Ultimately, the status of a stable complex system may be achieved. And sandwiched between the two poles—the start-up and the maturing phase—does a kind of spontaneous self-organization, again from complexity theory, keep the process of growth alive? The motor of complex systems may be invisible, but its power is plainly felt.

Ecological disasters threaten on several fronts. Unorthodox thinking beyond conventional rules of rationality and bolder innovative actions are our only hope. So problems of environmental protection are treated in this manner in Chapter 12.

9

Earthly Space–Time Trade-offs

Time will run back, and fetch the age of gold
John Milton (1608–74)

Something of a puzzle today is a spontaneous sprouting of innumerable, ill-defined electronic community entities. They seem to parallel artificial life. Be they mundane associations of medicos, scientific networks, the Inuit of Alaska comparing social problems with Aboriginal peoples in Australia, *ad hoc* industrial alliances or semi-permanent transnational groupings, they grow and flower, and sometimes wilt. How do these flimsy federations come into being in the first place? How do they self-organize and manage to survive? Moreover, how do they keep adapting and prosper? When these unorthodox social and business constellations began to make their appearance, many were generally viewed as an offshoot of what was then known in the United States as computer conferencing, or electronic communities. Some are centred on workers inside one corporation with extensions to suppliers and clients via telecommuting or teleworking. While the information and telecommunications systems, in particular the Internet, provided the motor nerves, the heart of the matter lies elsewhere. Clearly digital technology, for all its power, does not alone account for the mushrooming of virtual communities, nor for their changing topologies.

Initially, the ideas of the interchangeability of space and time, as a philosophical outlook, applied almost exclusively to the extraordinarily large scales of the universe and the minute scales of the atom. But they were regarded as basically irrelevant to ordinary life. The perspective changed radically during and just after the Second World War. Partly as a result of the increased rate of discovery and wider penetration of new technology, our perceptions of the notions of distance, time, speed, duration and lifecycle differ radically from those of our ancestors and even our parents. For us, space–time has shrunk. Global communication is instantaneous, automatic, interactive and taken for granted. Satellites circle the earth in hours. Crossing the Atlantic in three hours is a mundane, daily event, if expensive in fares and ecological tolls.

Virtual communities have their roots in a modern human-level interpretation of the philosophy of a space–time continuum. Down-scaled space–time has opened the way to innumerable permutations across a planetary dimension through globalization. And it is more than physical. Relocation of factories and places of work requires continuous 'upskilling' to provide the local skill levels the outplaced jobs demand. Raising the level of work and skills impinges upon traditional lifestyles and leisure time. Older hierarchies and orders are destroyed. Such space–time trade-offs follow the ideas of chaos theory and of the ever-greater complexity mode (ever more apparent in our modern life) because they increasingly occur by chance encounter between hitherto improbable partners.

Moreover the second- and third-order effects of space–time interchangeability are also of interest when supplemented by chaotics. These effects emphasize the advantages of modular service creation or manufacturing and assembly, rather than integrated operations, in response to ongoing market fragmentation and the need for customized local services and products for local markets. For instance, Cygna Life in the USA has its insurance forms processed during its night by 80 staff in a village in Ireland. The processed forms are transferred by fibre-optic cables across the Atlantic to await Connecticut's morning. Space–time interchangeability also bears on partnerships, cooperative networks and intricate webs of alliances in a crescendo of growing organizational complexity—modular dispersed operations, systematic outsourcing and subcontracting and so on. For instance, outsourcing of main information systems will double in the USA by 2000, so the percentage of US corporations outsourcing their core information systems will go from 20 to 40 per cent.[1]

Paradigms from space–time for chaotics show a faster pace of life, and a faster pace for time

Just what has chaotics got to do with any of the space–time concepts brought out in the special relativity theory? Little directly in mathematical terms. But there is an interesting point in philosophical terms. Against the 17th-century Newtonian theory of a mechanistic space, at the start of the 20th century, Einstein and others upheld the philosophy that space is a system of relations that includes time.[2] They added that distance is measured between events (and includes time in these measurements) not just between points in space. From the conceptual and theoretical point of view, the unifying idea of space–time—in place of the former idea of space, with time separate—is among the most important recent advances in mathematics.

To many people the notion of a four-dimensional universe has the appearance of a paradox. It goes against our shared ingrained conception of reality. Take the problem of measuring distance—we determine length with a ruler or some other measure. Seldom do we have to measure the position of a body in continual motion. However in the universe that surrounds us, the measurement of distances and times does not reveal the attributes of the things measured, but only relations between the things and the measurer. And these measurements are affected by the way the observer is moving. In particular, differences of perspective, or differences of size as we perceive it due to differences of distance, are attributable to the standpoint of the observer and generally not ascribable to the object observed. So the spatial and temporal properties of physical occurrences are found to be essentially dependent upon the spectator. And neither space nor time separately may be taken as strictly objective. Only the mixture space–time becomes valid.[3]

Chaos theory expects that erratic behaviour is natural to both the states of the observer and the observed. The space–time theories concentrate more on regular motion and states and less on how the universe appears when the things being observed behave in a highly random and erratic way and when the observer's own behaviour is apparently random. Our observations of society and our relationships also depend on the relative motion of the objects being measured. A brutal acceleration of so-called progress, perhaps more of chaotic change, has occurred in the last 30 to 50 years. It is so brutal that it would be difficult to find a parallel in the past, not even in the first Industrial Revolution. So a fast moving time, such as we are now in, demands that we rethink an initially simpler space–time paradigm derived from ideas for a more regular universe. And thus in our age more than any other, all measurements of distances and times, their effects and the relations between them become doubly subjective. To someone in another country, with a different perspective on time and distance, such social and personal changes may be far smaller, or far larger. Some truly astonishing changes of lifestyle tempo have occurred. For instance, the first fairly free, and democratic, election in the 5,000 years of China's history took place only recently, in spring 1996, and then in only one offshore enclave—Taiwan.

Flexible space–time mix: a new platform, in a nutshell

Using a backdrop of the notions of space–time we can move forward on several fronts. Such notions force a reappraisal of a whole range of relevant distances and geographical locations in business, e.g. the distance to markets, to sources of supply, to daily work by commuting, to pools of skills, ease of access to services and so on. Space–time in a world of chaotics compels decision-makers to put the mechanism of trade-off in the most general sense into perspective, and in particular trade-off alternatives between space–time coordinates as virtual substitutes for each other. So the postindustrial world is gradually dismantling many cherished images and symbols. Although we still use the term 'markets', they are no longer predetermined places or physical foci as they were up to the Middle Ages. Markets in the sense of where we operate to sell a service or good extend locally, nationally, regionally and globally. Trading in commodities, stocks and shares, currencies and other financial instruments is now done electronically and instantaneously, via networks that span the earth and operate 24 hours a day. Electronic markets will soon expand to include global education and work markets. Also, the famous stamp 'Made in . . .', which used to signal the country of origin and give a hint of the quality of the merchandise, has lost most of its sense. Complex products are nowadays assembled anywhere from components fabricated in a score of countries. Up to 70 per cent of a car's value may be in outsourced components, and the components from one component or car company may be made elsewhere, even on another continent.

Take the factor of time for instance. Consider its fuzzy connotations. Everybody sees that time is work in some way. Time is money (earned or wasted) and any service or product is wholly time-dependent—because it is demanded at a specific instant or within a closing time-window (e.g. in order not to miss a market) and because eventually it becomes obsolete. The difficulty starts as soon as an attempt is made to translate common wisdom into operational concepts.

Let us illustrate the essence of the time problem as individual 'time poverty'—an issue with which Western civilization is increasingly confronted. Daily commuting from home to work and back is the lot of millions all over the world. Aware of the problems involved, 29 suburban communities in the Paris region banded together in 1990 to act as a lobby to deliver time itself. Their core target was 'to commute in under 60 minutes', irrespective of how this was achieved. Time is the basis for this group, not distance to city centre. The aim is to deliver on quality of local road systems and rail, subway and bus connections. Going further is the lateral induction. Why commute at all? Should we be emphasizing telecommuting? Jack Nilles of JALA Associates, Los Angeles, predicts that over half of 'knowledge workers' in the USA will telecommute part-time by 2020.[4] This underlines our starting assumption that space–time is not alien to many contemporary, human-scale issues with which we struggle daily but is a fundamental concept when addressing them.

Faster disparities: but in which direction?

Our acceleration of lifestyle tempo has been driven by the combined impacts of high technology, mostly telecommunications, new capacity for production, modern biotechnology and health care. But it has also brought major economic and social disparities between peoples and countries. Humanity's recent trajectory has received vastly expanded knowledge and information plus a universal craving for new freedoms. As recently as 1,000 years ago (small in our biological time-frame) humans all over the world could be assumed to be much the same in social organization and economic conditions. Our history since then tends to suggest an uninterrupted flow of events, a steady progress towards so-called civilization, with a growing disparity in living standards, philosophies and notions of time and lifestyle pace. Even in the Victorian era, Gauguin and Robert Lewis Stevenson were attracted by the massive change in lifestyle pace they found in the South Seas compared to their native Europe.

But the case for progress is highly disputable. Have we progressed in meaningful ways? Are we civilized in meaningful ways? Moreover, change has not just been forward, gradual and continual. Rather it has been stop–start, a few steps backwards. Maybe it is going rapidly backwards in the countries usually considered the leaders of progress. The FBI recently announced a major victory, that the USA had reduced its murder rate by 8 per cent to 21,400 a year.[5] But per head of population this is at the level of deaths from car accidents (4,000–5,000 per year) in the UK.

Take the health care systems, since these often reflect progress in their society. In the USA, for instance, the health care system treats fewer cases of the common fatal communicable diseases than it did 70 years ago, but it now treats more car accidents and an ever increasing number of gun-shot wounds. But against this trend, some serious communicable diseases such as tuberculosis are beginning to reappear, while over the last ten years AIDS has been an enormous absorber of intensive care and research resources. And fewer and fewer Americans may be able to afford health care plans in the future, and so fewer will fully participate in the system. Cancer and heart decease, the killers of the middle classes, are increasing and dominate the system's diagnostic and emergency services. In contrast, in Africa, the health care situation is just not comparable, except that with a 'poorer' diet based far more on vegetables the incidence of stomach cancer is fortunately lower than in the USA. So just where is 'progress', in this one small area? Progress shows little gradualism, more step changes and turning-points, but in both directions.

Turning-points, catastrophe rates, grey hair and legroom

What we expect increasingly are turning-points that open entirely new chapters in humanity's short history. World population, which stood at 1.7 billion in 1914, has now quadrupled, driving changes faster than before, but in both directions. Of course, such changes may slow as contraceptives sweep the Third World, eventually driving birth rates down.[6] The current rapid increase in population density has not only translated into development of all kinds of natural and artificial products and projects; it has modified the breadth of the modern person's worldscape, spread ideas, changed outlooks on everything from accepting the political status quo to food expected on the table. Interestingly, it has recently pushed advances in equality of the sexes, as career prospects for women have brightened.

But a crowded world is considerably more exposed to the consequences of each natural catastrophe, and the number of such catastrophes is increasing (more about that below). Since the 1960s, the number of people killed, injured or displaced by tropical storms, famine, volcanic eruptions, flooding, droughts, earthquakes and other calamities around the world has increased by 6 per cent per annum, almost three times the growth of overall population over the last 30 years. The trends displayed in Figure 16 speak for themselves.

Rapidly changing demographic trends over the last half-century have profoundly altered our perception of the destiny and evolution of the human race. Thus, life expectancy in the Western world has doubled, generally exceeding 70–80 years now. Even in the less developed countries it has risen considerably. Compare this trend to India, where not so long ago life expectancy could be as low as 45 years for the poorer classes. The total effect is a general greying of our planet. Before 2030, the number of Americans over 60 may very well outnumber those under 18.

And we are changing physically in ways that would have been impossible to predict. For instance if you are of average size and under 40, you may sometimes feel uncomfortable at an office desk or in a factory or kitchen, without being able to say why. It is essentially because so much industrial and home equipment is designed to the standards of 50 years ago, when people were 10 cm, or a full 6 per cent, shorter on average than our generation. Oddly, the required upsizing of physical standards is badly lagging behind us humans. Thus, on counts of physical size and average lifespan, our evolution has been extraordinarily rapid, particularly when measured on the scales of Darwinism. In other words, we are disturbing or distorting natural selection processes with a powerhouse—perhaps greenhouse—for forced change through innovation, and all driven by reproduction.

Workstyles are changing the fastest

Our interpretation of the world and outlook have of necessity also been seriously affected by our rapidly changing relationship to the environment, workstyles and lifestyles. Workstyles are changing faster than ever before, and so are changing our lifestyles, especially as the Western work ethic becomes a foundation for lifestyles across the globe. Let us take some key instances, showing the trends and their effects.

First, the majority of salaried people in the Western world work significantly shorter hours than preceding generations. In Western countries, the figure lies

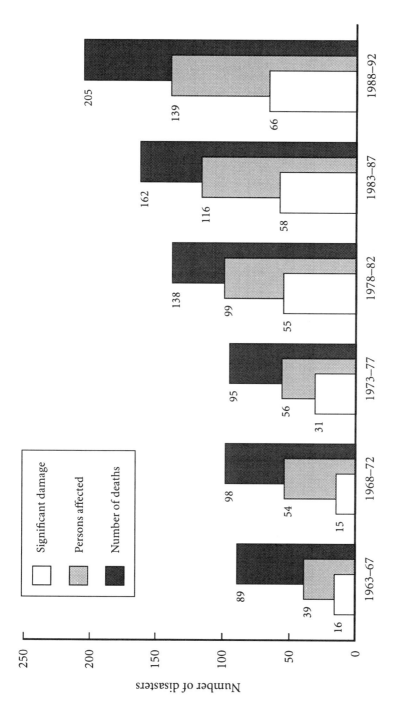

Figure 16. *Major disasters around the world, 1963–1992—significant disasters based on damage, persons affected and number of deaths*

Source: World Conference on Natural Disasters Reduction, Yokohama, Japan, 23–27 May 1994, *Disasters around the world: a global and regional view,* information paper no. 4 (April 1994).

between 1,600 and 2,000 hours per annum. This is half the average 19th-century figures. Combined with longer life expectancy, it provides the foundation for the 'free-time explosion' for many today. But the real consequences are still emerging. 'Small is beautiful': Schumacher's observation that less than 5 per cent of time, of all total lifetime in the population in the Western world, is now spent on work is a key factor. This percentage highlights the majority in our population who are too young to work, or are retired, or have no paid work. And behind that is the ratio of those supported in some way, and the growing proportion who are not supported, to those having paid work.

Work is changing radically in nature. Whereas in the 1960s, over half the workforce in OECD countries produced goods, 30 years later perhaps less than a fifth of them do so, because of the expansion of the service sector, which has coincided with reduction in manufacturing employment as a result of automation with computerized production and the spread of robots for repetitive manual tasks. Even in Germany, 70 per cent of GDP is in the service sector. This migration of work and skills (to the services sector, while blue-collar jobs migrate overseas), combined with 'upskilling', further changes our demands for education, our personal goals and our social interactions. Similarly, in the Asian Tigers with the arrival of blue-collar jobs work has moved away from agriculture. Industrial manufacturing has replaced it in such countries as Thailand, Malaysia and the Philippines, while Hong Kong and Singapore have moved their balance towards less trading and more advanced manufacturing.

Our master: time . . .

Perhaps philosophies of space–time trade-off, and complexity, can throw fresh light on the concept of time in the ordering of events, and more particularly, on time as a means of synchronizing processes that are often spread over global distances today. Competing in time has become synonymous with ever shorter response time. Many of our tools for time-based competition—just-in-time manufacturing and inventory control, flexible manufacturing, robotization of production processes—have come from Japan more than from the USA, while the West has perfected MRP II (manufacturing resource planning), CRP (customer resources planning for sales and marketing) and electronic data interchange to hook up suppliers, transporters, distributors and customers interactively with the producer.

All these are a far cry from the essence of the notion of time in work of the 1920s—the time-and-motion studies of scientific management.[7] But perhaps, seen in a longer-term perspective, our current views of the place of time in our work and competition are still far removed from what is in store. Are they just a curtain-raiser on practices in the 21st century? If that is so, are we (and are our children) prepared to adapt to perhaps an even more feverish tempo and frantic behaviour that might be the hallmark of the next decade and beyond? Have any psychologists, social researchers or politicos given serious consideration to work and lifestyle practices and policies for coping with a time-compressed, space-compressed world? Because the world of work is already baffling. Almost everyone seems to be doing some kind of support task, component activity or ancillary work. Very few—be she or he a hotel manager, rental car agent, truck driver, farmer, engineer or laboratory assistant—seem to produce the complete service or goods. Anyone who works is conscious of how mysterious production processes have become. The whole chain from inbound supply to outbound delivery is understood by few. It is as if the very complexity of the work process is hidden from our sight by an invisible, silent synchronizer of the myriad production tasks, with final consumption some distant objective.

Looked at from the point of view of the producer, the key indicator to watch across all these processes can be summed up as one parameter: response time—the interval from purchase order to final delivery. In retrospect, there has been some considerable room for improvement. Going back to manufacturing in the 1940s and before, only about 10 to 15 per cent of the production cycle might have been spent on dedicated working on the customers' orders. The remaining 85 or so per cent was taken up by waiting: waiting in a backlog of orders, waiting for components to be shipped in, waiting in temporary storage for completion of complementary assemblies, waiting for decisions. The same is true in the service sectors, especially finance and insurance. Processing an insurance claim can take months. Actual work on the case may be days or hours, even minutes. Most of the delay is spent in 'handovers'—the time between attention by the various actors in the flow of work. Reengineering exercises in such firms focus on obliterating the 95 per cent of an insurance claim's processing time spent waiting in in-trays, out-trays or internal mail. To keep the response time to a minimum has now become a core aim in many businesses to increase market share, even to avoid going under—as in parcels delivery and stationery wholesaling. Thus time (not distance) is the 'value dimension' for our 21st-century agenda.

Elemental space–time trade-offs

The reality of time compression is especially striking in certain industries—computing, telecommunications and a few related areas. Today many teenagers are familiar (at least superficially) with instantaneous on-line information searches and interactive video, both of which are dependent on real-time processing. However, in assessing the total impact on society and the individual of space–time trade-offs combined with telecomputing, we are confronted by an iceberg. We are just beginning to distinguish its hazy contours.

For instance, working at home via a remote terminal was initially seen in the 1970s as a substitute for travelling. The solution was deemed eminently suitable for mothers with small children and the handicapped. While this type of employment has retained its special attractions, it has not yet lived to the high expectations of its early promoters in the 1970s and 1980s in terms of volume and the number of people concerned. Today, the situation and outlook are very different. First, new networking technology has brought subtle changes to the way we work. We are constantly reminded that time-based performance is paramount. In addition, companies and most employees are changing their ways of working, often fundamentally. Third, our ageing demography and the reshaping of the family away from the nuclear model favour home-working far more. And our networking habits support lifestyle changes that are often space–time substitutions.

Take the most obvious substitution mechanism, that of electronic mail for paper, correspondence and documents. It is delivered instantaneously, i.e. usually without any perceptible lapse of time. But it is asynchronous. It can be read and acted upon at once or later. People at widely dispersed places can work on the same assignment at different times as long as their terminals are connected. The once pivotal role of the physical office is dwindling as more and more companies reduce their permanent staff and hire mobile and/or part-time workers instead. It is a two-way track. Typically, experts with narrow specializations may work for several employers simultaneously or on a part-time basis or under temporary contracts. These people have a new form of loyalty towards their transient employers. Just as an expert or consultant sells her or his know-how a bit at a time to different firms, there are specialized jobs that do not require the presence of a full-time, highly paid technician. So in the end, everybody seems to be better off. The company saves on both permanent staff and office space. The teleworker's earnings may exceed those in a fixed job, especially if corporate downsizing means that there is no longer a fixed job. The overall gain is increased productivity and a gain of a livelihood. Far from being an esoteric concept, remote working might become an important driver of economic and social progress.

Other kinds of working 'topographies' are becoming popular. When two, three or four architects, physicists, lawyers, auditors, etc. band together to form a joint venture, it is not only with the aim of providing a better service to customers. Often their prime motivation is to reduce overheads, typically by sharing a semi-professional assistant or clerk. Some real or virtual communities have found it to their advantage to hire older, retired people—of a certain calibre or reputation—on a part-time or a retainer-fee basis. Time-sharing used to be a buzzword in the early days of computing (and a label for doubtful holiday apartment deals). Since then, the formula has spilled over into innumerable human occupations, notably in the service industries. The spectrum is vast, from all transport operation, canteens and machinery servicing to telesales and building maintenance down to window-cleaning as well as the outsourcing of complete departments running the corporation's computers, network and databases. The Outsourcing Institute of New York expects US outsourcing spend to hit US$100 billion in 1996.[8] Of this, 30 per cent will be in blue-collar areas of plant and property management and 30 per cent in white-collar pursuits of finance, sales and customer services, with the major 40 per cent portion in information technology management and services.

Altogether, these highly flexible patterns tend to squeeze and cut traditional cultures, intermediate products and especially roles, from secretarial services to middle managers. And the trend is fostering rapid growth in different trades and specialities, from cabling system installers to alarm and security equipment makers, with the consultancy segment among the fastest-growing. Few sectors will be left unaffected by the new conditions. In banking, the fire at the Credit Lyonnais headquarters in May 1996 acted as a destructive creator, forcing operations into a virtual mode. Without a physical headquarters, operations continued the next day via remote back-up facilities for key database computers. The fire demonstrated how the whole bank could be operated from anywhere, with no physical centre, just computer links to key deciders and operational staff.

The most spectacular of changes in space–time patterns have taken place in the relations between different countries and even continents. Decisive cost advantages have induced corporations in the USA, Europe and Japan to set up off-shore production units or to form overseas subsidiaries, first in the Far East. At the time of writing, India and China—after Hong Kong, Singapore, South Korea, Taiwan and Mexico—are slowly becoming the main theatre of Western industrial decentralization, with the Philippines, Indonesia, Eastern Europe and even Russia and North Africa emerging from the wings. AT&T, IBM, Hewlett-Packard, Oracle, Texas Instruments, etc. have set up software factories or contracted with local companies in several parts of India because it offers a large, well-educated workforce, too often underemployed and underpaid. Essentially India's success boils down to the key fact that a first-class Indian programmer earns at best one-sixth of an equivalent American programmer's wages. Again, the interactive on-line network has proven catalytic. Thanks to the global time difference, computer workers in Madras writing program code or inputting data for a software firm or a database operator in the USA can execute changes and corrections requested the previous working day by their client or headquarters half-way round the world.

Cost is not everything; there is still much higher risk in many developing economies today. But the international distribution of labour will continue to change beyond recognition following further development of rapid, reliable communications globally. The net effect may be termed globalization, the shrinking world, or the coming of a global village. But the key effect is that the interdependence of nations, firms, customers and suppliers has diversified and accelerated dramatically in the past couple of decades, with many secondary effects. It is at the root of trade between nations and continents. Essentially, all these forces point to future space–time relationships that might be quite different from today's. For instance, one consequence of the increase in global trade, the value of which has steadily exceeded the sum of national GDPs since about 1950,[9] has been the acceleration of goods transport. Already more than a quarter of international trade in commodities is now by air. Current air cargo capacity is roughly equivalent to the total prewar shipping capacity.

Re-orchestrating business structures, tenets, practices and processes: towards smaller, concentrated units and variety at low cost

What is at issue is whether decision-makers will clearly see the need to rethink the whole of the value chain, production methods and operations in the light of new time pressures, not just primary cost pressures. Let us take one example. The degree of change trauma can be deduced from the overhaul pushed through by Compaq to move from the high-price end to the low-price end of the PC market. Compaq managed to cut its production cycle by a full 40 per cent and reduced the number of components in its PCs by a third. This implied redesigning not only the product but a complete new supply and manufacturing process. And it resulted in 50 per cent reduced factory space for production lines.

In such examples, older and unchallenged economic theories lose their appeal. For instance, for the last two centuries, economies of scale were supposed to be the very foundation of capitalist growth. This theory is no longer accepted without reservation. Smaller and medium-sized firms are gaining in almost every market, both in America and Europe and in other parts of the world. In service industries, the ideas of a workflow of paper with many handovers are giving way to the caseworker who follows an account transaction, a credit request or an insurance claim throughout its passage through the firm, reducing processing time from months to hours. That basic tool of mass production, Ford's assembly-line, has begun to recede into the background in the last five to ten years as high automation/robotization has given way to using small teams to build a complete item in one spot in certain industries, including the motor industry.

At a corporate level, the same is happening. The demise of the large company is at hand, as small and medium companies flourish and become the key economic drivers. This contrasts with the 1958 crystal-ball gazing of the *Harvard Business Review*, which surmised that computers would revolutionize American industry. Computers would lead to overconcentration in, and dominance by, a few giant corporations. What has occurred is the opposite, especially as computers with telecommunications lower the cost of control and management. Comparatively small firms (under or around US$10 billion in revenues) often call the tune for a whole industry with many hundreds of billions of dollars in total sales. For instance, in the computer industry, Intel and Microsoft set the pace while the larger suppliers of systems (IBM, HP, Fujitsu etc.) follow as best they can. Other industries follow the same pattern. While some ailing firms are taken over by or merge with their competitors, the movement is offset by increasing instances of break-up, as large conglomerates divest those subsidiaries and divisions outside the core business. The sense of 'synergies' and verticalization is less and less evident. Witness the break-up of AT&T into three companies, or the break-up of ICI into chemicals and pharmaceuticals with the formation of Zeneca as the new pharmaceuticals spin-off.

Because the notion of scale is being reassessed. The struggle is now to produce variety, at low cost. In this struggle, the very tiny firm is often able to provide a service or specific product more efficiently than a giant enterprise. Small process chains or production batches, rather than long series, can have distinct advantages. In manufacturing, smallness can eliminate the large stocks of half-finished products pending future (uncertain) orders. Customer's orders for smaller quantities can now be considered easily, as flexibility comes with smaller scale. Thus, the principle of economies of scale is slowly yielding to economies of variety. From the standpoint of the supplier, it requires a cleverer marriage of modular production delivery with bespoke creation of the product or service.

Contract alliances for fractured markets: coopetition mirrors complex systems

Moreover, the various segments have each become more fragmented. Be it in banking, cars or computers, specialists emerge successfully and generalists generally decline. Car assemblers have grown out of total car manufacturers. Assemblers such as Toyota in Japan now add less than 35 per cent of the value of a car during assembly. The rest is in bought-in components. European and US car manufacturers have not matched this yet. General Motors produces far more of its components internally than the average, which has been identified as a possible source of its troubled financial performance. On the subcontractor side, a typical model is auto-parts manufacturer Magna International Inc., which supplies all the big three in the USA with items such as sunroofs, seating systems, metal parts and airbags. In addition, the Canadian-based firm acquired majority stakes in auto-parts companies in Germany and Austria in 1994. The lesson is typical. Having mastered the intricacies of a few component parts, the subcontracting firm is able to produce them by the million and still get rich on very slim margins.

No PC vendor manufactures any semiconductor components in-house, apart from IBM. Most computer manufacturers, including ICL, Hewlett-Packard and Tandem decided in the early 1990s that a most efficient way to cut costs was to get rid of underutilized expensive manufacturing facilities and replace them with 'outsourced' facilities. Thus, offshore contract manufacturing has become the model, while the computer 'big names' specify designs, assemble the parts and market finished products.

Clearly, contract manufacturing in the high- and medium-tech industries is often the next step, reducing the costs of components for the assembler, while securing a bigger and more stable outlet for the subcontractor. Contract manufacturing is already the fastest growing segment of the electronics industry in Europe. In 1995, the contract electronics market was expected to be worth close to US$40 billion. Several major players, such as Texas Instruments, have set up separate subsidiaries to compete for contract work, basically playing the role of a subcontractor.

As services and products become more specific, more customized in response to market fragmentation, so component producers for such high-variety products, wittingly or unwittingly, are pushed into cooperative networks of added value. Such value chains tend to supersede the single, centrally controlled organization with much verticalization. They are highly parallel to the formation of stable complex systems. These trends force surviving giant corporations to adopt new attitudes and abandon earlier profiles of insular dominance. Two otherwise rival corporations may decide to act as partners in a specific area or for a specific purpose, while still fighting it out between themselves in other lines of business—a duality that may have been unthinkable several decades ago. Ray Noorda, once of Novell, defined this as 'coopetition'. Japan has flourished on 'kyōryoku shi nagara kyōsa'—competing while cooperating—since the 1950s. The new partnerships and cooperative networks between ever smaller business entities know no national borders. Increasingly, their allegiance to a particular location, or country, is weakened, as their markets and management grow internationally minded. So sweeping are the changes expected in all sectors that it is difficult to imagine existing social patterns will not also be remoulded.

In all of this we see the signs of break-up and chaos but also the support element of cooperative complex systems, limiting the randomness, to provide protective associations in which survival of the fittest is balanced by survival with a little help from friends.

NOTES

1 John W. Verity, 'Let's order out for technology', *Business Week*, 13 May 1996, p. 31.
2 Bertrand Russell, *ABC of Relativity*, rev. edn. (London: Allen & Unwin, 1958).
3 Why and how are the two 'dimensions' of space and time related? *New Scientist* assures us, quite simply, that the reason is because light travels at some 300,000 km per second. So one second in time is said to be equivalent to 300,000 km in space. (John Gribbin, 'A

special theory of relativity', *New Scientist* 'Side Science' supplement no. 49, 21 September 1991, pp. 1–4).

4 Geoffrey Nairn, 'Teleworker army will grow to 200m worldwide by year 2016', *Financial Times* Information Technology supplement, 8 January 1997.

5 'US crime on downward trend', *Financial Times*, 6 May 1996.

6 For instance, in Brazil the size of families has been reduced by more than half within a generation: the average number of children born to Brazilian women dropped from 5.75 in 1970 to 2.35 in 1993 (*International Herald Tribune*, 3–4 September 1994). Moreover, education is strongly linked to birth-control usage.

7 See Box 4 (on scientific management) in Chapter 6 above.

8 Peter Martin, 'In-out shake it all about', *Financial Times*, 16 May 1996.

9 Michael E. Porter (ed.), *Competition in Global Industries* (Boston: Harvard Business School Press, 1986).

10

Antidotes to Unemployment

*'If everybody minded their own business,' said the Duchess in a course
growl, 'the world would go round a deal faster than it does'*
from *Alice's Adventures in Wonderland* by Lewis Carroll

Around one job in ten disappears yearly, according to the OECD. In the 1950s and
1960s, the total number of unemployed recorded in the 24 OECD member
countries oscillated between 8 and 10 million. Between 1972 and 1982 this figure
tripled. After a short-lived improvement in the late 1980s, it started shooting up
again, in spite of ever more government money being poured into preventive
measures.

Whatever the contributing factors—be they entrenched protectionism, dis-
couragement of small and medium enterprises, short-termist downsizing, rapid
technology change, changing consumer demands or competition between low-
wage and high-wage economies—the world is witnessing a wholesale destruction
of many jobs. There is a tempting comparison for this monster of joblessness in
Greek mythology. The Hydra was a many-headed serpent that grew two heads in
place of each one cut off, unless the wound was immediately cauterized. (It was
finally slain, by Hercules.) The nightmare is particularly striking in countries
where unemployment approaches and exceeds the social crisis point for OECD
communities—the 10–12 per cent level.

30 per cent of world's potential workers are un- or underemployed

The problem is so perplexing that many wonder whether unemployment will
ever go away, or whether we are faced with high-tech élites ruling a jobless nation.
So judged by our traditional Western set of values, unemployment and underemployment are widely regarded as the most disturbing phenomena of our times.
They are seen as an unwarranted waste of human resources. They underline the

fundamental inadequacy of the economic system and represent a constant threat to social peace and harmony in local and geopolitical relations.

Public opinion is increasingly sensitive to long-term unemployment, because it takes such a widespread toll. It forces idleness on over 25 per cent of school-leavers and continuously removes middle-management positions and middle-class salaries, while whole classes of occupations disappear, especially the menial jobs for unskilled labour. The semi-skilled professionals are on a dwindling demand curve as métiers such as barrel-making or valve-grinding become obsolete competencies. In countries where the creation of new jobs lags behind unemployment growth, as in Europe, the wider division of classes and the emergence of a marginalized lower class, a lumpenproletariat, are ever more ominous.

Complicating this in Western countries is the welfare state as whole, with its crucial support for unemployment, retirement and health care. It is acting more as a barrier to employment than an enabler. And it has become an anachronism for five main reasons:

(1) The design of the system is no longer valid. Jobs are far scarcer, especially for the young, and the demography and family make-up of those needing unemployment support has changed with the relative growth in the numbers of the aged and frail, and with the break-up of the nuclear family. In many OECD countries, 15 to over 20 per cent of families are single parent, with the UK leading Europe in 1994 with a 21 per cent rate. In France, for instance, 36 per cent of all births took place out of wedlock in 1995.[1] Single-parent households are growing far faster, five times as fast as two-adult households in France. Demand for child-support benefits is growing, while governments deliberate about cutting off the poorest in the economic chain.

(2) Benefits and care systems are breaking down due to underfunding and overload. In the USA, the two main government programmes supporting a greying population—health and retirement, funded through a 2.9 per cent payroll tax and a 12.4 per cent payroll tax, respectively—will be unable to make repayments after 2012 without running deficits.[2] And the combined 15.3 per cent payroll tax also reduces the income available to save privately for the future.

(3) There is little to show that current systems of social protection really optimize the social benefit–cost ratio for those in need.

(4) The range of benefits is defined in an arbitrary fashion. Often dental care, hearing aids, eye care, etc. are excluded and left to the private sector.

(5) The overall burden of current systems of social security can become a drag on economic growth. They may act as a primary contribution to unduly high costs of labour, especially in Western countries. Consequently, national competitiveness in global markets is seriously eroded.

The key question is simple, but difficult

On the demand side for jobs, things are simple but difficult. Here, the key is how to generate extra employment opportunities, going further than just innovation-related jobs, but with the proviso of operating under two constraints, namely:

- Unlike the Great Depression of the 1930s, governments are saddled with huge budget deficits. They are in no position to launch vast relief-work programmes.
- Lowering overall welfare benefits is not a viable solution since it may court social unrest.

The answers do not lie in exhorting governments and industry to slow innovation—technology both creates and eliminates jobs. And a partial return to protectionism in foreign trade would be a double-edged weapon. We are left with one conceivable effective path towards a breakthrough. That is to reassess the whole range of social versus private risks and so define new priorities by discarding criteria that have become obsolete and counterproductive.

A microcosm of this problem is France, with around 12 per cent unemployment between 1992 and 1996. The French state has made some jobs appear through its centralism—its *dirigisme*—and it can prevent the slimming of bloated corporate structures as at Air France and Bull for years. But it cannot sustain and expand real employment, since this comes today essentially from the small and medium company sector, where for historical reasons its policies are a barrier and all hope for new employment is lost. The 'primeval soup' for small company entrepreneurialism cannot exist in France.

Full employment is a moving target, which Keynes hit, at first

For the better part of the 20th century, the issue of work and non-work was dominated by John Maynard Keynes.[3] Everybody has some idea that Keynes performed some profound work, perhaps even astonishing achievements. However, as time goes by and the problem looms even larger, few know exactly what it was that the English economist did.

Keynes's reputation basically lay in his repudiation of classical economic theory. He attempted to show economists, business leaders, government officials and the general public that our economic systems could be 'in equilibrium', even with a large volume of unemployed or underemployed resources. Previously, economic theory had focused on the distribution of wealth rather than the volume of national product. It assumed that whatever unemployment might occur it would set into motion self-correcting forces to restore equilibrium. In this view, unemployment in whatever form was to be attributed to institutional rigidities in the price–wage system. Hence, the primary objective of government policy was considered to be to reduce or eliminate these rigidities. Often, as we now realize, this policy works, at the cost of inflation, which debases wage-rates and subsequently pauperizes the working classes. Keynes worked out a policy recommendation aimed at promoting large-scale public works to generate expenditure that would remove unemployment (and thus maintain demand at a level that creates full employment). He accepted price inflation as a possible consequence, provided it was limited to under 2 per cent per annum. Keynes's radical remedies proved a boon to the capitalist countries of the West in the terrible Depression of the 1930s. The theory worked. It was implemented by the vast rearmament programmes, launched first by Nazi Germany, Fascist Italy and imperialist Japan. Western Europe, America, and the Soviet Union soon followed. But what Keynes and his followers have tended to overlook was the emergence of a new kind of rigidity, especially in the labour market. This came partly as a result of the application of Keynesian theory, and as a byproduct of the new welfare states created after the Second War.

Piecemeal therapies have proved fruitless

There is a striking parallelism between the state of affairs that our generation is faced with and that situation prevailing when Keynes attacked the interwar Depression. Now, as then, a piecemeal therapy advocated by the 'establishment' for alleviating unemployment is proving totally inadequate. Only a bold departure from both conventional wisdom and official thinking has any chance of reversing the descent of an ever larger segment of the population below the poverty line. The historical comparison deserves more than casual treatment.

When the national economy is able to offset the disappearance of obsolete jobs by generating new viable jobs, as in the United States recently, all seems well and good. However, this entails painful social adjustments, career turmoil and most frighteningly a slow slide into lower-paid occupations—'MacJobs'—for many, and overwhelmingly for the young, and a slide into part-time work.

The basic tenet of government policy destined to combat the many forms of joblessness, particularly in countries with high unemployment, is the assumption that 'there is no single recipe for full employment, but there is a menu of measures' that can help improve the situation. This is always piecemeal, a set of weak solutions in disguise.

The issue of work and non-work is comparable to the states of attachment between cellular automata in complex systems when in a dynamic stable state. Of late, the dynamic order/disorder paradigm has been the subject of intense debate both at national and international levels. So far it has been inconclusive. For instance, the experts of the OECD, which groups the richest nations, have recently reviewed the policies applied in member countries. The result is a document called 'Strategy for jobs'. Unfortunately, there is little new or convincing here. The report makes a quick reference to macroeconomic, structural and cyclical policies to promote growth without inflation, to foster innovation and disseminate technological know-how and to develop entrepreneurship. The OECD experts sound more convincing when they poke fun at such 'quick fixes' as across-the-board work-sharing to be enforced by law, a 32-hour working week as a model, or a replay of Keynes (in the disguise of a grandiose pan-European fast-transportation system, at a truly astronomical cost). The rest of the recommendations are couched in rather evangelical terms. Cautiously, they suggest that minimum-wage laws could perhaps be made less constraining (part of the social security contributions for young, unskilled workers could be paid out of the public purse) and that hiring of labour would be accelerated by relaxing redundancy payments.

But this does not really attack the inflexible labour laws on hiring or the cost to employers of social security, the protective plans for retirement, unemployment and health. The cost of social protection itself is an increasing barrier to employment in many Western countries, such as Germany, France and Italy and perhaps the USA. Reducing this barrier means attacking the price–performance ratio of social security, to give better benefits where required while reducing its cost to the employer and the employed. According to Jacques Calvet, chairman of Peugeot/Citroen of France, European labour laws on factory hours allow a production capacity of 1.9 million cars. US labour rules of three shifts, six days a week would give a capacity of 3 million cars.[4]

The solutions suggested so far seem fairly limited: either welfare becomes a safety-net only for the poor or there is an across-the-board citizen's income, tax free. The latter is interesting, but since taxes have to increase exponentially to pay for more people, more benefits have to come from less employment, and more expensive care must also be paid for. In the UK, 8 per cent of GDP was spent on welfare in 1951, but 19 per cent in 1995.[5]

A collapse of deterministic social models

Little wonder that our current vapid policies lack results. But understanding the general causes of the failure of most policies requires a short historical digression. We also need to examine how Keynes tackled a similarly complex issue in the context of his own time. Without making a clean break with classical economic theory, Keynes would not have been able to formulate his then revolutionary policies for ensuring so-called full employment. Likewise for us, there is no way forward without a radical reassessment of the woes that beset contemporary economy and society. And it is at this point that chaotics, with its rejection of certain forms of determinism, could be invaluable as a guide during analysis and in making recommendations.

The crux of the problem is that deterministic ideas of social superstructures still dominate our thought and policies (originating from the entry of reason into science in the 17th century). This is all the more puzzling when one considers that mainstream science has, after three centuries of blind belief in the immutability of the laws of physics typical of the Newtonian model, espoused the view that many concepts are far fuzzier than was previously imagined. And all axioms become arbitrary. It is fair to acknowledge that the connection between the key scientists Copernicus, Galileo and Newton and Hobbes, Descartes and Rousseau, the most influential philosophers of the 17th and 18th centuries, is not obvious at first sight. But real and deep-seated similarities exist in a common basis for their thinking (see Box 7).

Box 7. *Sociological thinking and philosophy grow from science and technology*

There are striking similarities between the advances of science in the 17th century and the rise of contemporary philosophy, and the world's landscape in the 20th century. Today, and in the 21st century, each and every new form of a discipline or field of activity does or will partake of one aspect or another of chaos and complexity, in much the same way that the concept of determinism cemented the 17th-century union between avant-garde scientists and the thinkers:

• It all started with Nicolaus Copernicus (1473–1543). The Polish ecclesiastic and astronomer believed the sun to be the centre of the universe, with the earth following a yearly rotation about the sun in addition to its diurnal rotation. The Italian Galileo Galilei (1564–1642) discovered the importance of velocity and acceleration in dynamics, and enunciated the law of falling bodies. The achievement of Johan Kepler (1571–1630) was the discovery of the three laws of planetary motion. The crowning touch was Isaac Newton's (1642–1727) work. He codified the three so-called laws of motion—the first two of which were discovered by Galileo. This spelled out his law of universal gravitation: 'every body attracts every other with a force directly proportional to the product of their masses and inversely proportional to the square of the distance between them'. Pure mathematics flourished. Coordinate geometry was worked out and popularized by Descartes (1596–1650). Differential and integral calculus was invented separately by Newton and Gottfried Wilhelm von Leibnitz (1646–1716). And the first logarithmic tables were published by John Napier (1550–1617). Great strides were achieved in the area of scientific instruments, with the invention of the compound microscope, the telescope, the thermometer, the barometer and the air pump and advances in magnetism.

• 'Knowledge is power' was the motto of Francis Bacon (1561–1629), who pioneered the use of the inductive—as opposed to the deductive—method of reasoning. He attempted a logical systematization of scientific procedure. Thomas Hobbes (1588–1679) transposed scientific thought into the discipline of political science.

• Descartes is rightly regarded as the founder of modern philosophy, a body of doctrines symbiotic with the then new physics and astronomy. Little wonder that we find Cartesianism rigidly deterministic. In his view not only dead matter, but all animals and indeed all living organisms, were governed by the laws of physics. The core of Descartes's theory of knowledge was the famous saying 'Cogito ergo sum' (I think, therefore I am). The process by which the conclusion was reached is called 'Cartesian doubt'.

• When put in perspective, our 20th century appears to have produced a greater explosion of scientific and technological advances, but comparable to the intellectual fireworks of the 17th century. Moreover, this has forced a dissipation of scientific 'certainty', a process analogous to dissipation of energy, in every discipline, from physics to genetics. It has become the recurring theme of the 20th century. But in spite of the spread of this aura it is possible to discern a new common denominator—chaotics.

• By contrast, the sudden explosion of the Soviet Union and the final downfall of Marxism are events too recent to sink into the minds of our contemporaries with the realization that social determinism has reached the end of its useful life.

Let us remember an often-overlooked fact that has caused much trouble. By and large, in their endeavours to classify observations, all the social sciences define suitable categories and try (and fail) to create meaningful typologies as the prerequisites for understanding, based on inspirations from the hard sciences. In their quest for respectability, the 'soft sciences' have overemphasized the old scientific process of logic, with its dividing lines and use of contrasts to validate and infer results. Thus in classical economics, capital was thought of as an economic factor, distinct from labour. Land was different from all other factors of production, leisure was opposed to working, and public enterprise and private interest were kept separate. Economics was essentially mathematical, and perfect economies in which markets obeyed perfect market rules were the basis for study, just as if they were electrons obeying calculable atomic forces.

Likewise, the social ladder was conceived of as rigidly fixed. Witness such classifying terms as the third estate, the propertied classes, the bourgeoisie, the proletariat, and the persistence of castes in some countries. The dichotomy criterion was all-pervasive. In an old English tradition, the people in the humanities have been regarded as the carriers of civilization and the scientists have been regarded as the plumbers. In many instances, these schema are plainly obsolete. Mixed economies (public with private enterprise) are widespread. Exchange-rate fluctuations, far from being 'pure', are in fact 'managed' (usually not very adeptly) by central banks. Wages and salaries are increasingly supplemented with income from capital invested, or from stock options that come with the job in such countries as the USA and Japan.

In key areas this penchant for classification and explanation based on opposing actors or states still lingers on. Today we have a binary division of the population into the gainfully employed on the one side and those out-of-work, drawing unemployment benefits on the other. Moreover the imbalance is growing steadily worse. As long as joblessness is portrayed as a negative state contrasted to full employment, the dichotomy appears as a choice between two clear-cut options. Confusion and feelings of helplessness are bound to prevail, because solutions cannot be found.

We need a new paradigm.

In search of that new paradigm

So far, we have reasoned in terms of a binary function—discrete dual states or situations. The argument takes on a new significance when we consider the rigidities that exist at the institutional level, because the answer may lie in between, with a mix of both. A short historical digression is in order, as it provides useful insights into the stubborn resistance to social and economic change.

Thomas Hobbes's *Leviathan* (1651) was the earliest, yet still-enduring, transposition of prevalent scientific ideas into the realms of political science. A rigid determinist and an applied mathematician, Hobbes professed a thorough materialism. Inspired by Galileo, Hobbes visualized human society as a replica of the physical world governed by eternal laws of nature, which the scientists of the time had deciphered. For him, life was just a motion of the limbs and therefore automata had an artificial life.[6] In the final analysis, Leviathan was a commonwealth based on a covenant, supposedly made by the citizens with each other, to obey whatever ruler the majority chose. The worst despotism was deemed better than social chaos.

A century later, the French philosopher Jean-Jacques Rousseau rebelled against this Hobbesian concept of an all-powerful state. He held it to be characterized by a vast bureaucracy, a machinery of coercion, exercising totalitarian control over its citizens.[7] A proposed new model of social organization is laid out in his celebrated essay 'Le Contrat Social' of 1762. However, Rousseau also asserted that society had originated in a contract. This was also defined as a covenant, firstly between the members of the society, and secondly between the community and the ruler, with specific definition of the rights and duties of each. But once the agreement was made these relations were supposed to remain intact for ever without variation.

This historical flashback provides an insight into some of the more influential preceding institutional frameworks and, most importantly, their inherent rigidities and lust for everlasting power as a metaphor and means for stability. But here lies a basic fallacy. No human communities have come into being—or could ever be created—by way of some covenant, whether called a social contract or not. The analogy with our present conditions is striking. Some of the 20th century 'Leviathans' are semi-scientific, semi-philosophical constructivists, but as sclerotic as their 17th- and 18th-century counterparts.

Defining a new therapy that works is a tall order. The situation varies from country to country and between continents, so new policies must fit local conditions. Sadly the piecemeal treatment of these ills has been a dismal failure. Clearly the structural mismatch between a dwindling demand for labour and a growing supply of labour in quantitative and qualitative terms calls for a radical approach. Any strategy must be targeted at basically rethinking both sides of the supply–demand equation. An attack mounted on such a broad front must anticipate strong resistance, as persistent opposition to even minor reforms of the sensitive area of social security and public welfare has amply demonstrated.

In the Keynesian world of the 1930s, attaining full employment was a top priority. In contrast, in a world recognized as chaotic, the focus must be on diversity of employment patterns, and on cooperating corporate strategies among smaller companies or 'coopetition' (as in stable complex systems) to spontaneously create new employment. Likewise, public policy and individual attitudes should be geared to a constantly better-trained, adaptable work force. This will become a prerequisite for the USA and Europe to compete on equal terms with the newly industrialized countries of East Asia and other continents.

But chaotics teaches us to forsake traditional classifications and all forms of determinism, especially long-established models. For instance, in Europe, where unemployment is dramatic, with 24 million 'officially unemployed' in the EU, a comprehensive job-creation and occupations-fostering policy might be based on flexible employment encompassing part-time work, intermittent employment, on-the-spot acquired know-how, upskilling and downskilling, sabbatical breaks, philanthropic work and so on. Such a structure demands retraining facilities for people of all ages.

The chaotics model also highlights the fact that positive conditions for survival include cooperation and 'getting by with a little help from our friends'. Cooperative complex structures are much more successful than pure *laissez-faire*, be it at the level of cellular automata or of types of capitalism.[8] We first discuss why we should proceed in this manner and then how to proceed in concrete terms.

An example may illustrate the thrust of this argument. Let us assume that a country decides to overhaul its social legislation and begins to provide housing to all, free of charge, be they natives or new immigrants, anyone under the poverty line. This is provided in return for a commitment to partial repayment at some future date, if and when the tenant's income increases. In view of the extra costs, some other benefits would have to be scaled down for the recipients, or in general, e.g. giving up compensation for short illness, limiting reimbursement of certain drugs or closing under-utilized hospitals.

Four vital interrelated goals could be attained:

- Overall public welfare is increased, since the overriding need for lodging prevails over less essential social objectives.
- Production costs for all sectors go down locally, as labour-related costs are lowered by the drive to lower-priced housing. This attracts more work and so more employment.
- Social cohesion within the country is enhanced and the integration of an immigrant population facilitated.
- The building and associated industries create new jobs; this sets in motion induced growth across the board through knock-on employment effects and increased disposable incomes.

Several real-life examples are cited below to show that sometimes daring changes can modify stagnant policy and work structures or practices. The key point is that overall gains exceed the total sum of individual benefits, but a triggering action is necessary to precipitate the motion.

We mentioned briefly how overall public welfare might be enhanced by cutting less essential benefits to provide seed money for a new housing-for-all scheme for the needy. This suggestion, a form of modified Keynesianism, is not as far-fetched as it may sound. Shortly after gaining independence, Singapore adopted a scheme designed along these lines quite successfully. Ever since, the scheme has ensured peaceful and friendly coexistence among its different ethnic communities. Granted, Singapore is a small country and its example would have to be reworked for a larger nation. However, one logical step in improving the present welfare state in a key area could lead to other fundamental reforms more easily. We have tried to avoid presenting this case in terms of politics. A truly multipartisan approach is a prerequisite for dismantling obsolete social and economic legislation.

The concept springs from chaotics in the sense of enabling a stable set of (socioeconomic) conditions to occur through cooperation. Individual initiative and entrepreneurs are not restricted by state capitalism or *dirigisme*, but *laissez-faire* capitalism of the 19th-century variety is not unleashed. The basic premise is to aim at a balance in the stability area for complex systems, the 'edge of chaos', not going over and not declining into rigidity. By supporting some basics—principally a roof over your head for those without—while enabling free operation of commerce, we aim at key life-enhancing support to encourage free job-creation and so fight unemployment.

Our conclusion above of balancing welfare with job-creation cannot be taken as a comprehensive programme of reform, only as a signpost to typical new directions in social thinking. An overhaul of social policy and legislation as a lead antidote for unemployment is a prime task as we prepare to enter the 21st century. It is a key item for our agenda.

Far more consideration of private plans may be part of this, but few political parties have the strength to attack this. Current systems are not likely to return anything at the level required to those who have paid all their life. Take the case of Medicare in the USA. The average annual payroll-tax payment for Medicare is $1,000. Investment of that sum compound over 40 years at 7 per cent would produce capital for the payer of $200,000. Leaving the capital intact would produce an after-tax retirement income of four times as much as the average Medicare hospitalization bill ($3,000) at a 15 per cent income tax rate.[2] So we could pay for some medical costs, possibly some retirement, and avoid the breakdown of the current system without raising payroll taxes, which destroy employment.

What is the value of work? and retirement?

A part of the social overhaul is a sea change in our philosophy of living. Creating many new jobs, however desirable, will not provide all the answers to the widespread anxieties of contemporary society, especially in a world where jobs may commonly be shared and transient. So a primary element in chaotics thinking would be to reevaluate the social standing of work. Salaried work did not acquire its prestige value in the eyes of society until quite recently, in the 19th century, and at that time only in the West. Before then, a variety of activities or occupations, from nun to knight, were thought far more praiseworthy. Definitely on the cards is a progressive blurring of the boundary between so-called gainful occupations and a whole spectrum of business activities, research, social work and teaching, as well as self-education. So far from being a disgrace, a 'lifestyle sabbatical year', or a period on support to retrain for a new assignment, or widening one's cultural background will be regarded as normal and as a plus. Eventually it will be rewarded. It is likely to be one hallmark of the 21st century. And retraining throughout life will be necessary as one moves between skills, careers and employers.

Another basic rethink on lifestyle values is due for the concept of retirement. Frighteningly for many, a wide range of retirement plans will not deliver enough support as we enter the 21st century. Fewer younger workers are entering the schemes to pay for the next generation of pensioners, just at the point when the greying numbers are due to expand enormously. This implies that retirement may be a lifestyle phase and practice of the past. And the sooner ordinary people (and governments) realize this, perhaps the better for everyone.

Inklings of brave ideas for a not very brave new world: based on risk concepts

Just to think creatively, we have to concentrate on changing our outlook, to eradicate our enduring phantasms. Much woolly thinking and the current random social legislation is ascribable to a traditionalist, muddled approach with fundamentals from the 17th century and 19th-century details and laws. The latest ideas on social contracts are still too close to these concepts.

From the perspective of chaos theory and complexity, social organization comes to be viewed as a balance of two risks. Risks may be equally found in the chaos of social strife with no real support and in the strangling rigidity of an expensive social security system with major contributions from the firm, the personal poverty of overtaxation and the constraints of legislation. Thus new social thinking might centre on the many facets of the two risk types and their containment or compensation. Below we set out some areas for rethinking, but they are only a first pass in this new vein.

New thinking on social policy and legislation should focus on risk

A systematic reevaluation of group versus individual risks and their treatment and apportionment is overdue. New thinking for policies on welfare—health and social security systems—should focus on self-help, not dependency. For the first time in the history of unemployment training, the theory of self-organizing agents in chaotics points to the need for job courses in self-reliance, independent operation, initiative, attitude, social networking and out-of-the-box thinking.

In a complex system, time in unemployment (being attached to a semi-stable structure, or free state, before migrating to a more stable one) becomes another full-time job (of searching for that more stable attachment). Thinking on employment benefits from the chaotics view would consider unemployment as a work process to find a new job, not a period of enforced idleness. So chaotics would focus us on reducing the risk of not finding a new job, and perhaps the need to find several positions at once if part-time work was all that was available. Thus, unemployment becomes a highly structured occupation—an organized job-search-plus-retraining period with far more encouragement and active guidance from employers in the recruitment process, which the employer could be paid for. The unemployed person does not have the stigma or loss of confidence, since the phase is effectively fully active and is viewed as an acceptable social state, rather like actors 'resting' between parts.

The acting profession usually has 90 per cent of its members unemployed at any one time and so is used to organizing other work and non-work around the 10 per cent portion spent in the core skill. Paid retraining should encourage new-skills acquisition. But more value and lower social budgets may come from training where the unemployed person uses savings or loans to buy that training, as an investment in her or his future. And for on-the-job training, should some part of unemployment benefit then be paid to employers for the first months or year of employment? All of this implies a non-means-tested approach, because means-testing encourages dependency (as support is withdrawn as more is earned). Also, saving is discouraged by means-testing because any accumulated wealth counts against benefits, so the drive is towards spending, as quickly as possible.

Cultural obliteration and unemployment— and the chaos from its spread

A further, complex 'soft' issue attached to risk is the effect of culture on mental drive and attitude to unemployment. Again, using ideas on cooperating systems, a strong cultural basis is essential for building attitudes of confidence and personal drive. The links between risk, personal outlook and group culture are usually ignored. Chaotics forces us to bring them together because culture is a key part of the supportive 'glue' of cooperation and risk-reduction. Studies of black immigrants against black natives in the USA have shown that the continued destruction of African-American culture within the USA since slavery, combined with a process of alienation, has removed much personal drive to normal economic success.[9] The self-ability to advance has been obliterated. Those educated in the Caribbean or Africa have been found to have a far stronger toolkit for success in their cultural backgrounds and mental attitudes. This toolkit delivers a higher personal drive for employment and a more intact two-person family structure (for more earners per household). In 1995, they enjoyed a 50 per cent lead in income per person over native black people. And in New York City, Caribbeans on average did slightly better than comparable white households on net income.

The holistic view of chaotics would point out that culture and mental attitude are equally linked to security and crime rates as much as to employment potential, because the microscopic (personal) is often the macroscopic decider. The conclusion for America is that to revise its crime- and violence-ridden structure is a key requirement to keep up in the world of the 21st century, since such behaviour is multiplying fast and progressively destroying more and more of the USA.[10] Risk-analysis from chaotics would imply that the major problem for the USA is not competition from Japan. It is its inner race to rebuild and reinforce the culture of its marginalized millions, to obtain a better mutual cooperating system.

Because complexity theory points out a frightening major event. If this alienation effect is not stopped—and it is growing rapidly—at a certain critical point, the lack of cooperation will halt the whole system. Very quickly, it can slide over the 'edge of chaos' into complete chaos.

NOTES

1 William Drozdiak, 'Stigma fades for out-of-wedlock births in France', *International Herald Tribune*, 17 May 1996.
2 Paul Craig Roberts, 'How social security and Medicare rip off Americans', *Business Week*, 27 May 1996.
3 At the peace conference at Versailles at the end of the First World War, Keynes was the chief British Treasury representative. Keynes first won world fame when he resigned in protest over what he considered to be the inequitable and unworkable provisions of the Treaty of Versailles. History showed that he was right in foreseeing that Germany's economic weakness stemming from the Versailles covenant would eventually engulf the whole of Europe in ruin and war. In the aftermath of the Second World War, Keynes took a leading part in the Bretton Woods conference (1944), from which emerged the International Monetary Fund and the World Bank. The latter's role will be taken up in Chapter 11 in connection with problems of underdevelopment.
4 Stewart Toy, 'A talk with Peugeot CEO Jacques Calvet', *Business Week*, 27 May 1996.
5 'Thinking the unthinkable; the welfare state in Britain: behind current arguments over tax lurks the thorny question of welfare reform', *The Economist*, 27 April 1996, p. 44.
6 Bertrand Russell, *History of Western Philosophy*, new edn. (London: George Allen & Unwin, 1961), pp. 531–41.
7 Ibid. pp. 660–74.
8 Will Hutton, *The State We're in* (London: Vintage, 1996).
9 'Black like me', *The Economist*, 11 May 1996, p. 57.
10 Joseph Weber, 'From memory lane to mean streets: letter from Newark', *Business Week*, 27 May 1996.

11

The Coming Take-off of the Third World

*There are but 2 families in the world, as my grandmother used to say, the
Haves and the Have-nots*
        from *Don Quixote* by Miguel De Cervantes (1547–1616)

In the next ten years or so China, India, Brazil, Indonesia, Bolivia and South
Africa may follow in the footsteps of South Korea, Taiwan and Singapore. They
may succeed in escaping from misery and backwardness. Three billion human
beings who live under the poverty line are directly concerned. The face of the
world will change as never before in history, since a radically different geopolitical
balance will emerge. This take-off justifies serious consideration as a priority item
on our agenda for the 21st century.

Perhaps with the help of modern evolutionary modelling, specifically insights from chaotics, we can try to explain how the vicious circle of underdevelopment could be broken. Already a handful of previously backward economies
appear to have done it, and their histories seem to support our contentions by and
large. But it may be well into the 21st century before we understand quite why so
many have misjudged the potential of nations in the Third World for sustained
economic growth when starting out from a very low level. Interestingly, chaotics
also suggests that the reverse process is possible—certain OECD countries could
be sliding backwards towards misery.

Chaotics implies, via chaos theory and the proposition of self-organization
of complex systems, that economic take-off is initiated by a trigger phenomenon.
However trifling it make look at first, growth appears, and is sustained, when
certain simple laws are allowed to operate. What is involved is fairly unpreced-
ented. So we seek a radically different scenario of how an evenly spread economic
development could be achieved globally to explain this. A comparison between
the chaotics approach and typical earlier views of the root causes of persistent
underdevelopment may be useful here. Our comparison should reveal any
failings on the part of policies based on neoclassical macroeconomics. The
approach is to use an explanatory model based on the artificial life of computer
simulation. Ideally, this should not only highlight the symptoms and causes of

failure, but also the directions for solutions. We shall thus dwell on balancing contemporary 'industrial Darwinism' with self-organization, since growth increasingly tends to proceed by way of successive competitive mutations, more or less as envisaged by Charles Darwin. The old-new evolutionary ideas closely fit the concepts of chaotics—both the conditions for the emergence of chaos and the behaviour of complex systems as they grow more intricate.

A modest question of principle: is development meaningful?

However, at base there is a question of principle, too rarely taken seriously in the development establishment. Does the Western model really imply meaningful 'progress'? Is it beneficial, especially socially, culturally and spiritually? And also, is it even materially beneficial to the mass of the people in reality? We must ask whether consumer goods and the Western lifestyle are worth the unemployment, drug problems, pollution, urban shantytowns, brutalist tower blocks in the wastelands of freeways, diseases from TB to AIDS and social dislocation that come with our idea of 'development'. The value of the governing concepts for our society comes into question in a 'less-developed' nation. For instance, unemployment is a characteristic of an employed society. For many developing nations, work has traditionally had a less important, less central place. Taxes, such as the poll tax in Nigeria in the late 19th century, were even introduced in Africa to force people into the colonial monetary economy of work, just as the Romans did on conquering a new people who had no need of their economy. New concepts of development should seek a far more flexible model, for meaningful progress, with only partial take-up of the Western concept.

This has not been the case so far. During the 1950s and early 1960s, moulded largely by Keynes, the West's leading economists set the two underdeveloped thirds of humanity on an unfortunate track, with the best of intentions. And since then, the same old models and recipes have been tried repeatedly to transform the 'developing world'—those countries between innocence and misery.

Samuelson's Alertia model

Professor Paul Samuelson of MIT has offered perhaps the most comprehensive traditional analysis of this path available in the literature. The first American laureate for the Nobel Prize for economics composed an erudite scenario entitled 'Alertia on the march' in the penultimate chapter of his best-selling, and now classic, book *Economics*. Alertia was meant to rhyme with inertia. It stood for a typically undeveloped country. The main thrust, in the words of the author, was 'to remind' Alertia's leaders of 'how the older capitalistic nations' had proceeded to break away from their own 'vicious circles'.

In describing underdevelopment, he quite rightly stressed population problems, e.g. the density of population, excessive birth rates, widespread illiteracy, the shortage of skills, the excess of unskilled labour, malnutrition, the precarious health situation, and so on. Land distribution has always left much to be desired. And on the whole, whatever development of natural resources had taken place may have not pushed forward a healthy growth economy in the Western sense. However, while there is no doubt that the level of savings remains too low in the Third World, the assertion that there is a chronic shortage of capital, domestic and foreign, as most economists including Samuelson have been saying, is more debatable. Investment flows are influenced by actual and anticipated rates of return (a key variable), and recently the developing world has offered high-growth, if risky, returns—and so major capital flows have occurred.

As for access to modern technology, another crucial element, for a very long time production methods and processes then in use in the OECD nations were unsuitable for the fabric of Third World societies. Although acknowledging that no master plan can fit all underdeveloped countries, Samuelson and others did not shy away from across-the-board remedies: revamp the tax system; invest heavily in infrastructure and public utilities; move away from staple crops; launch an industrialization drive, backed by low-interest loans and generous subsidies to such white elephants as giant steel mills and national airlines. On top of everything, erect a protection wall for the infant industries, by sky-high tariffs and strict import quotas—a measure that was very popular in South American countries from the 1970s. Relying on the neoclassical analysis and diagnostic, and backed by funding bodies under the aegis of the UN, Alertia's leadership had every reason to feel safe in implementing the recommended therapy. Foreign aid was available to them for the asking. Massive grants, cheap loans, technical assistance, local training facilities, overseas scholarships and innumerable foreign experts plus highly paid consultants sucked in several trillion dollars in aid over 40 years, yet 60 per cent of the world's population lives in poverty.

Only now can we identify some key fallacies in the whole approach. The precepts of a *laissez-faire* economy, fairly free of government interference, put the USA, Britain and Holland on the road to industrialization a couple of centuries ago. In contrast, economic experts urged that the Third World start by drawing up a plan for development at government level. On closer scrutiny, it turns out that this particular schizophrenia was due as much to the then widely held belief that the Soviet system of centrally planned economy was relevant to the under-developed countries as to the infatuation with Keynesian macroeconomics. In *Economics*, Samuelson saw no value in 'the virtues of the Invisible Hand', once the central piece of Adam Smith's work (and of modern political economy). The net effect was to debase microeconomic concepts and its cardinal rules. Thus, adapting to changing user wants and new technology, providing incentives to be productive, adjusting output and input and price fluctuations were effectively ignored. The planners, it was believed, knew better. The Third World has paid a heavy price for five decades for such thinking.

Moving away from centrally planned development

Nineteen ninety-four marked the 50th birthday of the founding of the World Bank, a sister organization of the International Monetary Fund. Both were born at the Bretton Woods conference at the end of the Second World War. The scope of the Bank's operations is mammoth. Its loan portfolio exceeded US$140 billion in 1994, spread over 100 countries. Yet the anniversary was not a happy one. The Bank's annual *World Development Report* charged the governments of the Third World with economic and financial mismanagement. But a growing chorus of critics asserts that the various funding agencies must also rethink their policies, practices and organization.

In the aftermath of the Second World War, most of the ruling classes and intelligentsia in Third World countries were ill prepared to set up and operate an efficient, corruption-free government. Countries squandered billions of dollars on capital-intensive projects—dams, highways, power plants and other infra-structure toys—without ensuring the maintenance and build-up of human capital through education and the local micro-infrastructure of roads, schools and essential social services of health and birth control. Such countries lived beyond their means while the masses were, and are, miserable. They need a driblet of the benefits of a freer capitalism. Tentacular bureaucracy, outsized military establishments and limiting government regulations put major obstacles in the way of the (few surviving) entrepreneurs. The Third World was also encouraged to ape the consumerist behaviour of the West and move into large cities with a lifestyle of consumer goods, while rejecting their own traditional lifestyles and local produce. For instance, one tragedy is the undernourishment of new-born babies in the Third World because mothers are encouraged to feed powdered milk to babies in lieu of their own, far more healthy milk. And while export-oriented strategies advocated in some of these countries have made the rich richer, every-where the well-to-do tend to benefit more than the needy from heavily subsidized health services, generally paid for by Western donors. On the economic front, soft loans to government have tended to halt the pursuit of private capital and have thus prevented local governments from adopting free-market policies.

Excessive commercial suffocation through regulatory rigidity has been the lot of three billion people since the beginning of the postcolonialist era, with grave effects on the creation of small and medium enterprises. For instance, in

New York, a new company can be set up in four hours; in the UK, in one to three days; in France, in three to six weeks. In South and Central America the same process can take over 200 working days to deal with the red tape.

In summary, it seems that four parties are involved in the current condition of the Third World—our traditional economists, the funding agencies, the donor countries and the receivers. But if they have erred, perhaps it has been essentially due to the lack of a robust back-up strategy to fall back on when the traditionalist approaches fail.

Escaping government control: what a little magic of deregulation can do

Perhaps the biggest stumbling block for economic take-off in the Third World has been government control of the economy, specifically of the private sector—and often in what is the early dynamo for growth, manufacturing industry. Practices have ranged from short-sighted regulation to widespread corruption and fraud by politicians and bureaucrats, in the guise of state planning and managed economies. Firms depend for their survival on public procurement and government tolerance. This situation was worsened when underdeveloped countries launched import-substituting industrialization policies, under prodding from the funding agencies. These resulted in further raising barriers to foreign goods. But often the new domestic industries proved inefficient and so were in need of continuous, costly subsidies and even heavier protection—Brazil being a prime case in point. Thus, misdirected investment added an extra drag on an already overstrained budget—all in the name of sacrosanct, rigid planning policies.

In contrast, consider what even a partial relaxation of bureaucratic government can achieve. Indonesia is the world's fourth largest nation. In 1965, when the former army general Suharto seized power, the country was one of the poorest, with a gross national product per capita of US$70, half that of India. In 1993, Indonesia's GNP per capita exceeded US$700, more than double India's. Deregulation, partial privatization of bloated industries and liberalization of trade, under the GATT rules, have taken the economy far.[1] In comparison, India's tighter control and bureaucracy have not allowed economic development to flourish at the same level.

Removing the yoke of government interference has especially dramatic results for the development of any country that has been held under long repression, as in the heavier colonial exploitations. With freedom and the right conditions of autonomy, we often see a sudden economic 'miracle' as the effects of liberty spread. Cases in point include Korea (freed from 40 years under the Japanese in 1945) and what is occurring in Central Europe (after 45 years of Soviet presence).

Assuming free enterprise is released from the deadly twin constraints of government control and Fordist rigidity of production, just what could happen? And if economic development emerges and spreads, what will be the reactions of the more advanced countries? Will the evolution be harmonious or produce social unrest and more geopolitical squabbles?

Economic models using artificial life

Setting broad goals for economic development and growth has always been easier than reaching them. Part of the problem has been a lack of understanding, because there is no meaningful way to model growth out of underdevelopment. It is made more difficult because development keeps moving its goalposts as it proceeds and appearances are deceptive. What is going on beneath the surface is immensely complex. Far too complex to be captured in a set of equations, however elaborate, despite the attempts of economists to see this as somehow meaningful. Algorithmic approximation may go some way to bridging the gap. But this technique soon runs up against inherent limits in real-life applications. So far we have had to resign ourselves to be trapped in a kind of limbo, between crude naïve extrapolations and sophisticated paradigms that are largely meaningless. They are based on algorithms whose accuracy and 'efficiency' goes to zero rapidly, long before the complexity of the problem approaches reality.

Until recently, the predicament was further compounded by the mainstream physicists and philosophers. Their reaction to a revival of scientific interest in Darwinism and in evolutionary theories over the last decade has been quite tepid. Induction-based Darwinism at best provides only a clue to how the complex process of economic take-off develops. Social theorists and speculative thinkers in the late 19th century made abundant metaphoric usage of Darwinism. Some distilled Darwin's theories into popular travesties of the struggle-for-survival kind.[2] Oversimplified justifications for racism, militarism and imperialism were the result. Others emphasized their kinship with biology, peaceful coexistence, labour relations, *laissez-faire* capitalism or socialist economy. Small wonder that all this theorizing and speculation had so little practical impact on 20th-century society, or on Third World underdevelopment.

We need more than this. Professor Thomas S. Ray, a plant biologist and computer expert at the University of Delaware, produced 'the first logical demonstration of the validity of the Darwinian theory of evolution'.[3] In 1990, he devised an imaginative computer program named 'Tierra', Spanish for 'earth'. Ray's achievement had two effects. First, it conferred credibility on the work of a few pioneer biologists who have hypothesized about running the evolutionary clock backwards and then forwards again. Second, it provided an inducement to a small core of unorthodox researchers to apply massive computer simulation to problems of evolution across very different fields. This proved that simulation can capture and investigate phenomena hitherto unknown or even unsuspected.

The essential ingredient for new concepts is a theoretical framework or model based on contemporary scientific thought. Modelling has the advantage of forcing us to identify clearly the conditions for survival of our ideas, the initial conditions and external forces, the validity of our thought processes. We have to spell out in detail prerequisites, limitations, consequences and secondary impacts. Models closely related to chaotics and its two root components (the theory of chaos and the theory of complexity with its principle of self-organization) would be best here.

Guided by analogies from molecular biology, Ray created a computer program illustrating the process of self-replication. His starting-point was a set of simple, mechanical rules—80 of them altogether—that specified how an ancestral creature could reproduce itself. Tierra replicated spontaneous self-induced genetic changes. No limitations were imposed on how the organism might mutate, or what kind of descendants it might produce. It passed the mutations on to the progeny and evolved new species, whose interactions aped those of real observable evolution and ecology. After a few computer runs encapsulating thousands of 'generations', the menagerie of creatures in Tierra comprised tens of thousands of 'descendants'. New species emerged, some larger, some weaker than the ancestors. Some of the progeny turned out to be predators and prey, hosts and parasites, advanced offspring and plain failures. Furthermore, the digital eco-system would fluctuate in its composition. At times it would be dominated by a few robust types, at other times an incredible diversity was displayed. The similarity between Tierra's virtual bestiary and terrestrial biology is striking. Hence the name 'artificial life' by which this approach relying heavily on computer simulation has come to be known.[4]

Artificial-life programs have been applied in a variety of fields. Linguists have used interactively self-reproducing systems to gain insight into the development of language. Danish pioneer researchers have studied how a population of computer routines might assist in simple problem-solving and decision-making.[5] And the artificial-life approach can even explain the occasional spontaneous breakdowns of telecommunication networks.

Our digression on artificial-life experiments was not an aside. Computer-based artificial life has direct relevance to the key issue, economic take-off, particularly under the conditions in Third World countries. The model highlights the prerequisites for creating and sustaining a momentum in economic expansion:

- specific initial conditions
- size effects
- trigger mechanisms
- supportive environments for self-organizing cooperative agents
- governing rules for self-organizing cooperative agents

Note that all are fundamentals of chaotics. We look at each of these in order below.

The problem of initial conditions: why reinventing the wheel each time in each country can be a *good thing*

Historical precedent tends to corroborate a fundamental tenet of chaos theory—the paramount importance of initial conditions and of making the right choices to ensure early growth. Initial conditions for development are quite different in the Third World from those in the West, and also differ between developing countries.

During the recovery from colonization after the Second World War, those who were supposed to be the intellectual and political vanguard in the developing world clutched at any palliative straw in the economic wind. Early on, the belief that backward countries could be spared the effort of reinventing the wheel, or of inventing a wheel of their own, was uncritically endorsed.

It was taken for granted that the developing nations were in a position to copy up-to-date technology created and practised elsewhere. It is beguiling to believe that 'the new lands do not have to develop still unborn Newtons to discover the law of gravity . . . they do not have to go through the slow meandering climb of the Industrial Revolution: they can find in every machinery catalogue wonders undreamed of by the great inventors of the past'.[6] But is it really so—or could it be just the reverse?

Our Western-type industrialization has been a hard, long learning process, over two hundred years, as ancient royal and feudal organizations were gradually superseded by new paradigms of industrial organization and production in the limited company. And it took another hundred years for organizations of the postindustrial revolution to form. In German industry, the first coming of professional managers to replace the family owners of Siemens—the Siemens brothers—marked a new era, at the beginning of the 20th century.

The problem in developing countries has been how to move almost overnight from prevalent patterns of agriculture with craft production to heavy industry and mass production. Granted that Germany and France joined the industrial race relatively late in the 19th century, followed by Czarist Russia and Japan, all were able to catch up with Britain, Holland and the USA. But it does not follow that the Third World between the late 1950s to the 1990s could do likewise with similar results. Everything is different—the competitive situation, the global trading balance, technology, the production processes, the scale of operations, the market and the environment. All have changed beyond recognition from the late 19th century, when trading patterns, power balances and cultures were at a more primitive stage of emergence.

In theory, the model of development of the 1950s was to be driven not only by an imported assembly line, but by a large-scale solvent demand nationally. But this was simply not there. For the same reason, whatever foreign investment occurred, it went primarily into export-oriented production, largely of raw materials. These commodities were about the only growth sources that emerged spontaneously without local government or funding agency intervention. However difficult it may be to adapt advanced foreign technology to an under-developed country's own use, an interaction does exist between technological change and economic development. But the interplay is far more complex than is generally realized. For instance, as chaotics points out, the initial conditions (as in education levels and cultural tradition) are crucial. And that interplay is the key issue in development.

Thus the concept and mechanism of 'technology transfer'—the apparent panacea for Third World take-off—has turned out to be little more than a catch phrase. Some conventional development economists did note this, and Samuelson said:

> Time and again, experience has shown how easy it is to get a foreign loan to put up a model factory in Turkey or Burma. Often it is imported piece by piece from abroad and embodies the latest wrinkles of Western technology. Yet, with what results? With high production and sales exceeding costs, so as to yield comfortable profit which can be ploughed back into further industrialization? Only too rarely. Often such grandiose imported projects turn out to be extremely unprofitable. The factory that is an optimal investment for New York may in Ankara or Rangoon be a fiasco.[7]

For a recent major example of the importance of the initial conditions of traditions and culture, we take the break-up of the Soviet Union and its former empire. Poland's GDP grew to 104 per cent of its 1989 value in 1996, while Russia's sunk to 56 per cent in the same period,[8] because Russians do not remember a market economy and had few glimpses of alternatives. So, over 60 per cent of the new business class with power and riches are largely the former masters, the old communist bureaucrats, because they had the networks, the knowledge and the culture of power, plus the habit of taking the initiative. Poland had a progressive change over 10 years, under the influence of Solidarity, a cleaner and clearer break, plus a more recent experience of free markets. Most import-antly, Russia's initial condition in 1989 was a militarized economy, with 70 per cent of GDP being government expenditure.[9]

The importance of size: the nature of the firm and technology transfer

In many ways, the striving for progress by underdeveloped countries reached a watershed with the collapse of the Soviet Union and its centralized planning system. There is fairly common agreement that developing countries should move closer to the free-market model of the economy of the USA and Western Europe. There is one useful parallel here. During the first Industrial Revolution, the preponderance of small and medium-size firms ensured decision-making was diluted among a myriad of decision centres. Major strategic blunders, which inevitably accompany increasing scale of operations and their complexity, were avoided.

For the development process and evolution to take hold spontaneously, the essential requirements can be summarized as the existence of a large number of different sizes and sorts of player able to act fairly freely. This is the precondition for randomness to operate. The plurality prerequisite should be taken in a broad sense. It applies not only to individual firms, plants and other production units, but also to distribution chains, service providers and every kind of intermediary, so that bottlenecks cannot develop and prevent an initial economic ripple from spreading further.

A corollary to the problem of maintaining a sufficiently large dispersion of firms is that of the size of the firm in relation to an initially limited domestic market. Small size should be the rule. Giant size—with or without foreign funding—should be the exception. This is not because small is beautiful, but more simply because small works better, and is in line with the consumer power in developing markets. Small manufacturers and service providers in developing countries can remain in business only if they make a profit most of the time. This condition can be met more easily with a philosophy of small batch, modular production, using flexible technology and imaginative engineering: the law of return on volume can be broken. This newer pattern of organization is more suited to the Third World. It demands limited production resources, ingenious adaptable staff, little capital per unit of output and fast turnover.[10] Also it engenders cottage industry subcontracting as a cheap form of extension of its established capacities. Producing more value with less is the dominant theme. We might call it 'the triumph of the small fry'.

Making a virtue of necessity in the second blue-collar flight, with variety at low cost

If the traditional technology-transfer process is a failure, is there a solution? In looking at space–time trade-off patterns in economics and the social sphere, in previous chapters, we focused on a new philosophy of production with more flexible systems of corporate organization, virtual rather than fixed. This is likely to be supplemented with a network of international alliances. Such a changeover is rapidly taking hold worldwide and is in line with development demands.

Why do we take manufacturing production as important, when most Western economies are at least 70 per cent in the service sector? Because the next destination for industrial production, beyond Korea and Taiwan, is the Third World. It is of special significance, since one future wave of development may come from absorbing a percentage of the blue-collar jobs first passed from OECD countries to the newly industrialized countries.

On the organization and supply side we see 'flexible' or 'lean' manufacturing, just-in-time production, integrated supply chains, small-batch processing, back-office reengineering and continuous incremental innovation. In short, 'a dynamic and continuously evolving system' is appearing.[11] This could be far more suited to the traditions, conditions and mentalities of the Third World than the earlier, rigid assembly-line methods of Henry Ford. Furthermore, use of far less expensive modular machinery that can be changed over for new production runs or models without costly delays reduces the need for heavy capital outlays. Production changeover is performed simply with increased mobility of tools and improved machinery layout.[12] It is hardly surprising that most of these production approaches should have been first initiated and tested in Japan and other smaller Far Eastern countries. Firms there are constrained—by costly factory space, lack of raw materials, limited skills supply, small-size markets, expensive licensing agreements, high royalties on foreign patents and so on. Paradoxical as it may look, the very limitations—as we Westerners see it—of space, know-how, supplies and outlets have proved to be a boon to the nascent industries of East Asia.

On the demand side, market fragmentation and the trend towards custom services and goods to cater for niche markets open major opportunities to the developing countries. As variety at low cost becomes paramount, their lower cost-base becomes a critical success factor.

It may also be a blessing for service sector activities. From the standpoint of the developing countries, such operational pressures are positive inducements to adopt new production methods. We can abandon the repeated unsuccessful attempts to copy the rigid Fordist mass-production system.

The importance of size II: returning to microeconomics—and increasing returns on human capital

Taken together, these interlocking features tend to prioritize microeconomic considerations over the excesses of macroeconomics. The latter deals with unspecific raw aggregates like investment, consumption and savings, rather than with particular items, and focuses on their relationships. Microeconomics is more modestly concerned with particular firms, households, individual prices, wages, incomes, family budgets and the like. Consequently, the tools of demand and supply micromarketing—marginal costs analysis, the practice of business in the firm and the industry—come into their own. Instead of blindly increasing international aid and local government spending on (half-baked) prestige projects, relative prices and shortages, both in the capital stock and in consumables, indicate resource allocations.

A key factor is the effect of the microeconomic level of investment of capital. This gives increasing returns if the investment concept is broadened to include human capital, not just technology, as shown by Paul Romer in a 1986 paper,[13] so the law of diminishing returns on capital no longer applies. The consequence is that growth can exist without technological progress and with imperfect competition. The traditional model from the 1950s and 1960s argues that progress requires technology and that the markets and competition must be perfectly efficient. But nothing is perfect in this world, least of all the competition between producers, sellers and intermediaries. The chaotics model is based on increasing returns, with a microlevel of encouragement and the reality of imperfect markets and competition. The conclusion is that governments should invest in human capital and a stable environment, at a microeconomic level, to ensure that the existing resources are used well and, most specifically, that the human resources are not squandered. The focus on microeconomics for development will be a key item of our 21st-century agenda.

Triggers, climates and mutations

From chaotics, the recipe for development appears to be to allow a certain amount of chaos, or freedom, at a microeconomic level. Chaos promotes creativity. It allows entrepreneurs to flourish. Companies can fail as well as flower. But the state does not allow free enterprise to become banditry, as it has done in Russia recently, or in the USA at various periods from the railway robber-barons of the 19th century onwards. Thus, chaotics points out that long term macroeconomic planning is not a reasonable exercise, because the business environment is highly comparable to the weather process. Disturbances that upset weather or business forecasts are equally common, and long-term planning at a detailed level is not practical.

In contrast, setting the conditions for a general 'business climate' can be far more beneficial. Setting free the markets and players allows growth, within certain limits. The key trigger mechanism may be a single act or a stimulus, often inconsequential at first sight. Some chaos is essential to entrepreneurial creativity for take-off. Rigidity would never allow this. Alliances with improbable partners, a chance meeting with an unsuspected customer or a risky opportunity provides the 'spark' that ignites spontaneous take-off. However mysterious, the hidden chemistry does work, and growth gathers momentum through continued repetition and mutation of smaller businesses into larger ones. Mutation then again sets in, slowly modifying the behaviour patterns of the players, pulling them together, or drawing them into conflict, just as on Professor Ray's Tierra. Take-over bids and mergers ensue between predators and prey. Weaker alliances dissolve and are replaced by new ones. With evolution, the economic fabric of the developing country grows in complexity. The production of services and commodities diversifies, markets fragment further, users become choosier. New services and products are stimulated by the expansion in types of demand. As the newly industrialized countries of East Asia know well, this process may result in explosive growth and so plays havoc with neat long-term planning.

Industrial Darwinism and Solon: balancing natural selection with self-organization

And if the competition mechanism is to operate at all efficiently there must be a penalty for failure in the Third World. Far from being a waste of resources, a rapid winding-up of failed companies is more beneficial socially than keeping them going. They absorb precious public subsidies continuously, as France's support of Credit Lyonnais and Air France has shown recently. Only through fighting it out in the market, in a microeconomic contest, can producers and vendors significantly contribute to sustained growth. But blows delivered at a macroeconomic level weaken both the giver and receiver.

Another economic limit is key here and has been known for millennia—the damaging effects of a concentration of accumulated assets, which are effectively frozen, often linked to compound interest debt. For instance, on taking power in ancient Greece in the 6th century BC, Solon set up initial conditions for growth by limiting accumulation of land and capital and by redistributing the excess. The state that we know as Athens was the issue of his success. Also, to limit the damaging effects of compound interest and accumulated debt, Solon used a key instrument—cancellation of long-outstanding, spiralling debts. Is this biblical guideline—it appears in the Old Testament—in reality applicable to Third World indebtedness? We shall return to these powerful mechanisms in the next chapter, as a metaphor for controlling environmental damage.

Again, a recent example is Russia from 1990 onwards. Unstructured *laissez-faire* capitalism, mixed with ex-communist corruption, has allowed the situation to be that that confronted Solon in the 6th century BC. A few very rich are getting richer—often through business as banditry—and the rest of society is sinking fast, with nothing in their bellies but bitterness.

Supportive environments for self-organization: 'structured freedom' and the four states of capitalism

We thus have a situation where freedom with supportive limits, positive feedback and self-organization may create the basic evolutionary process—this might be termed 'structured freedom'. What we really seek at an implementation level is a balance whereby initial investments in human capital can be harvested by small business. It may be useful to consider this state as perhaps one of four states of capitalism, similar in socioeconomic terms to the Steven Wolfram's four states of chaos, as explored by Chris Langton.

The first state of capitalism might be termed 'unstructured rigidity'. It is perhaps closest to the first state of Wolfram's model. Everything is frozen, but in ways that do not and cannot cooperate effectively for the country's economic good in a sustained manner. Everything is rigid, but in no progressive way, and nothing changes. Creativity as entrepreneurialism is stifled because central planning rules. A key example is the former Soviet Union, where state planning failed its population and 70 per cent of the economy was tied up in the military industrial complex. Corruption is generally rife. India and China are breaking out of related moulds.

The second state might be termed 'structured rigidity'. It is close to the second state of Wolfram's model. Although all is carefully organized, there is little, usually too little, entrepreneurial creativity, because state capitalism rules and creativity means some freedom, some chaos. The costs of such inefficient systems are high, and business is too taxed to be profitable without major protectionism and privileged groups. This situation also leads to a more hidden corruption. Several countries are close to this model, including France and Germany, but with different levels of semi-free agent. France has a more rigid form, with concentration on large state-orchestrated businesses and so could not escape its 12 per cent unemployment rate from 1992 to 1996. The state can only give bureaucratic positions or generate artificial demand, but it cannot create meaningful, profitable jobs. Germany's system of Mittelstand, of medium-size companies, gives a better form of this model, but it too is breaking down. Italy's booming black economy of small enterprises is a successful reaction to a state apparatus in the red-tape model with enormous state enterprises, and stifling business restrictions. For example, while IRI, the state holding company, built up tens of billions of dollars of debt over the years 1991–6, Naples became the centre of Italy's highly successful wallet and leather goods industry. But official tax returns show almost no such factories in the area.

In development and politicoeconomic terms, chaotics points to a state of balance where development can occur, but pure chaos—anarchy—does not reign. This key state for development is 'structured freedom', where sustained 'economic life' can reign. Some chaos is allowed to give creativity in a capitalist sense—entrepreneurialism. The ground rules and initial conditions favour strong independent commercial growth, especially for small companies. This has been the way forward for Taiwan, Hong Kong, Singapore, Korea, Thailand and now Indonesia. The Italian grey economy has this model. Groups of small companies may be favoured, to build the initial sustainable business momentum. We have seen this act with some benefits in the postwar *keiretsu* structures of Japan and the *chaebol* in South Korea. But the mistake in both cases has been to allow them to start off too large, and to let them grow larger and more powerful, so that the cardinal error in chaotics terms, rigidity, has sometimes set in. The trick is to limit such groups in size and power.

Culture and cultural background can also be important as a framework for structured freedom. The Japanese have shown that 200 years of peace in the Edo period in structured rigidity, as a semi-feudal state, gave a unifying cultural background on which to develop rapidly. And the Edo period itself was a reaction to going over the edge of chaos, with constant civil war raging for years. Israel's development also mirrors a transition to structured freedom. The sell-off of state enterprises has coincided with an influx of highly qualified immigrants from Russia to provide the human capital for a booming economy, while a strong cultural heritage has produced the basis for cooperation and caring.

As we move away from a stable state of artificial life, we go closer to 'edge of chaos'. Just before we go over may lie a region of 'unstructured freedom'. This is a region where the economy can go either way very easily—specifically, backwards to chaos, over the edge, in a process of 'reverse development' under certain conditions. The key example here is the USA. Capitalism takes a fundamentally different form in the USA from the form in Germany, France, Japan or the UK. It follows an American creed of classical liberalism, based on earlier religious sects who rejected the official churches.[14] While many Americans are intensely moral, US capitalism is uniquely anarchistic and suspicious of central government. This leads to a limited sense of cooperation and group responsibility, and so to less care for the unfortunate, or awareness of how their condition holds back the whole economy. It is thus easy to see why US social groupings work well up to the levels of tens of millions, but not beyond. New York and Louisiana seem to be different countries, not just different states.

On our chaotics journey, we see a progression of chaotic states from which development cannot spring, with one state favourable to development. At one end we have unstructured rigidity, then structured rigidity, through to structured freedom and into unstructured freedom. This is not an all-encompassing truth, always applicable, just a framework for seeking a solution; but it deserves a place on our agenda as a way of thinking about capitalisms for development.

Evolving a political framework for sustained development

We have now reached a point where we could consider the question of what is the best type of political regime for economic take-off and sustained growth. A leading personality and thinker from Singapore recently asserted that 'All over the world, institutions, that evolve in response to the needs of an earlier period of industrialization are no longer adequate'.[15]

The supporters of unconditional *laissez-faire* private enterprise believe that only a truly democratic regime can create, enforce and maintain free-market conditions. In contrast is the resounding success of the East Asian Tigers. None of these is a democracy in the Western sense. What do these countries have in common? The answer is, to varying degrees, authoritarian governments that pursue a strong development policy and impose social order and a tight discipline. Such governments have carefully created a favourable macroeconomic environment for microeconomic freedom. They provide sound public finances, an adequate level of national saving and investment, and policies with legal teeth to control inflation in prices, wages and land values. For example, in 1996 Singapore enacted laws to end speculation in property and land by foreigners, deliberately to halt the inflationary spiral seen in the UK, Japan and the USA following such property price inflation. These governments have often tended to build an economic framework through favoured players—imperfect competition. Examples are the *chaebol* in South Korea and the Chinese diaspora families in Indonesia and Thailand. In some ways these structures copy the postwar Japanese *keiretsu*.

Chaotics tells us why. To build wealth nationally, certain cooperating forces are necessary. The 'Game of Life'—a computer game for autonomous agents—shows us that limited cooperation, balanced with competition, is far more successful for survival. It forms a 'tempered industrial Darwinism', with imperfect competition, but open markets, encouragement of education but low government spending as percentage of the GNP, and an influx of only the most suitable foreign technologies.

So the critics of Western-style democracy contend with some justification that liberal democracy by itself does not necessarily promote growth. It might or it might not. Its supporters reply that a dictatorship that has shown itself lenient to free-enterprise capitalism can always be brought down and replaced by a tougher one—South America offers some key examples. In principle, a democratically elected government should be in a far better position to ensure economic development in the long term. At the present time this argument is still inconclusive.

As part of this, it will be instructive to watch the race between China and India as they move through the tumultuous change from command economies to free enterprise. The richer of the two in natural resources, China has taken the lead so far in dismantling its systems of state controls and is currently enjoying a substantially faster rate of growth than India. But India is now poised for take-off.

It holds more key cards—a more democratic government, an efficient legal system, a trained managerial class and a surplus of first-class scientists and engineers plus emergent financial institutions and familiarity with Western styles of business. The people of Asia are changing more radically under the impact of Western ideas than they have for 2,000 years. Cultural mutation is taking a strange form—a mixture of capitalist consumerism, despotic business groups and watered-down socialism. But in neither country will the way forward be simply to graft liberal democracy on to centuries-old traditions. The question is whether this hidden transformation will produce a new model of society that has more general applicability?

Fragmentation of the nation-state: the reemergence of the city-state

We have spoken often of the giants of the Third World, India, China and Indonesia. However, over two-thirds of the members that make up the 160 or so 'United Nations' have a population of 10 million each or less. They are often forgotten because world politics and economics are dominated by fewer than two dozen 'powers'. These bigger powers call the tune at the International Monetary Fund, the World Bank, the World Trade Organization, the UN Food and Agriculture Organization and the Bank for International Settlements. In other words there are some 120 countries in the Third World in need of suitable and different policies. Economic success has escaped them, so far, because their development route has been wrongly mapped. What is missing most are potent strategies for dealing with specific cases, for example small tropical areas, sub-Saharan Africa and so on. Meaningful geographical groupings, or subsets, with common features and complementary interests should be the basis of specific policies.

To take the third state of capitalism, structured freedom, further towards implementation, the vision of a smaller self-organized unit could be seen as an important message on size from chaotics. Certain business people and politicians in the Far East, and a number of political economists from American universities, are also considering a specific political entity on this scale.

They believe that the old concept of the city-state with its rural hinterland, or a small regional entity, could provide a more appropriate framework for economic take-off and sustained growth. The idea has found a sympathetic echo in Europe, where there is a long tradition of small self-governing communities. China and Russia also seem to be favourable. We attempt to bring together the various arguments to make a case for a city-state framework in modern guise.

Historically the city-state has represented a successful form of organization in economic and social terms. Ancient Thebes, Athens under Solon, Sparta and later on the Italian city-states of the Renaissance marked a significant advance over the surrounding, debt-ridden peasantry. In the Middle Ages the prosperity of the Hanseatic league towns signalled the downfall of feudalism. According to de Tocqueville, the strength and growth of the USA could be traced back to the jealously autonomous, close-knit American communities of the 17th and 18th centuries, which grew in the 19th century into the powerhouse of 'small-town America'.

The large nation-states are not immune to the current yearning for diversity —ethnic and cultural, economic and the fragmentation into self-governing regions and subregions. The recent, spectacular growth of the Chinese economy is traceable to the new administrative splintering of China into city-regions, each with a population of 2 million to 10 million people. These new, human-size administrative units enjoy a large degree of self-determination. They are encouraged to solve their own problems of urban and rural planning, new industries, raising capital and operating educational and training facilities. Not so in Russia, or the Ukraine, although Alexander Solzhenitsyn has strongly expressed the view that for political and economic reasons the reconstruction of the nations of the former Soviet Union must begin at the grass roots level by creating highly decentralized small territorial entities. Budding democracy in small units is increasingly perceived as a stepping-stone to local economic take-off.

Fragmentation of large centralized nation-states has a parallel in the devolution of decision-making within giant corporations and multinational companies towards smaller profit-centres and semi-autonomous units. The implosion of very large industrial organizations is accompanied by the rise of alliances between smaller, more human-size firms who share certain common objectives but compete fiercely against each other in other areas.

Economic reshuffling also leads to the emergence of new sources of growth located in the fringe and overlap areas of the economies or territories of many countries. They are often based on a commonality of interest or complementary resources—skilled labour versus favourable location or proximity to a major market or exceptional transport facilities. Example are Singapore, which has grown to be the crossroads of East and West, and Hong-Kong, with a similar role. But tomorrow the crossroads may not be physical (shipping lanes or roads) but electronic, just as Bangalore is growing to be a software powerhouse—and so an extension of the USA or European economy.

The corollary is a slow erosion of the authority of nation-states. They are forced to bow to intraregional interests that tend to transcend national borders. Thus, the concept of rejuvenating a unit of the size and form of the-city state ought be on our agenda for the 21st century.

Urban versus rural development

However, a delicate part of this development concerns just where progress is focused geographically within a city-state or other structure: it cannot just be as an urban development. In 1900, 90 per cent of the world's population lived in the countryside. As we move into the 21st century, we find that over 50 per cent of the global population will live in large cities. Over the next 30 years, 90 per cent of urban growth will be in the cities that lack every facility for decent living—those of the Third World. In contrast, both Japan and South Korea based their original postwar 'aims' (not so much plans) around development of the countryside and taking account of an agricultural local economy. Today Japan is still fiercely protective of those native rice-farmers. By concentrating on relieving pressures on urban society, they have been far more successful in avoiding dramatic change in cultural values and the resulting urban decay and violent crime. Japan and South Korea tried to avoid the development model we see today, in Africa and South America, of an expensive high-rise capital city completely divorced from its country. They aimed to spread development across the country, as in the German postwar model. In contrast, China has generated a key problem with the reversal of its support for the countryside. By centring growth in the coastal cities, 100 million former peasants now roam China looking for work, and the final effects may be turbulent as traditional cultures and the fabric of their society are broken up.

Negative development: going backwards

In the early 1970s, *The Economist* peered searchingly into 'The next 40 years to 2012, from 1972' and even beyond.[16] Closing his eyes to the perils of linear extrapolation, the survey's editor concluded that it was 'logical to suppose that practically all of man's remaining economic problems ought to be solved' within the next 80 years. America's average family income would climb to around US$250,000 (at 1972 prices). And 'two-thirds of mankind should be raised from intolerable indigence to something better than the comfortable affluence which the other third of us already enjoy'. This speaks of incessant progress in monetary and development terms, everywhere. However chaotics suggests development can go both ways, by viewing economics as an environment in transition between states, all of which are quite possible at any time.

Development becomes reversible if cooperation and self-organization break down. This effect is being seen in some OECD countries, which are sliding backwards—the 'negative development' effect. A most sensitive area to push progress backwards is in the stock of human capital, skills and education. For example, in the UK, social decay and the failure to spend on education over the last 15 years—in comparison with the previous 30—means that illiteracy has risen. In the UK 1 person in 7 is now illiterate at 21 years, and 1 in 5 is innumerate.[17] Just after the Second World War, the UK had the largest GNP in Europe. It is now ranked fourth, having fallen behind France and now Italy over the last 15 years. With its growing population of homeless and jobless, the UK is receding towards the wealth levels of Eastern Europe, but below its education levels. Could the UK be overtaken by the Scandinavian community, Spain and the Benelux community next, if current (but opposite) education and economic trends continue in each country? The key lesson here is that running down the human capital stock today indicates a state of backwardness for tomorrow, with a gradual reversal into uneducated, unskilled masses. Increasingly the future is towards a society based on knowledge-workers, especially in OECD countries.

Other areas of critical sensitivity are the gaps between rich and poor and the general conditions to create insecurity, especially violence, both of which reduce business confidence and halt investment and growth. For instance, in the USA the number of children of the working poor (defined as those bringing in less than US$11,800 per annum for a family of three at 1994 prices, with at least one person working) had increased by 65 per cent from 3.4 million in 1974 to 5.6 million in 1994, and the number of children in families receiving welfare had also increased, from 7.9 million to 9.6 million in the same period.[18] These are the conditions for marginalization and social decay to occur, with the spread of violent crime, so the USA offers the highest murder rate of all OECD countries, with 23,300 murders in 1995. Thus while the USA makes much better use of its capital than Japan, or Germany, it will be passed in overall size of economy by Japan around 2005.[19] The lesson is that even a position of an enormous superiority in wealth and in vigour of capitalism can be eroded if cooperative support does not extend fully into the majority.[20] We can easily go backward in our state of cultural development. A key example that shows the resultant condition is the situation inside US schools. In 1995, the key issues in US schools were handguns, drugs, pregnancy, rape and in-school violence; whereas in 1940, the big issues were talking out of turn in class, not waiting in line, and chewing gum.

NOTES

1 The positive judgement on the performance of the Indonesian economy is not to be construed as an apology of the regime of General Suharto.
2 Paul Crook, *Darwinism, War and History* (Cambridge: Cambridge University Press, 1994); cf. *New Scientist*, 10 December 1994.
3 Malcolm W. Browne, 'Computer "creature" mutates and wows scientists', *International Herald Tribune*, 29 August 1991, quoting a statement by Dr Graham Bell, Professor of Biology at McGill University, Montreal, Canada.
4 The first conference on artificial life was organized in 1987 on the initiative of Dr Christopher D. Langton of the Los Alamos National Laboratories in New Mexico. Of course, artificial life is not to be confused with artificial intelligence, which pursues other aims and uses other techniques.

5 Under the leadership of Dr Kristian Lindgren of the Nordita Laboratories (*source*: 'Frankenstein's friends', *The Economist*, 6 April 1991, pp. 81–2).

6 Paul A. Samuelson, *Economics*, 5th edn. (New York: McGraw-Hill, 1961), pp. 729–37.

7 Ibid.

8 Martin Wolf, 'How the West failed Russia', *Financial Times*, 7 May 1969.

9 John Thornhill, 'Russia's unfinished revolution', *Financial Times*, 30 May 1996.

10 According to an MIT study, modular-oriented producers use 'half the human effort, half the manufacturing space, half the investment in tools, half the engineering hours to develop a new product in half the time' and furthermore their method 'requires keeping far less than half the needed inventory on site, results in vastly fewer defects, and produces a greater and ever-growing variety of products'—quoted in J. Womack, D. Jones and D. Roos, *The Machine that Changed the World* (New York: Maxwell Macmillan, 1990). These savings are found in particular in computers, software, electronics, machinery-building, steel-making, car parts, some chemicals, and also in the production of garments, shoes and toys. OECD, *Globalisation and Regionalisation: The Challenge for Developing Countries*, by Charles Oman (Paris: OECD, 1994), pp. 83 and 93.

11 OECD, *Globalization*, p. 86.

12 Ibid. p. 129 (fn. 241).

13 Paul Romer, 'Increasing returns and long-run growth', *Journal of Political Economy* (1986).

14 Seymour Martin Lipset, *American Exceptionism: A Double-Edged Sword* (New York: W.W. Norton, 1996).

15 George Yeo, Singapore's minister for information and the arts, in an article published in the *International Herald Tribune* under the title 'In Asia and elsewhere, smaller will be the better way to govern'.

16 Norman Macrae, *The next 40 Years: 2012–1972*; reprinted from *The Economist*, n.d. (?1971), pp. 1–45.

17 Will Hutton, *The State We're in* (London: Vintage, 1996).

18 Annie E. Casey Foundation, Baltimore, USA, 1996, report on the state of children in the USA.

19 Stefan Wagstyl, 'US financial short termism finds favour', *Financial Times*, 7 June 1996.

20 Lipset, *American Exceptionism*.

12

An Environment in Search of Its Guardians

Let none admire that riches grow in hell;
that soil may best deserve the precious bane
                    from *Paradise Lost* by John Milton (1608–74)

Chaotics delivers a clear message on disasters: nature's normal stable state is always that of recovering from the last natural disaster. Species reorganize and learn to adapt and live with such disasters. Up to a point. But over the aeons, animals and plant types, whole species, have disappeared following natural disasters they could not adapt to. For example, dinosaurs suddenly replaced the predominant water-based life-forms, as quickly as they themselves finally disappeared. So past a certain point in the disruption of the environment, and our ability to respond, we humans may well decline. And very quickly. Chaos theory indicates there could be a bifurcation point in the rate of disasters where we will transition into a phase of more accumulated pollution, accidents, floods and typhoons than we could handle. Are we approaching it?

A recent UN study found that the casualty rates caused by natural and manmade calamities keep rising steadily, by close to 6 per cent per annum.[1] Moreover, the actual count of natural disasters, be they earthquakes, floods or typhoons, has risen slightly over the last 10 years as the earth warms up. Disasters of all types, excluding wars, displaced over 26 million people in 1994, up from nearly 10 million in 1984. Disaster relief has had to treble between 1990 and 1994, to U$3.5 billion, to meet the escalating catastrophes. In 2000, natural and manmade calamities may displace 40 million people, according the International Federation of the Red Cross and Red Crescent.[2]

Is overdevelopment a prime cause of our plight?

In the previous chapter, we considered underdevelopment and how to ensure economic take-off and growth. Conversely, could the present ecological disaster be the result of 'overdevelopment', as suggested by Derek J. de Solla Price, a scientific historian, years ago.[3] There has been hardly any limit to man's megalomania and the damage inflicted on our environment—near destruction of the ozone layer, the dying Siberian taiga, the death-throes of the Caspian 'Sea', massive deforestation of Amazonia and Malaysia, desertification in sub-Saharan Africa. More cars jam our roads each year. Our cities are more overcrowded. The congestion of airspace, the piling-up of industrial waste and now nuclear waste, all scream that the human–ecological balance has collapsed. From ancient China to the Midwest in the USA in the 1930s, to most of Africa today, overfarming— rather than the lack of rain—has led to widespread destruction of soils. All are catastrophes brought about by man upon himself. The net effect over the last 50 years has been to go from Hiroshima to Chernobyl.

For instance, work has just begun on the colossal Three Gorges Dam on the Yangtze river, which will create a reservoir 400 miles long, roughly equivalent to one-quarter of the Mediterranean Sea in length. It will force more than a million people from their homes. Its turbines are to have eight times the capacity of the Aswan High Dam on the Nile, four times greater than any power station in Europe. The giant Chinese project is supposed to combine flood protection and power generation. Moreover the potential environmental damage has still to be properly assessed. Not only is there a major risk to all the ecosystems in this huge chunk of continental China, but Chinese engineers have themselves warned that if the dam is operated at full capacity, its reservoir could fill with silt within 20 years. No lesson has been drawn from a similar, unhappy experience when the Egyptian Aswan hydroelectric dam was erected.

A further example is the catastrophic flooding in northwest Europe in January 1995. The extent of the damage was arguably more than the inevitable consequences of usually heavy winter rains. Rather, a combination of urbaniza- tion, modern farming techniques and navigation streamlining has rendered the low-lying areas increasingly vulnerable. By systematically removing bends and loops to speed up navigation on the Rhine, the Moselle and the Meuse our engineers have contributed to making the flooding of West Germany and Holland worse. Moreover, out of every 100 houses inundated in the floods in France, year in year out, 75 are dwellings built in the lowlands in the last 40 years and only 25 are older structures erected on higher ground, the standard practice since time immemorial. Today 12.5 per cent of Germany lies beneath concrete or asphalt, and every week 1,500 acres more are covered for streets, parking lots and other urban development. Some 480,000 miles of hedges, says the French Ministry of Environment, have been ripped out since the 1960s as part of a monumental scheme for regrouping long-splintered farmland. Once the protective hedges and other natural barriers have been removed, urban areas and open farmland do not absorb water as effectively as land in its natural configuration.

Chaotics would suggest that we have to take the environmental problem far more seriously. We must find a way of limiting man's insatiable 'development for destruction' before we go over the 'edge of chaos'. But our relatively recent efforts to integrate environmental protection into the very fabric of daily life can be characterized as at best an uneasy balance between procrastination and utopia.

Manmade destruction of our own society has to be included

The full concept of our environment should also go beyond the safeguarding of the natural ecology. Countering the rise of nuclear accidents, drug addiction, AIDS, urban decay and other horrendous woes is a key part of this attack. Leaving a kilogram of plutonium in the open air at the heart of a city would make the whole region uninhabitable for generations. We clearly need far better protection against the smuggling of nuclear materials, for instance. The Ukraine's nuclear accident has a countable cost in its widespread environmental destruction and a hidden cost in the mutational affects on future generations and the thousands of skilled professionals who have fled the Ukraine for pastures less radioactive.

Concern for personal security has never been higher this century. In the USA, the strongest economy in the world today, major urban areas are 'no-go' areas for most of the population and the authorities. We are faced with the un-ravelling of society, traceable to the quasi-universal crisis of identity.[4] The US state is challenged from within by 'militias', since the lack of proper gun-control laws fuels lawlessness. Social dislocation and personal exclusion go with the erosion of the jobs, homes and security and the break-up of the community.

What can be done about this decay-cum-disintegration of our social environment? The former Secretary-General of the United Nations Boutros Boutros-Ghali kept pleading in favour of a more active approach to development, the elimination of poverty, and a reduction of disparities among social classes, ethnic groups and nations. Pet remedies abound. Upholders of order urge their governments to enact stricter laws, strengthen the police, impose heavier prison terms. The Churches repeat their exhortations against permissiveness. As always, defective analysis begets inoperative prescriptions—in flowery terms.

In search of 'sustainable development': the links between growth and the ecology

Environmental degradation is not a chance result of minor deficiencies in the process of economic growth. The attack on our ecosystems has its roots in the economic process itself. More specifically it depends on the types and levels of productive activity and the decisions made in the key areas of total energy usage, generation of waste, toxicity of products, byproduct production and methods of waste-disposal. Common misconceptions abound on 'sustainable development' for economic growth, stimulated by wishful thinking and convenient blindness. What is called 'management of the environment' (in theory achieved by integrating economics and ecology) often amounts to little more than piling up untested equations on gratuitous assumptions.

The first serious attempts to mitigate the consequences of disorderly economic growth were made in the USA in the late 1960s and early 1970s, followed by Western Europe. Dubbed 'technology assessment' they were concerned primarily with large-scale public and private projects. The stated purpose was to guestimate the first-, second- and *n*th- round impacts of new technologies on a case-by-case basis, but with no formal framework. The real aim was either to kill a project deemed harmful to people or the environment, or at least eliminate its most dangerous features.[5] The following two decades witnessed a blossoming of studies, proposals and counterproposals, ingenious schemes for containing overzealous inventors and unscrupulous promoters. With a sigh of relief, many observers greeted the consensus on the concept of 'sustainable development' from the Brundtland Commission—the 1987 meeting of the World Commission for Environment and Development.[6] Here, it seemed was a realistic objective worth pursuing.

Any rejoicing was short-lived. The underlying premise of sustainable development using economic incentives/disincentives to control pollution and destruction is not proven. Such measures include pollution charges, subsidies, various monetary inducements, and penalties set by direct regulation on standards, rationing permits, enforcing zoning rules and markets in pollution permits to validate their economic value. Can these really be relied upon to achieve the desired objective(s)? While one OECD publication in 1994 saw 'a new stage in international environmental policy', another OECD study issued the same year claimed that 'the idea of sustainable development has become quite controversial'.[7] Grandiose plans are not adhered to by industry and are rarely backed up by government.

For instance, a Mediterranean Action Plan to clean the sea and its shores and protect its ecosystems was agreed over 20 years ago, in early 1975, by the governments concerned. Yet despite the active collaboration of hundreds of scientists and environmentalists, this visionary international attempt to save the Mediterranean has simply failed. Industrial overdevelopment, unchecked pollution and excessive fish catches, among other factors, have dealt fatal blows to the whole area. The net results directly affect 130 million people living along the 30,000 miles of coastline, not including an extra 100 million yearly visitors. For instance, the mercury content of fish is one of the most alarming consequences of the rise of the Italian and Spanish chemical industries.

Just as dubious as grandiose agreements is the feasibility of developing reasonably accurate estimates of the economic value of environmental goods and services. A coherent policy aimed at protecting the environment and enhancing the quality of life requires information. Most current measurement techniques are inherently biased. Even the 'best' proxy indicators that are used are highly subjective evaluations (*faute de mieux*). In Box 8 we look a little more closely at some of the proposed 'environmental indicators'.

There is, however, another overriding caveat. Whatever model is finally chosen, the number of variables and likewise the number of parameters are of necessity very large, perhaps too large. Their interactions can however only be guessed at, and even the guesswork is ephemeral. In many ways, the problem is similar to the early attempts at modelling and hopefully predicting (even controlling) the weather, which have failed.[8] In both instances, the problem is far too complex to be amenable to mathematical analysis. The underlying dynamics are still unknown, a '*terra incognita*'.

Box 8. *Assessing environmental impact: indicators and the concept of value in quality of life*

A coherent policy aimed at protecting the environment and enhancing the quality of life requires information. Unfortunately environmental information is notoriously inadequate. Most of the time the data is unreliable, or simply unavailable. Existing monitoring systems are at best rudimentary. Much remains to be done to agree internationally even on basic definitions and standards.

Broadly speaking, environmental monitoring is concerned with:

• the detection and localization of 'hazards' and 'nuisances' and of their sources, e.g. abnormal radiation levels, air pollution, water pollution, noise, oil spills, etc., due to emissions, leakages and waste;
• the measurement, or at least an indirect estimation, of the observed volumes or levels of emissions, leakages and waste; and
• the quantification of the resultant change(s) in the use or usability of land, lakes, sea-shore, etc., from abandonment (as in the Ukraine) to recovery.

The units used are usually expressed in biophysical terms, to which monetary values are subsequently applied allowing at least a rough theoretical calculation of cost–benefit ratios. The major areas of application in the USA and Western Europe are all connected to health risks to animals, plants and humans: air quality, water quality and supply, conditions for fishing, wildlife preservation, surveillance of natural parks, etc.

Natural damage assessments are often based on a so-called PPP (polluter pays principle), despite disagreement over which damages and which costs are to be included. In cases of major disasters, such as oil spills at sea from tankers, it is generally left to the court to make the final ruling, often after years of litigation.

Over the past decade, emphasis has shifted from reducing the effects of environmental catastrophes to prevention and improving the quality of life. Creating positive environmental services and goods—e.g. public gardens, protected sea-shore, playgrounds and recreation areas, and ornithological reserves—is the new focus. In parallel, efforts have been made to develop a range of sophisticated valuation techniques to determine how much better off, or worse off, we as individuals or households are, or would be, as a result of a specific change in environmental quality.

'Contingent valuation' studies attempt to elicit respondents' preferences for a specific future (so far non-existent) service or good. Surrogate market techniques look at markets for some other good related to the environmental benefits and costs. So-called hedonic pricing proceeds by comparing property values supposedly related to differentiated streams of benefit (e.g. cleaner air, less noise, etc.) to be enjoyed by the occupants of houses *A* and *B*, in relation to houses *C* and *D* in another zone.

On top of everything, there are two further problems. First, how to make given site findings 'transferable' to other similar sites. And second, what time-discount formula is to be applied for length of suffering when measurements are so subjective.

Small wonder that these theoretical exercises have run into scepticism. Most realistic observers, together with practical environmentalists, argue that attempting to assign arbitrary economic values to non-market goods, such as the air we breathe, serves no useful purpose. Others believe current measurement techniques are unreliable and so demand better measuring rods. Clearly the present state of the art leaves much to be desired.

Using economics as a metaphor for the ecology?

Can we use economic metaphors to understand ecological disasters? In both cases, the eternal tendency of humans to overreach themselves is to blame. A review of the enormous literature on the subject and the output of innumerable conferences over four decades brings out two strikingly persistent but contradictory trends. First, outspoken advocacy of all-embracing (though plainly utopian) planning, which contrasts with the second trend—an equally strong propensity to equivocate and put off decisive action, pending an improbable consensus on what to do, how much to do, when and where to start.

The first approach produces visionary schemes, such as a universal, perhaps UN-sponsored, programme for returning to natural conditions. This would include a world government endowed with vast regulatory powers, for a catalogue of mammoth-scale rehabilitation projects and worldwide ecological monitoring. The alternative school of thought concentrated first, in the 1960s and 1970s, on technology assessment of major techno-industrial ventures (public and private). But later on it began emphasizing the need to investigate problems in depth. It therefore focused on developing a battery of measurements and instruments for so-called environmental economics.

What could be done to improve substantially the protection of the earthly environment? We will briefly review some of these techniques and the accompanying policies. However, chaotics makes us realize that the suggested measures and indicators may not be valid. Just as with weather forecasting, no matter how sophisticated our sets of mathematical equations are such approaches may come to little more than illusions. The real answer requires a prior understanding of how the process of environmental degradation sets in and then how it spreads unless kept in check.

The exponential law—better known as the compound interest curve—provides a revealing approximation here to what happens if no boundary, no obstacle of any kind, is opposed to unrestricted growth and similarly to cumulative degradation. Of course there are other growth models, but the message they carry is not fundamentally different.

Note that we are not particularly concerned here with compound interest in money lending, or mortgaging per se. Instead, we focus on the law of compound interest, since it provides a pattern for exponential growth in geometric progression. It is simply a very direct way to present the environmental case in mathematical terms, because it conveniently illustrates the risk of proceeding at the same pace indefinitely, without any guard-rail. Moreover, it offers a key insight into how to deal with it legislatively at the level of a whole society.

Deuteronomy on compound interest: a metaphor for run-away development

Compound interest's harmful effects have been known for two millennia. Ancient Hebrews and Greeks of the 6th century BC found ways of neutralizing the harmful effects of the compound interest equation while retaining the benefit of continued growth. Just how did they do it?

Deuteronomy, the fifth book of the Old Testament, written in the form of a farewell address by Moses to the Israelites before they entered the Promised Land of Canaan, contains several references to usury, or lending at interest, besides pillorying other sins. Biblical Hebrews and ancient Greeks knew something of exponential accumulation and the evils associated with its excesses. They had an inkling of the dangers of outsize growth and its companion, accelerated decay. While money lending to foreigners was allowed, and even encouraged, lending to fellow countrymen was in principle prohibited. 'Thou shalt not lend upon usury to thy brother.'[9] Islamic law was even stricter. 'Allah hath blighted usury', bluntly says the Koran.[10] In the Middle Ages, all interest was originally termed usurious and the strongest indictment of usury came from the Catholic Church, which prohibited the clergy from engaging in such practices. Yet the interdiction did not seem to prevent anyone (especially those at the top of the Church) from borrowing or lending money at interest. From the 13th century on, while the prohibition still stood, more and more people breached it than observed it.

In retrospect, the compound interest law has proved to be one of the corner-stones of Judaeo-Christian civilization. This is all fairly common knowledge—except for the most important caveat, which has long since been (most conveniently) forgotten. Just as sin, any sin, after an appropriate period of time, is to be pardoned or forgiven, *Deuteronomy* institutionalized remission, or the cancellation of the debts outstanding, every seven years.[9] Knowing human nature, the Hebrew legislator specifically forbad greedy moneylenders to charge still higher interest in anticipation of 'the seventh year, the year of remission'.

The provisions decreed by Moses had their equivalent in the early legislation of Athens. Solon (639–559 BC) was the first Greek statesman clearly identified and known to history as a giver of laws and as a reformer. Elected 'archon', or chief magistrate, in 594 BC, he found social conditions in Athens deplorable. Noblemen were all-powerful and the peasants were losing their lands and even their personal freedom because the newly rich capitalists had accumulated mortgages on prac-tically all small farms in Attica. The subsequent rise of Athens to power and fame owed a great deal to Solon's decision to annul all mortgages and debts, to limit the amount of land anyone might add to his holdings and to outlaw contracts in which a person's liberty might be pledged.

Drawing from chaotics, we see a twofold thrust. First, these laws were intended to limit the growth of lending at compound interest. This is equivalent to restricting the positive feedback effect of ecologically challenging activities to a minimum. Secondly the seven-year repayment halts a slide into the state of deathly rigidity through monopoly control with pauperization of the masses, by freeing large amounts of frozen capital in order to spark new commerce. Essen-tially Solon switched the community from an early feudal form of monopoly capitalism to entrepreneurial self-organizing units. The ecological equivalent is to periodically take stock and restore everything, before it goes irreversibly too far into the embrace of catastrophe. This includes detecting and breaking up any major drivers towards disaster. How could we do the equivalent on a massive scale for our ecology and so halt the slide over the 'edge of chaos'? An ambitious large-scale solution is called for to reverse the present trend to self-destruction. And full-scale effective protection of the environment cannot be had at bargain prices.

Breakthrough solutions from chaotics

What is needed is bold new thinking, a shock therapy on several fronts. We also need to understand more of the detailed damage inflicted by the ever-expanding production of material goods. The repair job of restoring and robustly protecting our earthly ecology can be expected to occupy several generations, possibly even more. And a major departure from current practices and policies is called for to reach breakthrough solutions. Chaotics may provide some of the key pointers here, by reassessing our priorities and pointing out how resources could best be used or, more importantly, reused.

But any overblown programme would be doomed just as surely as all the grandiose attempts have failed in the past. To maximize the chances for success it would be wise to select a few highly visible objectives and then marshal overwhelming resources, and if possible work from bottom-up. Whatever actions are undertaken, they should be prudently targeted and aimed at cooperation at all levels—local, regional, national and international, and both public and private.

Proactive guardianship for the environment: an environmental health care plan

Chaotics suggests that we reevaluate our options around our resources, in a decomposing then a recomposing cycle. The consequent solution may at first seem naïve. It is to give serious thought to recycling the better part of the huge excess subsidies spent each year on agricultural production worldwide. Instead of excess production, the money would be spent to hire a percentage of the dwindling rural population to act as ombudsmen and wards of our global environment. The goal would be to redirect a whole range of human endeavour to care for the environment. Part of the new services would be analogous to the conventional health care schemes, developed after the Second World War in response to the growing concern for bodily and mental well-being. But this would be a health care industry for the environment. We would make environmental protection one of our most valued occupations, equivalent to a medico. Standard wages for specific jobs would be paid. A new labour force would be formed by continual training in balances in the ecology, to produce a deep understanding of dependencies and cycles in nature. The social-psychological benefits should not be ignored. Instead of subsidizing alienated farmers with no future ahead of them, we would create motivated environmental workers and officers skilled in safeguarding nature and the environment. But it depends on changing our mental model of the environment into one of a life-support resource, as precious as agriculture, health or manufacturing, and to be invested in, protected and nurtured.

The tasks and duties to be entrusted to the 'guardians' are enormous: atmospheric quality, from air pollution to ozone layers; water quality; forest management; animal and insect husbandry; enforcement of forest laws and hunting and fishing regulations; surveillance of rivers, lakes and sea-shores; reconstruction of dikes, hedges and windbreaks; maintenance of firebreaks; control of gene mutations; wardship of parks, wildlife preserves and experimental farms. Further tasks would include ongoing research on natural dependencies and food chains plus creation of the early-warning systems for comprehensive monitoring of earthquakes, flooding and natural disasters.

Human swords into ploughshares: a taskforce for disasters

Guardianship of the environment will increasingly require a well-funded, permanent emergency global taskforce for combating natural disasters, from oil slicks and oil fires to floods, hurricanes and earthquakes. Again, using the chaotics approach of reevaluating our surplus resources in a decomposing then a recomposing cycle, an extension of the concept above is to create a disciplined operational force for rapid deployment to protect the environment and aid disaster victims.

Also, chaotics points out that the taskforce should focus on the most uncontrollable and perilous parameter, to combat the greatest danger. It should act as an extension of the current nuclear monitoring agencies, as a taskforce specifically focused on the lifecycle of nuclear materials, to ensure safe storage, monitoring of standards and a halt to the smuggling of radioactive materials. Using the chaotics principle again, of decomposing then recomposing cycles, it would be based on reusing, via retraining, redundant military personnel worldwide. It would also ensure that environmental protection measures, remedial care, preventive measures and monitoring are carried out.

We must also reemploy the redundant military industrial complex (both armies and arms manufacturers) in the East and West following the end of the Cold War. Impossible you say; hard to believe that any army could become the civilian reconstruction and emergency disaster force of the future. But it is already happening. To reconstruct Bosnia, the US army has the 353rd Civil Affairs Command, which consists of environmental engineers, public transport managers, electrical supply experts and telecommunications engineers, even emergency bankers. Interestingly, when asked if the unit used the *Managing Chaos* book, their commander, Brigadier General Thomas Matthews, said they were writing it. And then he said something even more profound: ' The art of War is very mature. It goes back thousands of years to Sun Tzu. The art of peace is much newer . . . we're learning about it here'.[11]

A moment's reflection shows this has some inner consistency and logic, because it fits several needs at the same time. Somehow, we must slow down the massive migration to the overcrowded cities, even reverse the rural exodus and the subsequent depopulation of the countryside. And the resources required to launch such a forward-looking social policy are at hand, in the agricultural subsidies.

Responsibility, banking and disaster insurance for the new ecological risks

The concept of man's environment as we understand it goes beyond the simple safeguarding of our ecology. US banks have been held legally responsible for lending to firms that have polluted land. The argument is that funding institutions are responsible for financing the ventures that cause the manmade disasters. In all of this we see the conflict of giant industries. While insurers may pick up the bill for disasters, other industries make their living from warming up the planet. Cars and the energy industry in general are the two major generators of carbon dioxide and sources of its influence on global warming (and incidentally of accidents affecting much of the population, from nuclear spillage to vehicle deaths and injuries). Thus, the World Energy Council, representing the energy industries of 100 countries, has strongly criticized a report from the International Panel on Climate Change linking man with global warming, mainly from fossil fuels.[12]

The UN Environment Program (UNEP) calculates that between 1987 and 1993 there were 16 catastrophes linked to the environment, each of which cost directly over US$1 billion. Of these, over 80 per cent were due to windstorms, while the rest were due to earthquakes, oil spills and fires. The insurance industry's total pay-out for these catastrophes was of the order of U$50 billion.[12] US insurers have been the hardest hit by environmental claims. They have tried to exclude environmental risks from their contract conditions, but have only found themselves in lengthy lawsuits over contaminated land.

Insurance and reinsurance companies have finally realized that global warming is steadily increasing the number and seriousness of natural disasters, and the cost of the damages they pay out on. Moreover there is a huge new set of insurance problems due to manmade disasters, new hitherto unknown risks against which we are virtually defenceless. Chernobyl and Three Mile Island have given stern warnings. We need a new and innovative taxonomy of the whole insurance principle to offer a higher degree of protection. The chaotics solution would be to take the situation away from the 'edge of chaos' by reorganizing around new strategies for insurance.

The time has come to rethink the instruments of insurance in this light, specifically the function, contents, stipulations and forms of compensation. Perhaps this rethinking could be based on the concept that future insurance policy conditions should promote and partly pay for the new guardian services. In 1996, 60 major insurance companies held a conference to debate the environmental risk problems and their own future policy.[12] There is also a small but growing body of fund managers, led by insurance industry investors, who feel that business must be ecologically responsible; they will not invest in environmentally unsound ventures. Ultimately this could have a major leverage effect on share values. The market price of those companies that endanger the environment will tend to fall as fund managers avoid them.

Effectively, we are beginning to see that the financial and insurance industries could end up as the true 'regulators' of our ecology. A new set of concepts, structures and roles, for the insurance industry in particular, may arise in the 21st century, from a relationship with guardianship.

Rural development: reversing the exodus

A further concern for ecologists is the exodus to the cities over the past three or four decades, which has taken place on a vast scale in the Third World. The UN Population Fund expects a huge urban growth, with Africa, the least equipped to cope, expected to have the largest growth.[13] In 1950 only one city had over 10 million citizens—New York. In 1996 there were 14, with Tokyo having 27 million. A further 13 'mega-cities' are expected by 2015, when nearly 80 per cent of urban dwellers will come from the developing world. For many underdeveloped countries, reversing the trend to an army of jobless in the cities is a prime goal, because the UN calculates that by 2020, approaching 100 million new urbanites per year will flood their cities. The exodus empties the rural school-room, bankrupts local shopkeepers and service businesses and drives the young to emigrate. To revitalize the countryside permanently, it also is necessary to maintain and develop the essential infrastructure—local utilities, services and amenities, now undermined by emigration from the near-emptied countryside. In a vicious circle, dwindling demand for schooling, banking services, local trades and crafts puts pressure on the regional education authorities, electricity boards, water utilities and banks to close down altogether. While local branches lose money, their closure accelerates the depopulation trend.

Chaotics, with its emphasis on networks, relations and supportive interactions, provides a rationale for reviving our dying rural areas. We can see a way out of the vicious circle. The reversal would try to use low-cost technology to compensate for distance, to bring jobs to the countryside, reversing the trend of people moving to where the work is. International communications are gradually becoming universal with the deregulation of telecommunications. And very-low-cost home information–communication–entertainment appliances will be available in the 21st century. They herald a renaissance for our rural areas, globally. Modern telecommunications technology could return the home to being the workplace, as it was two hundred years ago, via networked access to other workers, information, cooperative work, electronic markets and procurement. Electronic documents, trading and consultation are cheaper and faster than their conventional counterparts. The network can support education and reskilling, medical care and care in old age. In the more developed world, it could also provide remote access to mundane lifestyle services, such as teleshopping, telebanking, teleinsurance, and legal and tax advice. Also modern technology has revolutionized the costs and forms of organization of production and distribution and made it possible for smaller organizations, alone or in alliances, to compete more on equal terms with major corporates who rely on economies of scale and size. Using chaotics, with its emphasis on decomposing and recomposing cycles, we turn to electronically networked infrastructure services—be they banks, utilities or tax services—wherever possible, to serve rural areas.

NOTES

1 UN, 'Major disasters around the world: a global and regional view', report from the World Conference on Natural Disaster Reduction, Yokohama, Japan, 23–27 May 1994 (New York: United Nations), ch. 5, fig. 1.
2 UN, *World Disasters Report 1996* (Oxford: Oxford University Press, 1996).
3 Derek J. de Solla Price, 'The expansion of scientific knowledge', in Peter Albertson and Margery Barnette (eds.), *Managing The Planet* (Englewood Cliffs, NJ: Prentice-Hall, 1972), p. 143.
4 Boutros Boutros-Ghali, 'Let's get together to halt the unravelling of society', quoted from a message distributed in advance of the World Summit for Social Development, Copenhagen, Denmark, 6–12 March 1995 (reported in the *International Herald Tribune*, 10 February 1995).
5 To relieve the congestion at Heathrow and Gatwick, London's busiest airports, the Civil Aviation Authority has studied various options for additional runways. While analysis showed a strong case for additional runway capacity, the projects were dropped in early 1995 because either 3,300 homes would have to be demolished to make room for a third runway at Heathrow and or the village of Charlwood would be seriously affected by an extra runway at Gatwick. Any future development, said the announcement, 'must take account of environmental impacts'.
6 The title of the Brundtland Commission's report was significant: *Our Common Future*; see OECD, *Managing the Environment: The Role of Economic Instruments* (Paris: OECD, 1994), pp. 12–13.
7 OECD, *Managing the Environment*, pp. 27, 47; OECD, *Project and Policy Appraisal, Integrating Economics and Environment* (Paris: OECD, 1994), p. 14.
8 Problems encountered in early weather forecasting are dealt with in Chapter 2.
9 *Deuteronomy* 23:19.
10 The Islamic law of transactions is dominated by the concept of ribā. Fundamentally, this is the prohibition of usury, but the notion was extended to cover, and therefore preclude, any form of interest on capital loans and/or investment, in addition to any kind of speculative transaction, e.g. gambling. In our time, however, usury is taken to mean fixed investment in any form, and therefore it is impossible to predetermine rates of return. Of late, these prescriptions have been considerably watered down, particularly in Egypt, Saudi Arabia and several other Middle Eastern countries.
11 Thomas E. Ricks, 'In postwar Bosnia US army reserves guide reconstruction', *Wall Street Journal, Europe*, 11 June 1996.
12 Leyla Boulton, 'Debate warms up', *Financial Times*, 29 May 1996.
13 UN, *UN World Population Report 1996* (New York: United Nations, 1996).

13

A Recap: Briefly, Thinking with Chaotics— for our 21st-century agenda

How do we think using chaotics? To recap and bring out the full force of chaotics, we summarize twelve key concepts of chaotics below. We then interpret these in business and real-world terms for our agenda, under three convenient headings:

- Seven deadly pitfalls in thinking about business and about our world
- Seven pillars of business dynamics
- New therapies for social decay

Towards a philosophy of chaotics

A set of twelve first principles for thinking with chaotics

1. Chaotics can be defined in terms in the four states of chaos—frozen, flexible or semi-frozen, life-sustaining and chaos. There are specific phase transitions between the states, sometimes giving choices of direction—bifurcations.

2. Real-world living systems can be modelled as a population of autonomous agents that interact through self-organization into groups, which reproduce, and which obey set laws of interaction. They can exist only in the third state of chaotics, so the battle is to keep from sinking back into rigidity or over the 'edge of chaos' into anarchy—both are deadly states.

3. Life and dynamic systems are about the organization of matter, not the matter itself. So life is about synthesis, not analysis—it is about the dynamics between things, not the things.

4. Mutations are evolutions, and the natural state of the world is a series of disasters, as the world is ever breaking up and reforming in new patterns and associations. So life is constantly adapting to the effects of the last catastrophe. This defines life—as survival. But the aim of survival is at the level of the species. And so the aim is to reproduce, to mutate and adapt, not to preserve the life of one single organism as long as possible in one lifetime.

5. The autonomous agents often do not organize their behaviour optimally

and the environments in which self-organizing agents interact may be liable to change, so behaviour has a random element of chaos. This is equivalent to imperfect markets and imperfect economic agents with imperfect behaviour.

6. Cooperating autonomous agents succeed best, but only when they interact along the lines of trust until a hostile act is encountered (when cooperation is withdrawn). This survival behaviour is far more successful than purely hostile, or purely friendly, behaviour.

7. Complex systems with chaos present are not open to deterministic laws in a Newtonian sense. And they mirror the real world.

8. Behavioural effects in natural systems are non-linear, but many power law systems follow a pattern.

9. Part of this non-linear behaviour is due to positive feedback, so chaotic systems show increasing returns, not decreasing returns, as the input is increased or prolonged.

10. With positive feedback, small chance inputs may rapidly build up an output, so deterministic laws do not apply. Thus initial conditions are crucial, and make accurate prediction hard or impossible.

11. Rules governing the behaviour of natural systems are bottom-up, based on relations between primeval agents. The group behaviour springs from the individual behaviour of the 'free' agents under their low-level rules.

12. Systems in chaos often show no effects of scale—for instance the fractal pattern features are true for all scales of pattern.

Seven deadly pitfalls in thinking about business and our world

1. Because the world's natural state is one of change, and of non-linear behaviour, simple mechanistic extrapolation has little value. Its milder version, 'business as usual', invites complacency and inertia, which can lead to major errors, since future projections fail as soon as conditions change. Antidotes for thinking in the mechanistic extrapolation mode should include a key ingredient —some chaos. Systematic dissent, provocative alternatives and fostering creativity in any way are some ways of adding a garnish of chaos.

2. Problems that grow at a compound interest rate, if unheeded and unrestrained, may well breed disaster. Examples are excessive farming, cumulative environmental damage, the debt load built up by South America in the 1970s and 1980s and in business, such as the bleeding of IBM between 1989 and 1993. Chaotics points out the need to reverse such trends by periodic reassessment, with suitable instant restraint and perhaps concentrating on the core business in hand.

3. A business rationale based on quantification of everything in the business process is a futile exercise, because estimations of the critical parameters are

prone to serious errors. The more sophisticated the 'indicator', the greater the risk. To recalibrate risky parameters, a modicum of intuitive thinking can be helpful. Resorting to higher-level views, or using induction and deduction iteratively, is likely to be more useful. At best, in long-term projection of business or socio-economic processes we can accurately predict the 'climate'. The 'weather', be it a supply chain or a political situation, can only be predicted with any accuracy for a very short term.

4. In forecasting (of technology, of markets, etc.) a prefabricated consensus may mislead, even when backed formally by 51 per cent of the experts, as in a Delphi survey. Mainstream views of future developments ought to be confronted, and compared with conflicting viewpoints. For true intuition, keep the most creative dissenting views, throw away the consensus.

5. Linear models that admit of only a single outcome offer no useful solution. Whether in social organization, economics or technology, it is far better to have multiple possible solutions by considering various non-linear paths.

6. When considering an economy or society, information cannot be encapsulated in static concepts, as implied by such buzzwords as 'information explosion' or 'mega databases'. Rather, information should be seen as a process, a spatial, dynamic process linking myriads of large information heaps via a network.

7. Rigidity is not stability; as the break-up of the Soviet Union has shown, it is deadly. So conventionality and conventional thinking must always be challenged, especially when they parade as progress, because they inhibit progress. Unsettling questions are the most welcome, since they help break up today's conventions, to prepare us for the unexpected.

Seven pillars of business dynamics

To nutshell, competitive pressure is increasing because there are simply far more alternatives (or bifurcations) today as business increases in complexity. This is due to more freedom, newer demands, new business models, more entrants and globalization.

1. Operating under increasing rather than decreasing returns is the baseline from which to start making many more business decisions (given the latest technology, the huge fixed costs involved and whether your business is ready and able to convert to this mode). The critical factor is the strength of positive feedback, which creates the self-sustaining snowball effect.

2. Trigger mechanisms are frequently the basis of business success. The triggers are often inconspicuous at first and thus difficult to identify and quantify—maybe it is a chance meeting with a new customer, an invention, a new process, the discovery of a sudden latent need. But chaotics emphasizes the

extreme sensitivity to initial conditions, so no effort should be spared in searching out suggestions of triggers, evaluating them (however fanciful) and developing ongoing business through focused and timely decisions.

3. Managers need to integrate a dynamic economic intelligence of turbulent markets into a flexible strategy and decision-making process. Success and failure are linked to top management's ability to understand and take advantage of spontaneous, self-organizing dynamics within the firm. 'Scientific management'—the command-and-control deterministic strategies, based on what happened yesterday and 'business as usual'—have to be discarded.

4. New forms of business organization are emerging under the impact of the chaotic trends of reverse scale effects combined with self-organization. In the future, tasks and projects of Herculean proportions will be beyond the means of even the biggest corporations. But they will be within the scope of 'schools of minnows'—smaller companies acting in concert. The self-organization principle points to a range of structures, from virtual communities to *ad hoc* alliances, with a global spread of partners across oceans and time zones. The advantages of small size, in focus, speed, much leaner operations, and flexibility, provide the opportunities of reverse scale for those business people and administrators with the right organizing talents. Competition relies on alliances in 'coopetition' and the edges of the firm blur.

5. Well-established corporations are increasingly being stunned, and suddenly, by an unanticipated competitor or product event, with massive bleeding of market share. Competitors are seizing the initiative with new competitive scope—going offshore, reorganizing, producing new products, making killer alliances or redefining the core business. As sound prediction of strategy becomes so difficult, so decision-makers become more dependent on fresher, accurate knowledge of today's market state, plus the talent for imagining tomorrow's changes. Internal communication must be far more efficient, and thus internal organizational structures must be simpler and flatter. The firm's optimal size will be set by the speed of a market it can less and less claim to control. Thus leaders must become more imaginative and more daring.

6. It requires a mindset change to go beyond current thinking and recognize an innovation in its future context. So picking the likely market winner in product or technology innovation cannot be left to mainstream expert wisdom. Relying on traditional futures has wildly underestimated the market and lifestyle impacts of the computer, the health club, the photocopier, the home PC and the fax. In the world of the 21st century, such mistakes will be increasingly common.

7. The mechanism of innovation requires a mix of the chaos of creativity in a framework for thinking—an example of structured freedom, but with the structure gaining in importance. While the discovery and take-up of penicillin could be likened to the 'butterfly effect' of chaos theory, NASA's ten-year programme culminating in man's landing on the moon illustrates the growing complexity of present research. The rapprochement of the two approaches in a deeper

complementarity is a key theme of chaotics. When successful, the result is usually large-scale techno-industrial systems.

New therapies for social decay

Three problem areas dominate the postindustrial landscape: unemployment, under-development and environmental degradation. They have several things in common. All three lie at the intersection of the business of wealth creation with public welfare. The ongoing social dislocation calls for non-conventional remedies:

1. In view of the advanced state of decay, we need a quantum leap in boldness of thinking, perhaps the equivalent of shock therapy. Our inherited conventions in how we see our world have become deadly rigidities. We must reconcile ourselves to the loss of our cosy certainties about the family and corporate loyalties, the right to a permanent job, the traditional place of abode, the ancestral attachment to land and our whole past cultural structure. Clearly, the conversion to the new philosophy of living implies acceptance of attitudinal flexibility, the willingness to unlearn and to learn afresh and a readiness to move to alternative occupations. Part of this, whether we like it or not, is the intrusion of a new global space–time equation into everyday life.

2. The unrealistic objective of full employment and the underlying rigid labour legislations will have to be abandoned and replaced by more flexible employment policies, favouring part-time and intermittent work, sabbatical breaks, philanthropic work, retraining, upskilling, etc., the aim being to keep people occupied and continually interested in their own progress throughout life.

3. We need to implement an imaginative scheme linking employment policies to new enhanced social benefits in order to generate widespread popular support. A key move here could be to institutionalize the right to literacy for all—young and old—the right to decent housing for those who live under the poverty line, the right to protection against excessive environmental nuisances. Each of these much-needed improvements in the quality of life would entail the creations of thousands of new jobs.

4. In order to stop environmental decay, one solution is to use a fraction of the agricultural subsidies worldwide to maintain a highly professional corps of guardians of the ecology—a comprehensive environmental health care plan on a scale comparable to the early health care schemes for the masses in Western Europe after the Second World War. The drift into urban overcrowding and cultural decay must be reversed and the countryside revitalized.

5. Self-organization with a 'tempered industrial Darwinism' could be a formula for the economic growth of developing countries, by precipitating structured freedom. This is a state of many players, free-competition microeconomics, micro-loans, investment in human capital and flexible technology, not bloated

macroeconomics, while imperfect competition and markets are the expected norm.

6. Cultural and social concerns, combined with entrepreneurial growth, favour new groupings in business and politics, with the notions of the city-state replacing the nation-state and the virtual corporation superseding the conventional firm.

7. While the advent of the 21st century heralds the opening up of immense new opportunities, it also implies the need to face up to a variety of new risks on a scale unimaginable by older generations. To compensate for this, a radical overhaul of our current insurance philosophy (and practices) is needed to assess the true risks.

APPENDIX 1

Computing under Chaotics:
Slow Decay versus Self-Organization

Where is the wisdom we have lost in knowledge
Where is the knowledge we have lost in information
... and where is the information we have lost in data

after T. S. Eliot, 1928

A fifth freedom with cherry-picking for science and technology

As we move into the 21st century, ever more intriguing and mysterious problems will open for exploration in technology and science, especially in the areas of computing, communication theory and network structures as well as in cognition, psychology, microbiology and applied mathematics. Thanks to chaotics, we are at a sort of watershed in thinking about these key areas, because the contribution of chaos and complexity theories is to bring new tools for understanding every facet of the world around us. Eventually these may even cast light on the origins and structures of our planet.

In the previous chapters we presented the ideas of a small set of diverse researchers who have ignored traditionalist thought to push the study of strange behaviour in a number of ill-assorted systems ranging from mathematical to social, wayward processes and abnormal phenomena. Collectively, their endeavours have led to the emergence of the first layer of a new-born 'science' complete with a first set of axioms, primary theorems, elemental models and a kit of analytic tools, and applications.

What will be the impact of chaos and complexity on science at large? Chaotics will stir controversy, especially in applied mathematics and may give rise to a new style of 21st-century-oriented engineering. With a fresh eye, we may revisit the basic notions of dimensionality, symmetry, mathematical transformation, equilibrium, stability, etc. In so doing, we shall uncover the growing interdependence between disciplines and begin to appreciate why, in addition to being first-class specialists, contemporary researchers are increasingly required to be generalists as well. In other words, cherry-picking in other people's gardens is to be encouraged (just as the so-called fifth freedom in aviation allows foreign airlines to cherry-pick passengers in previously protected domestic markets and so provoke new kinds of traffic pattern).

In this section, we wish to apply our conceptual framework to a specific case study, computing and software. There seems to be a mutually beneficial relationship between computer science, especially software engineering, and chaotics. Three key software areas could benefit from the interaction:

- how to detect software errors at an early stage, eliminate bugs, compress and decompress data beyond the present limits, and thus speed up the migration to multimedia
- how to make software engineering more flexible and more productive, both by playing on extreme modularity and reusability (alias 'atomism') and by anticipating a shift in emphasis from software production to data gathering and repackaging
- how to harness the phenomena of chaos and complexity for improved and radically new computing philosophy, paradigms and algorithms

The magnitude of possible impacts of chaotics on software productivity and computing alone might confirm chaotics as a universal science in its own right. But first we need a new mind-set for tomorrow's computing metaphors, whose size problem will be a major stumbling block. Because that worn-out cliché of 'today's information explosion' is dwarfed by the complexity of tomorrow's data volumes and computing loads. And a large enough quantitative change becomes a qualitative change.

Traditional progress in software seems to be going well. The number of patents for software issued in the USA alone rose to some 5,500 in 1995, in line with what is believed to be an exponential growth in new software ideas.[1] But how many of these patents really contribute to software engineering progress? Algorithmic gimmicks and titbit programming do not make truly innovative paradigms and a radically new computing philosophy. Consider the human genome, said to contain some three billion nucleotide building-blocks. Think of the job of collecting, analysing and collating the data to be stored in databases and distributed via interactive networks for practical exploitation in medicine and pure research. We also need a new mind-set to clear up some of the confusion that has gradually invaded logic theory. Boolean logic, based on either-or propositions, is of little direct use for many real-world problems, such as social questions or quantum mechanics. However, the fuzziness associated with newer computing techniques is closer and more relevant to the real world and especially to the typology of its data.

The Internet as a chaotic world—
with information as a dynamic process

The word 'information' conjures up too many explanations and ideas. Since the advent of the digital computer in the late 1930s, scientists and practitioners alike have struggled to come up with a definition of 'it', 'the thing' and its conflicting connotations. For instance, there is an enormous conceptual distance between elemental weightless, sizeless, colourless bits[2]—those 0s and 1s that travel roughly at the speed of light—on the one hand, and on the other, the Internet.

Data volumes grow ever more staggering. Back in 1986, we estimated that the volume of data generated daily by mail, newspapers, broadcasting, databases, remote sensing and other mass media at some 10^{14} bits (i.e. 100 million million bits).[3] In a matter of a few years the wired society of 'on-line' people has come to count in terms of megabits, then gigabits, and now terabits (10^{12} bits). Much more is now digitized. For example, a one-hour high-definition TV programme displays about 4 terabits of data. So the 1986 estimate of daily data is now out of date by a factor of many orders of magnitude. And nobody quite knows how many host computers are hooked into the Internet—any figure is out of date, since the net's popularity is exponential. With millions of individual and institutional users at any one time, the global net carries ideas interactively, in formats from simple one-liners to full-motion multimedia documents. Its interactive pattern is an extremely complex behaviour of groupings. With (semi-) open access to sources as diverse as protein databases, credit ratings of businesses, classical libraries and illustrated encyclopaedias, astronomical images, music, holiday attractions, restaurants, cartoons and films, its content and organization are just becoming an enormous guided chaos. Its freedoms of expression reach towards anarchy, and very diverse cultures. Alaskan Eskimos (Inuits) compare notes on repression with Australian Aborigines. And with a variety of media channels, it provides telephony and supports multimedia, even video-conferencing and see-mail videoclips. Whatever the fad of the day, it caters for it. And yet clearly the Internet is not at its zenith. We have a burgeoning chaotics system. The crux of its underlying problem is how to build better, more meaningful links between the tiny bits of disparate data that together make up the fathomless ocean of global information. Hot-links with hypermedia over the World Wide Web allow us to click on a reference and seamlessly jump to other databases elsewhere. We have a highly complex system, one filled with chaos.

But as compilers of databases and operators of networks know all too well, there is no simple, universal recipe for indexing—cataloguing, classifying and ordering the myriads of apparently trivial items, signals, measurements and more complex proxy indicators by straight reference to generic groups and species. However tedious and vast this sorting out may be, it is matched by the job of making a seamless Web navigator palatable to all classes of user.

A digression on computing in biology

To emphasize the scale of difficulties facing architects and designers of the future Internet and its successors, it may be useful to draw a parallel with work now under way on another scheme, also of near-Herculean proportions—mapping the human genome. The thousands of scientists who undertook the task of unravelling the genome's secrets thought that the project would stretch over the next 15 to 20 years and cost upwards of US$3 billion. The genome is made up of 3.5 billion molecular groups called *bases*, or nucleotide building-blocks, known as A (for adenine), T (for thymine), C (for cytosine) and G (for guanine). Human genes (and those of other animals and plants) are made up of tens of thousands of bases arranged in specific sequences. The genes are arranged on chromosomes, of which every normal human being possesses 46, in 23 pairs. At the molecular level the genetic material is comprised of DNA with its famous double-helix structure. Quoting these exotic orders of magnitude underlines the scale of the complexity of the task—owing partly to the sheer quantity of data and partly to the mammoth number of possible combinations. In 1989 the molecular biologists involved in the programme agreed to store their information for the genome map in a standardized way by using a system of labelling that would still require the storing of approximately 500 terabits.

That was the situation and outlook up to 1992. That year, a team of French researchers led by David Cohen stole a march on American and British centres for genetic research by piecing together a map covering some 28 per cent of the genome, including practically the whole of chromosome 21, the first chromosome to be almost fully mapped. This particular chromosome is connected with Down's syndrome, Alzheimer's disease and some forms of epilepsy. However, the complete human genome is too vast for geneticists to search through it every time they wish to trace an interesting gene or part of DNA. The French team's method of constructing physical maps of specific chromosomes solved the problem by carving the genome into a jig-saw of manageable fragments, searchable by computer. Thus, the problem became tractable and fairly easily solvable. The moral is a new approach to computing problems.

Practical philosophers wanted

This type of computing in the biological disciplines is relatively new and therefore it provided ample opportunity for innovative conceptualization of the data as a prelude to the formulation of logical inferences and working hypotheses. That is just what Cohen and his colleagues at Généthon have done. The decisive require-ment for this type of breakthrough is a researcher's ability to grasp the underlying logical connections between observation and theory. You need to be able to figure out the existence or likelihood of alternative paths or short cuts. And that is where chaotics—chaos and complexity theories—comes in very handy. As Clark Gylmour, Professor of Philosophy at Carnegie-Mellon University in Pittsburgh, has said: 'Programmers of computers are a dime a dozen, but what is needed are people who can take vaguely formed problems and find ways to make them precise enough to be programmed; this is what philosophers can do'.[4]

The occasion was the launch of a programme for a major new field of study, called 'Logic and Computation', back in 1985. Echoing Gylmour's statement, his CMU colleague Watts Humphrey put it bluntly: 'The scale of our largest software system will always stretch the limits of human ability. Software thus represents a new human frontier. The conquest of that frontier will require all our wit, skill and dedication'.[5]

Granted, the connection between philosophy and high technology is not easy to disentangle. Yet it is essential for further progress that we try. Most computer algorithms are traceable to a logical theory (possibly augmented here and there with a zest of psychology). But many foundations of computing—e.g. the von Neumann architecture of modern computers, artificial intelligence, or the concept of parallel processing—transcend even the most elaborate system of philosophical reasoning, whatever notation is used. So let us try to work heuristically by returning to the concrete example of the Internet.

Tracking down vital data

The Internet[6], as we have viewed it, embodies the fundamental vision of information—be it elemental or global—as a dynamic process. The original Internet was built a quarter of a century ago, as a US military experiment to design and test out a distributed computer network capable of surviving a nuclear onslaught. After two decades of uninterrupted growth, the system had become a top-heavy, unruly monster. With connections to an untold number of computers and databases in some 60 countries it had no central point for directing the user to the right source of data, and little advice on how to access it.

Among the Internet's users, the European Laboratory for Particle Physics in Geneva, Switzerland (CERN) played the crucial role by creating a new approach to information search strategies. Motivation came from CERN's growing need to transmit masses of data in-house, and worldwide between thousands of researchers. Two CERN specialists, Tim Berners-Lee, a telecommunications engineer, and Robert Caillou, a seasoned documentalist, came up in 1989 with the idea of supplementing the physical network with a layer of software now known as the World Wide Web (WWW), as an intuitive hypertext access to networked information. Hypertext techniques allows a user to summon any item highlighted without knowing how the computer or the connection works, or where the information comes from. Information anywhere can be 'browsed' using marked-up words and 'net browser' software. The WWW makes it simple to browse through the Internet's seemingly endless resources. According to Robert Caillou, the Web is the plain antithesis of the traditional top-down planning resorted to by governments and practised by old-fashioned corporations.

Democratic, free-wheeling, Darwinian—such are the epithets used by the Internet's evangelists. So commercial free enterprise over the Internet has turned it into an electronic market and a consumer channel. On-line providers such as America on-Line and Compuserve abandoned their hostility to it because the major telecommunications carriers such as AT&T competed with them in providing Internet services. New software battles in the interface and browser market have provided rapid product development, so millions of users have learned how to use and understand this world, even assembling personalized home pages on their own PC. There is a key lesson here. The two largest, most complex information systems—the World Wide Web and the genome project—have evolved in response to the users' needs as well as their constraints. The conclusion is a quite simple message—that users are more interested in the message (the contents) than in the medium, contrary to Marshall McLuhan. A radically different rationale for the information process is overdue. We can infer that the traditional approach of one-sided data-gathering and formal processing and dissemination of information, whether sequential or parallel, is far too simplistic. As computer networks continue to grow larger, completely new techniques for understanding and managing them will be required. Inexpert users will have to use the services of a intermediary,[7] perhaps an 'intelligent' software agent.[8] It is on that premise that Dun & Bradstreet and other professional information providers have built their business, by 'offering more than numbers'.[9] But too often, we feel that that 'more than numbers' falls short of what is needed, so the provision of information services will become far more sophisticated. The Web makes us realize that there is a specific logic that goes with the printed word, and another logic altogether that is in keeping with pictures and video. Besides the physical models of Newton and Laplace, there are biological microcosms, ecological archetypes, behavioural patterns, economic and industrial blueprints, and more, and they all coexist, interact and contribute to our informational surroundings. The dynamics of the information process in this situation can be nutshelled: a multilogic culture is the future. The Internet and the genome project herald its advent. They make us conscious that Boolean logic as used in computing is a far cry from the formal logic of Descartes; but it is not far enough, so 'fuzzy' logic and its successors in new logic (such as maximum entropy) must take us further.

The Web convincingly demonstrates that 'information highways', by giving easy, quasi-instantaneous access to a variety of resources not only permit and even encourage cultural diversity, but also emphasize the primacy of the individual user, preserving all of her or his idiosyncrasies. Computer enthusiasts keep predicting that, as a result of ever-cheaper computing power and storage, eventually 'all data will be on-line; everybody will be a user; everybody will be connected'. Perhaps on the contrary, the uniform pattern of usage is the least likely to prevail: everyone will have their own pattern. This confirms the finding that the value of information does not reside in its volume or comprehensiveness, but rather in its subjective pertinence (relative to the ultimate user) and its objective relevance (relative to the purpose or end-use). As a corollary, the user's logic may be at variance with the designer's intention, and vice versa. Initially the PC was deemed particularly suitable for the home; yet, office workers were the first to popularize it. Likewise, ARPANET's success was due to its e-mail facility, a feature that the network's designers and promoters failed even to mention in their initial offerings.

Slow decay, self-organization and fault tolerance

Let us turn to general computing and our dependence on it. Some specialists in computer systems risk-analysis are suggesting that, until we have a more precise scientific method of evaluating the dangers, computers should no longer be used at the core of critical applications like emergency services, nuclear reactors, and fly-by-wire autopilots. In a recent book entitled *Reinventing the Future: Conversations with the World's Leading Scientists*, the author, Thomas A. Bass, wrote, 'In chaos theory ... information equals surprise, and the more information you have the more surprised you are. This has been my overreaching principle in shaping this book—to maximize surprise'.[10]

W. Wayt Gibbs claimed that often systems crash because they fail to cope with the unexpected, and networks amplify this problem.[11] In a somewhat similar vein, John Casti, a mathematician at the Santa Fe Institute, considered that the cause-and-effect relationship, as reflected in hard data, can be anything from catastrophic to chaotic to lawless to ... surprisingly, unexpectedly expanding.[12]

There is growing concern in leading corporations and public organizations that, to be of real value, the organization's information technology (IT) strategy must be integrated into its business goals, culture and planning, as well as its everyday activities. IT and business strategy must be one. This is a severe challenge given the current methodologies and know-how deployed in the applications software development arena. Unfortunately there are many examples of dismal failure, where major systems have overrun cost and time estimates and have not met business requirements—approximately 40 per cent of all custom development goes this way. Many million-dollar information systems have been thrown out even before they have been used because of this type of shortcoming. Examples are rife in the banking and other financial services sector. The decision in March 1993 to abandon the centralized Taurus stock-trading system in the City of London, after investing about US$350 million, not to mention the loss of over 300 jobs, is just one very visible example.

And yet large numbers of systems are found to be wanting soon after they have been brought into operation. For instance the Central London Emergency Ambulance Service computer, used to direct ambulances immediately to people who are suddenly gravely ill or injured, became overwhelmed with calls in autumn 1992 just months after its inauguration. As a result, during a period of a few hours, many people in the metropolitan area died needlessly; the director of the service, of course, had to resign. But the real message is that the system design was seriously flawed, through lack of understanding, or even awareness, on the part of those who were responsible for its construction and acceptance of the weaknesses of digital computer systems, especially in non-linear dynamic situations. A small increase in the number of 999 calls caused an unacceptably large growth in computer response time, with disastrous consequences; chaos manifested itself in more ways than one.

Another example is the Bell Atlantic and Pacific Bell telephone network outages in the summer of 1991, which were subsequently traced to a typographical error in a software patch. And more recently the Denver Airport baggage system débâcle proves that the situation is not getting any better, despite its final success.

Biological engineering for tolerant systems

Given the uncertainty and unpredictability of the real information process and the real world, information systems ought to be designed to tolerate errors and abnormality, without jeopardizing the survival of the system. The underlying concept of tolerance should begin by minimizing errors. A key feature of fault-tolerant systems is their ability to adapt and survive. For success here, we can draw useful lessons from biological systems. This view implies a basic conceptual change, reengineering in the broadest sense, since business dynamics as well as technical design issues are involved.

We can take a leaf out of the book of nature, where living systems have evolved because of their innate ability to survive in hostile environments. Mutation and selection of the fittest, the two key elements of Darwin's theory, are only possible when organisms are robust and able to tolerate surprising change. Despite attacks from all quarters outside, and microorganisms within, such 'computers' as plants and animals continue to function more or less as they should. Their performance may degrade, at worst gracefully. From such battles with the unforeseen, biological systems develop improved resistance to invasion and evolve new functions and behavioural patterns. How do highly ordered, adaptable organisms like plants and animals come into being? What is the secret of their quasi-permanent status?

There are two main sources of difficulty with digital computers. First, bug-free programs, to all intents and purposes, do not exist. This is what we might call the microscopic road to chaos. Computer programs of the traditional kind, written for machines built according to the principles set out by Johan von Neumann some 50 years ago, only work when every single bit is in the right place and sequence. Digital computers use binary logic—a voltage is high or low, positive or negative, or again, a current flows or it does not. The reason is that, when they were first developed in the 1940s, physical devices with more than two stable states were too unreliable, so engineers chose to stay with two-state, or binary, logic, and this naturally lead to the representation of all data in terms of the binary digits (i.e. bits) 0 and 1. Technology for implementing multivalued logic could well be useful for the development of systems better able to tolerate random errors. Moreover, computers are being developed based on fuzzy logic, in which, instead of all decision values being true or false, black or white, there is a range of probabilities from 0 to 1. In order to make sense out of the stored bits and at the same time enable error-detection to be carried out, some agreed method of grouping them together must be established, otherwise there would be no way of knowing if a given isolated bit, say a 0, was correct or had been corrupted and should really be a 1.

There are sophisticated methods for detecting bit errors, such as longitudinal checksums and cyclic redundancy checks calculated with orthogonal poly-nomials. Some error-detection algorithms allow up to a certain number of bit errors in a given bit sequence to be corrected also, but there are penalties to be paid in terms of the number of extra bits added to the sequence. A common approach when an error is found is to go back and repeat a certain number of operations since it occurred, be they memory fetches in a computer or re-transmissions over a network. The supplementary computation and transmission costs for the various techniques have to be traded off against each other.

Two sources of these errors are so-called 'white' and 1/f noise (noise power is inversely proportional to the frequency—a power law) in, for example, semiconductor chips, amplifiers and transmission channels. The 1/f noise shows extensive temporal scaling behaviour, in the same manner that fractal coastlines exhibit spatial scaling. Thus, in the case of 1/f noise, on all time scales (1 hour, 1 minute, 1 second, 1/10th second, etc.) the ratio of error-free time to that during which noise produces errors is constant. Even during error bursts there are error-free periods. The behaviour of such temporal functions is weird, and is similar to the interesting Cantor middle-thirds set. As programs of hundreds of megabits are moved around between memory and processing units, and over networks, the probability of bit-corruption becomes quite high, added to which programmers are at liberty to make programs modify their succession of states in a way that is dependent on the data they receive, so it is small wonder that the occasional bit goes astray, with potentially catastrophic results. In other words, a tiny error, of whatever origin, can cause the subsequent evolution of a program to run wild.

The other problem is the sheer complexity of the computer programs and information systems that we attempt to construct. Given this enormous breadth of application, any problem expressible in algorithmic form, no matter how complex, can, in principle, be tackled with the help of computing machinery. Even if each program module in a very large information system was completely free of bugs and there were absolutely no physical error sources in processing, storage or transmission—in other words no microscopic glitches—it would not be feasible to map out all the zillions of possible states a given system could evolve to as a result of the interactions among modules and the effect of data. This may be considered the macroscopic route to chaos.

Can we use another route—analogue or 'analogue-like' (multistate) systems—since the real weakness of digital systems is that just one bit out of place can stop the whole machine, or possibly set in motion an entirely irrelevant piece of program code? Analogue systems suffer to a much lesser extent from this type of problem. And in the light of non-linear mathematics, we must be careful about using digital computers to explore the future evolution of physical, economic, social or information systems. Maybe hybrid methods (combining the best of analogue and digital) could be considered, or entirely new paradigms for 'analogue-like' multistate computation for complex or non-linear systems.

Sophistication in simplicity

To overcome this problem perhaps software modules should be developed as tightly specified, small entities that might be called 'restrained objects' or 'proven actors' or 'simple objects'. In the same way that low-order iterations do not 'reach' chaotic behaviour, small software routines are less likely to run wild as a result of either bit errors or undue complexity. Moreover, more than one of these 'soft' components should be available to the overall software system that requires a particular component to carry out its task, so that errors, when detected can be overcome through redundancy rather than in-line, i.e. immediate, correction. Such redundancy is applied in many engineering disciplines and commonly built into hardware, especially fault-tolerant systems, but rarely are software algorithms duplicated; on the contrary they are often made re-entrant so that many different applications can be using the same software module concurrently, increasing the likelihood of attaining unforeseen and unwanted computational states. Of course duplicate or multiple copies of software modules will demand more memory, but with storage costs decreasing annually at anything up to 50 per cent, is it not worthwhile to sacrifice memory for software reliability?

Let us be clear that we are concerned here with an analogy between the iterative evolution of non-linear dynamic systems and the containment of errors in algorithmic calculations by limiting their size in terms of number of instructions. A small module may still carry out a very large number of computational steps to achieve its desired result.

For fault-tolerance in complex systems, and chaotic systems, software should be developed in small chunks, or building-blocks. Each is completely specified, and can be proved in terms of its inputs, outputs and internal states. This resembles the object-orientated programming paradigm, but goes further by recommending the successive division of objects until they become 'safe'. By this we mean small enough for the associated algorithms to be formally verified and also having data persistence and protection with back-up (or redundant) modules.

Improved knowledge of chaos and its potential origins in software systems drives us naturally to the conclusion that the marriage of a number of reasonably well-established computing concepts could succeed. Objects, formal methods, data persistence, error detection and redundancy, with the deliberate constraint of keeping the algorithmic elements very small in number of instructions bring a new paradigm—'atomistic programming'. Schumacher coined the phrase 'small is beautiful'; we might add that 'small is serviceable, robust and anti-chaos'.

We are, of course, arguing qualitatively for a new approach to software production. We are not able to give a figure for the maximum number of machine instructions in a single algorithm. In all probability there is no such figure. It depends on the individual algorithm and perhaps the data sets to which it applies, and there is likely to be a distribution of optimal algorithmic sizes. What can be said with some certainty is that the bigger a program is the more likely it is to go wrong and the more difficult it is to debug. Large computing systems, in all their variety, should therefore be constructed from tiny, formally proven and standardized atomistic algorithms.

We are emphasizing here the application of the engineering adage 'keep it simple'. Just as in other areas of endeavour, in the software industry there are no trophies for boxing too cleverly and designing complicated algorithms. We may draw a parallel with RISC versus CISC technology for microprocessors.[13] Although there is as yet no clear winner between these two designs, no one can doubt the challenge of the former to the latter in the top-end workstation market, one of the fastest growing sectors today in the information, computer and telecomms (ICT) industry. Another advantage of atomistic programming is that it would facilitate the transition from software to firmware, when appropriate.

In this context we distinguish between complexity, a phenomenon of the interactions among a large number of simple (or otherwise) systems, and complicatedness, a characteristic of overambitious, entangled single systems. Complex systems, incorporating several or many simple systems, (which may, or may not, show chaotic behaviour) can manifest ordered, deterministic, static or dynamic behaviour, and be proved to do so mathematically; whereas the behaviour of complicated systems is nearly impossible to analyse and almost invariably unpredictable.

Even the most complex systems in industry and commerce can be constructed from a set of less complex systems, which in turn can be made by putting together simpler systems, and so on until we get down to the algorithms that can be encoded in (indivisible) atomistic programs. Complicated systems are less manageable, and therefore undesirable. Atomistic programming should close the software gap, so software engineering becomes worthy of its name.

NOTES

1 Charles Arthur, 'Nothing new in software?', *New Scientist*, 4 February 1995.
2 To borrow a favourite expression used by MIT's Professor Nicholas Negroponte ('In the Information Age, a new set of have-nots', *International Herald Tribune*, 14 February 1995).
3 Georges Anderla and Anthony Dunning, *Computer Strategies 1990–9* (Chichester and New York: John Wiley & Sons, 1987), pp. 247–51.
4 Elizabeth M. Fowler, 'Philosophers wanted', *International Herald Tribune*, 5 March 1986.
5 Linda Runyan, 'Escaping technology's tar pit', *Datamation*, 1 April 1986.
6 The literature dealing with the Internet is monumental. Readers might gain special insight from the following sources: 'The Internet: the accidental superhighway', (a survey by) *The Economist*, 1 July 1995; Kurt Kleiner, 'What a tangled Web they wove . . .', *New Scientist*, 30 July 1994, pp. 35–9.
7 The concept of intermediary or gatekeeper was explored at MIT as far back as the early 1970s. See Thomas J. Allen, James M. Piepmeier and S. Cooney, *The International Technological Gatekeeper* (March 1971; reprinted from *Technology Review* 73(5)).
8 Ellen Germain, 'Software's special agents', *New Scientist*, 9 April 1994, pp. 19–20.
9 Claudia H. Deutsch, 'Combatting information overload: Dun & Bradstreet aims to offer more than numbers', *International Herald Tribune*, 18–19 February 1987.
10 Thomas A. Bass, *Reinventing the Future: Conversations with the World's Leading Scientists* (Reading, MA: Addison-Wesley, 1993).
11 W. Wayt Gibbs, 'Software's chronic crisis', *Scientific American*, September 1994.
12 John Casti, *Complexification* (New York: Harper Collins, 1995).
13 The central processing unit of a computer has built-in logic circuitry for decoding and executing the instructions of a program. Examples of instructions are:

- add the contents of register 1 to the contents of register 2 and store the result in register 1
- if the content of register 1 is a negative number, branch to another address location in this program
- fetch the contents of a specified cylinder and track on a given disk drive

All instructions can be built up from a basic irreducible set of instructions—a sort of computer alphabet. But the designer of the arithmetic-logic unit can also include in hardware compound instructions in addition to those of the irreducible set; such designs are called complex instruction set computers (CISC). The alternative design philosophy is to build in hardware a restricted set of instructions (maybe a few more than the irreducible set); such machines are called reduced instruction set computers (RISC). Which design is chosen is a matter of trade-off and depends on the type of applications the computer is to be used for. RISC machines, in general, take less time to decode and possibly more time to execute program instructions than CISC computers.

APPENDIX 2

Playing Simple Games with Numbers

As far as everyday life is concerned, non-linear behaviour is not only more interesting than linear behaviour but also more useful in understanding our environment and society.

To examine this further, we are going to play an extremely simple numbers game. We shall compute successive values of what mathematicians call an iterative function and engineers call a feedback system. The equation we have chosen to compute with is deceptively simple; it represents a set of parabolas, each one different according to the value of a. A schematic illustration is shown in Figure A1, where i is the iteration number, starting at 0. You will note that iteration is akin to feedback.

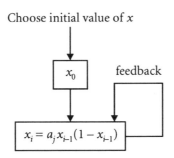

Choose initial value of x

x_0 feedback

$$x_i = a_j x_{i-1}(1 - x_{i-1})$$

Figure A1. *Iteration is akin to feedback*

Suppose for the moment that $a_j = 2$. Think of a number x_0 between 0 and 1; it will be a fraction of course, but do not worry about that. Calculate the value of x_0 times $(1 - x_0)$ and multiply by 2 to give a new number. Notice that x is raised to the power of 2 in this expression, which can be written $2x - 2x^2$. Now comes the iterative part of the game; you let this number you have calculated be a new value of x (say x_1) and use it again exactly as before by calculating x_1 times $(1 - x_1)$ times 2. You continue in this way, always feeding back into the formula $(2x_i(1 - x_i))$, for successive values of i, the new value that you calculate on each iteration. The fun is to see what the sequence of values of x_i looks like. To help visualize what is going on, we shall look at the details of the iteration. But, first let us define roughly what is meant by a function and the special variety called an iterative function.

A simple iterative function system

A function is a map that takes a member of a set of objects and uniquely relates it to a member of another set, which may be identical to the first. For example, if the both sets consist of the infinite set of all real numbers, then a function is a recipe for taking each and every member of the set of real numbers and calculating the value of another real number. Generally we may write $y = f(x)$, where x is a member of the first and y a member of the second set. For each value of x there is a unique value of y. The opposite is not necessarily true. (There are, of course, other types of function on the set of real numbers that we do not need to go into here.) An iterative function system takes a value of x, computes y and then feeds this value back into the functional relationship as a new value of x; so $x_{n+1} = f(x_n)$, where n is the iteration number.

The function $y = 2x(1 - x)$—you notice it is just a parabola—is plotted in Figure A2, which also shows the straight-line function $y = x$, at 45° to the x- and y-axes. The corresponding iterative function system is $x_{n+1} = 2x_n(1 - x_n)$, the one of the simple game we have chosen. In fact, the sequence of x values quickly converges to $x = 0.5$, and the reason why is illustrated graphically in Figure A2 for the case where the number first thought of is $x_0 = 0.1$.

For this value of x_0 you simply read off the value of y from the graph ($y = 0.18$), and that value becomes the input x_1 for the next iteration, which is obtained by graphically finding the intercept with the straight line $y = x$, as shown in Figure A2. Thus the iteration is represented by the stepwise path, A, B, C, D, E . . . No matter what value of x_0 you start with, you finish up at $x = 0.5$, which is where the straight line $y = x$ crosses the parabola and happens to be the maximum value of $2x(1 - x)$.

Table A1 sets out the sequence of numerical values of x as the iteration proceeds with $a_j = 2$, starting from different values of x_0, as illustrated graphically in Figure A3.

The only remarkable thing about this game is that, no matter what number you first think of (x_0) between 0 and 1, the final value is always 0.5. This amusing little algorithm is like a basin, and this point ($x_{final} = 0.5$) is like the bottom of it, attracting anything that is put into it—it is a point attractor.

This is quite interesting, but not so fascinating that you become excited. But there are other things we can do to try to increase the level of interest without altering the basic idea of the game. So far, we have focused on iteration of a simple function of x, a single parabola.

Instead we can consider a whole family of parabolas (see Figure A4), running

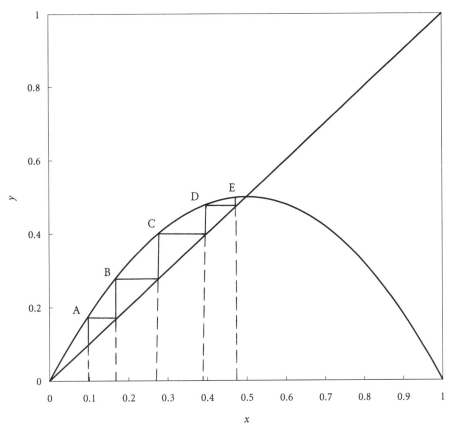

Figure A2. *A graph of the parabola $y = 2x(1 - x)$ and straight line $y = x$, showing the sequence of x-values for the game $x_{n+1} = 2x_n(1 - x_n)$ starting at $x_0 = 0.1$*

through a series of values of the multiplier a, and iterate the equation $x_{n+1} = a_j x_n (1 - x_n)$, $n = 0, 1, 2, \ldots$ for each given value of a. We call a_j a parameter. For each value of a_j we can carry out the iteration as before. The new idea we have introduced to make the game more interesting is the possibility of choosing different values of the parameter. So, the game now has two distinct mathematical concepts built into it: iteration and parameterization. We could introduce other variants like changing the shape of the function, but let us keep the game simple and see if there are any surprises that make it more than mildly interesting.

Consider the parameter value $a_j = 3.5$ (i.e. $x_{n+1} = 3.5 x_n (1 - x_n)$ is our iterative function). This, you will probably agree, does not look like a major change, but just playing with a parabola that sticks out a bit more prominently above the straight line $y = x$ makes things look very different!

Instead of the sequence of iterates of x tending to a single fixed value—what

Table A1. Iteration of $x_{n+1} = 2x_n(1 - x_n)$

Iteration	Starting value, x_0									
	0.1	0.2	0.3	0.4	0.5	0.6	0.7	0.8	0.9	1
1	0.18	0.32	0.42	0.48	0.5	0.48	0.42	0.32	0.18	0
2	0.2952	0.4352	0.4872	0.4992	0.5	0.4992	0.4872	0.4352	0.2952	0
3	0.416114	0.491602	0.499672	0.499999	0.5	0.499999	0.499672	0.491602	0.416114	0
4	0.485926	0.499859	0.5	0.5	0.5	0.5	0.5	0.499859	0.485926	0
5	0.499604	0.5	0.5	0.5	0.5	0.5	0.5	0.5	0.499604	0
6	0.5	0.5	0.5	0.5	0.5	0.5	0.5	0.5	0.5	0
7	0.5	0.5	0.5	0.5	0.5	0.5	0.5	0.5	0.5	0
8	0.5	0.5	0.5	0.5	0.5	0.5	0.5	0.5	0.5	0
9	0.5	0.5	0.5	0.5	0.5	0.5	0.5	0.5	0.5	0
10	0.5	0.5	0.5	0.5	0.5	0.5	0.5	0.5	0.5	0

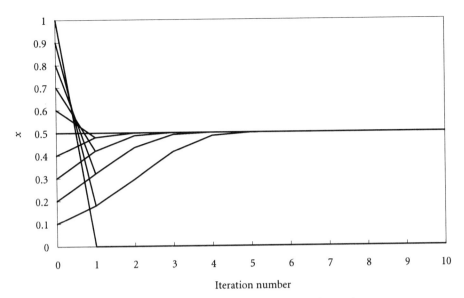

Figure A3. *Logistic difference equation iteration* $x_{n+1} = 2x_n(1 - x_n)$

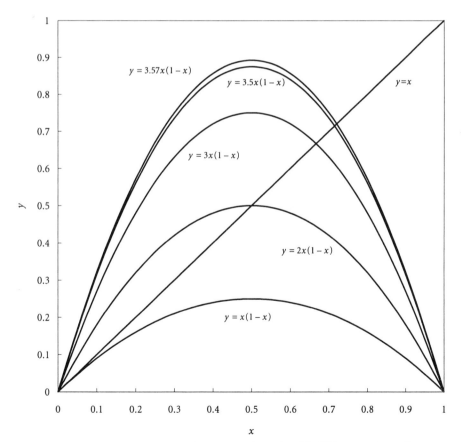

Figure A4. *Some parabolas of the form* $y = ax(1 - x)$ *with different values of* a

Table A2. *Iteration of* $x_{n+1} = 3.5x_n(1 - x_n)$

Iteration	Starting value, x_0									
	0.1	0.2	0.3	0.4	0.5	0.6	0.7	0.8	0.9	1
1	0.315	0.56	0.735	0.84	0.875	0.84	0.735	0.56	0.315	0
2	0.755213	0.8624	0.681713	0.4704	0.382813	0.4704	0.681713	0.8624	0.755213	0
3	0.647033	0.415332	0.759432	0.871933	0.826935	0.871933	0.759432	0.415332	0.647033	0
4	0.799335	0.84991	0.639433	0.390829	0.500898	0.390829	0.639433	0.84991	0.799335	0
5	0.561396	0.446472	0.806955	0.833286	0.874997	0.833286	0.806955	0.446472	0.561396	0
6	0.861807	0.864971	0.545225	0.486221	0.38282	0.486221	0.545225	0.864971	0.861807	0
7	0.416835	0.408785	0.867841	0.874336	0.826941	0.874336	0.867841	0.408785	0.416835	0
8	0.850793	0.84588	0.401425	0.384555	0.500884	0.384555	0.401425	0.84588	0.850793	0
9	0.444306	0.456285	0.84099	0.828354	0.874997	0.828354	0.84099	0.456285	0.444306	0
10	0.864144	0.868312	0.46804	0.497643	0.38282	0.497643	0.46804	0.868312	0.864144	0
11	0.410898	0.400213	0.871425	0.874981	0.826941	0.874981	0.871425	0.400213	0.410898	0
12	0.847213	0.840149	0.392152	0.382864	0.500884	0.382864	0.392152	0.840149	0.847213	0
13	0.453051	0.470046	0.834291	0.826977	0.874997	0.826977	0.834291	0.470046	0.453051	0
14	0.867285	0.87186	0.483873	0.500802	0.38282	0.500802	0.483873	0.87186	0.867285	0
15	0.402856	0.391022	0.87409	0.874998	0.826941	0.874998	0.87409	0.391022	0.402856	0
16	0.84197	0.833433	0.385199	0.382818	0.500884	0.382818	0.385199	0.833433	0.84197	0
17	0.465697	0.485879	0.828873	0.82694	0.874997	0.82694	0.828873	0.485879	0.465697	0
18	0.870882	0.874302	0.49645	0.500887	0.38282	0.500887	0.49645	0.874302	0.870882	0
19	0.393564	0.384643	0.874956	0.874997	0.826941	0.874997	0.874956	0.384643	0.393564	0
20	0.83535	0.828425	0.382928	0.38282	0.500884	0.38282	0.382928	0.828425	0.83535	0
40	0.826941	0.826941	0.38282	0.38282	0.500884	0.38282	0.38282	0.826941	0.826941	0
41	0.500884	0.500884	0.826941	0.826941	0.874997	0.826941	0.826941	0.500884	0.500884	0
42	0.874997	0.874997	0.500884	0.500884	0.38282	0.500884	0.500884	0.874997	0.874997	0
43	0.38282	0.38282	0.874997	0.874997	0.826941	0.874997	0.874997	0.38282	0.38282	0
44	0.826941	0.826941	0.38282	0.38282	0.500884	0.38282	0.38282	0.826941	0.826941	0
45	0.500884	0.500884	0.826941	0.826941	0.874997	0.826941	0.826941	0.500884	0.500884	0
46	0.874997	0.874997	0.500884	0.500884	0.38282	0.500884	0.500884	0.874997	0.874997	0
47	0.38282	0.38282	0.874997	0.874997	0.826941	0.874997	0.874997	0.38282	0.38282	0
48	0.826941	0.826941	0.38282	0.38282	0.500884	0.38282	0.38282	0.826941	0.826941	0
49	0.500884	0.500884	0.826941	0.826941	0.874997	0.826941	0.826941	0.500884	0.500884	0
50	0.874997	0.874997	0.500884	0.500884	0.38282	0.500884	0.500884	0.874997	0.874997	0

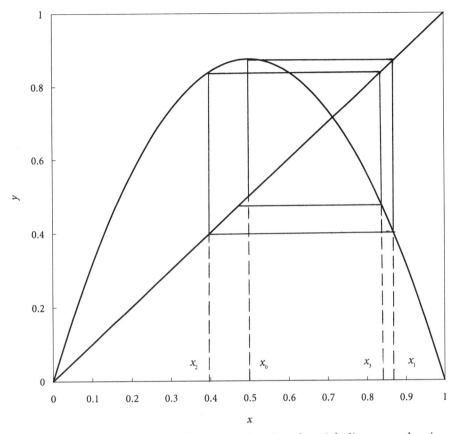

Figure A5. *A graph of the parabola* $y = 3.5x(1 - x)$ *and straight line* $y = x$, *showing the sequence of x-values for the game* $x_{n+1} = 3.5x_n(1 - x_n)$ *starting at* $x_0 = 0.5$

mathematicians call a limit point—after a few iterations to settle down, the sequence of values of x cycles through four distinct fixed values (approximately $0.383, 0.827, 0.501, 0.875$) and continues to do so for ever more. The details of the iterations with $a_j = 3.5$ are set out in Table A2 and Figures A5 and A6.

The variation of the parameter a_j in the game is clearly a significant element that both increases its potential to amuse and, what is more, indicates that something very interesting is going on in the system being modelled by this simple iterative equation.

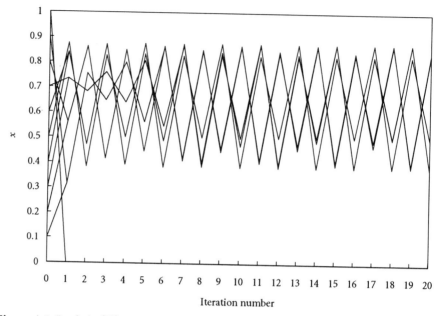

Figure A6. *Logistic difference equation iteration* $x_{n+1} = 3.5x_n(1 - x_n)$

Thresholds, bifurcations, attractors, equilibria and stability

In fact, if we choose a sequence of values of a_j and play the game for each of them, a remarkable pattern or structure emerges in the end-point values of x as a result of the simple iteration $x_{n+1} = a_j x_n(1 - x_n)$. It goes like this. When a_j lies between 0 and 1, the final value of x always equals 0 (a limit point). For a_j greater than 1 and less than or equal to 3, the final value is still a single limit point, though it depends on a_j; it is actually $(a_j - 1)/a_j$, which is why, when we chose $a_j = 2$ at the beginning, the iteration finished with x equal to 0.5 ($=(2 - 1)/2$). Although we have not demonstrated it, if a_j is greater than 3 and less than or equal to 3.449, the end-point of the iteration of x flips between two values, which is said to denote 'period 2'—a so-called 2-cycle—inasmuch as it takes two successive iterations for x to cycle back to either of its end-values.

If a_j is greater than 3.449 and less than or equal to 3.544, the end-point of the iteration takes on four values sequentially (a 4-cycle), as we saw when we carried out the iterative operation with $a_j = 3.5$. With a_j greater than 3.544 and less than or equal to 3.564 it becomes an 8-cycle, and so it continues doubling the number of end-points (8, 16, 32, and so on) at closer and closer values of a_j until, at $a_j = 3.57$, the iteration becomes chaotic and generates end-point x values randomly. The algorithm $x_{n+1} = 3.57x_n(1 - x_n)$ becomes a random-number generator for numbers in the range 0 to $a_j/4$, i.e. 0 to 0.8925.

If we plot the limiting values of x_n (n large enough for the values to have settled down) against the parameter a_j of the iterative logistic difference equation, we obtain the well-publicized picture of bifurcations (see Figure A7 on page 202) at ever closer thresholds: period doubling leading to a chaotic distribution of x_n values at and beyond $a_j = 3.57$. Even beyond this 'edge of chaos' at $a_j = 3.57$ the period doubling continues in narrow windows, as illustrated in Figure A8 (page 203) for $3.57 < a_j < 4$.

Each time the period doubles at a certain value of a_j, we say there is a bifurcation, and the values of x to which the iteration is drawn (or attracted) are called collectively the attractor. So the attractor in our game changes with the value of a_j. It can be a single point $x = 0$, or a single point that varies with a_j (according to $(a_j - 1)/a_j$), or a finite set of points (2, 4, 8, 16, etc. of them) or an infinite set of points when chaos set in, in which case it is called a strange attractor. This is summarized in Table A3.

Before leaving this amusing game, we should mention another important finding. The infinite sequence of thresholds, a_{jk}, at which period doubling (or bifurcation) occurs (k counts the value of a_j at which bifurcations occur, in sequence) is convergent, i.e. the values of the parameter a_{jk} get closer together as k increases until they reach the limit $a_{j\infty} = 3.57$, when chaos, rather than period doubling, sets in. Mitchell Feigenbaum, an American mathematician, showed that the ratio of successive differences $[a_{jk} - a_{j(k-1)}]/[a_{j(k+1)} - a_{jk}]$ tends to a limiting value of about 4.6692 as k tends to infinity, independent of the form of the iterative function used in the game, provided that it has only one variable—x in our case. This is a sort of mysterious, or we might say magic, number; it is another irrational number, like π (the ratio of the circumference to the diameter of any circle) or e (the natural base of logarithms).

Thus, we begin to perceive an extraordinary richness in the outcomes of a numbers game based on a deceptively simple iterative equation. What is more, this game has implications for the real world.

Table A3. *Attractors for various ranges of a_j*

Interval of a_j	Attractor
$0 \le a_j \le 1$	$x = 0$
$1 < a_j \le a_{j1} = 3$	$x = (a_j - 1)/a_j$
$a_{j1} = 3 < a_j \le a_{j2} = 3.499$	2-cycle
$a_{j2} = 3.499 < a_j \le a_{j3} = 3.544$	$2^2 = 4$-cycle
$a_{j3} = 3.544 < a_j \le a_{j4} = 3.564$	$2^3 = 8$-cycle
$a_{jk} < a_j \le a_{j(k+1)}$	2^k-cycle
$3.57 < a_j \le 4$	chaos with intermittent 2^P-cycles

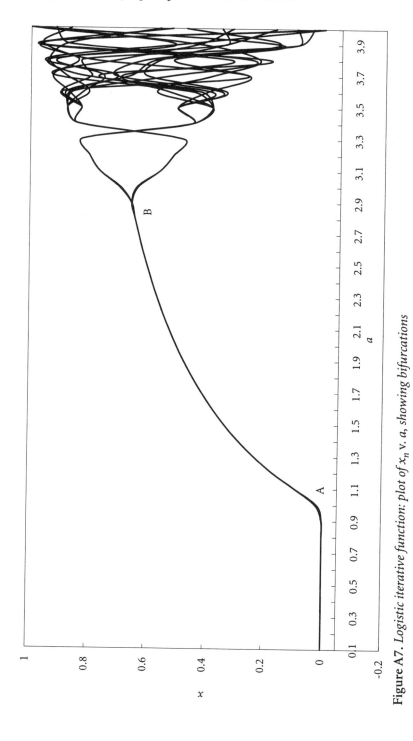

Figure A7. *Logistic iterative function: plot of x_n v. a, showing bifurcations*

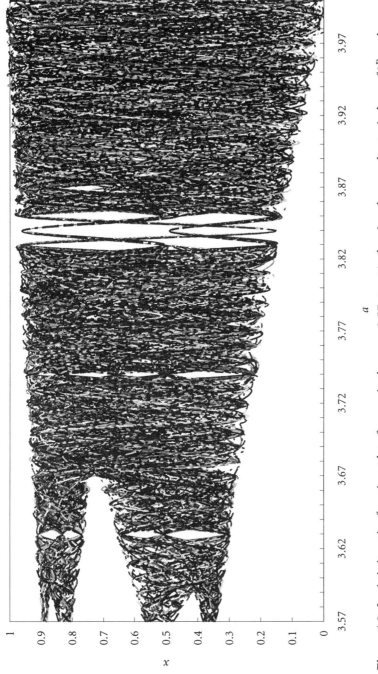

Figure A8. *Logistic iterative function: plot of x_n v. a in the range 3.57 < a <4, showing chaos and yet windows of 2^p-cycles (the white patches!)*

What's the time?

As it stands, the equation we have been discussing does not include the time explicitly. It could refer to a set of x that do not vary with time, and the iterative calculation would represent an algorithm for finding the local or global minima or maxima of the function $a_j x_i (1 - x_i)$. In practice, however, for the logistic difference equation, successive iterations represent succeeding values of x in time; they represent a time-series. This is where dynamics, especially non-linear dynamics, comes into the equation.

Bifurcation is, as we have seen, an erudite term for what is, at bottom, a simple concept, namely that of division into two branches. It crops up all over the place in the detailed study of the dynamics of systems where the variables are not related in a linear way. Bifurcation can lead to chaotic behaviour, as we have seen above for a particular simple iterative function. A fictitious example might be that future movements in the US dollar/Deutschmark exchange rate are a function of the square of its present value, the square root of the relative unemployment levels and the third power of relative industrial output levels. Such a relation could well lead to bifurcations in the evolution of the exchange rate.

Alternatively, we can imagine that the x-axis represents a variable in a non-linear dynamic system, for example the population of China or the market share of a given vendor's microprocessor chip, and the a-axis the growth parameter.

Rock solid or changeable

In many cases we desire the dynamic system to be in a steady, or equilibrium, state; e.g. population of a region, cruise control in a car (steady speed), rate of inflation, temperature in an office or oven. When the rate of change of x with time is zero ($dx/dt = 0$), the system is in a steady state or equilibrium. For our iterative numbers game, the equivalent is to have successive iterates equal, i.e. $x_{n+1} = x_n$.

In addition to equilibrium, another crucial concept is that of stability. By stable we mean that, if one perturbs the system by displacing x, by an external agent that is then removed, the internal driving force of the dynamic system will automatically bring it back to the (equilibrium) solution. It is as though the solution *attracts* the values of the variable. This is why the curve made up of the values of x for which $dx/dt = 0$, is called an attractor, a key word in the business of non-linear dynamics and chaos.

There are many everyday examples of steady-state solutions in dynamics. Many of them are unique and do not manifest multiple states or chaotic behaviour. A pea or radish placed in, or even thrown into, an empty classical parabolic salad bowl will come to rest at one and only one position—the bottom of the bowl—irrespective of its initial position and speed. On the other hand, a rigid

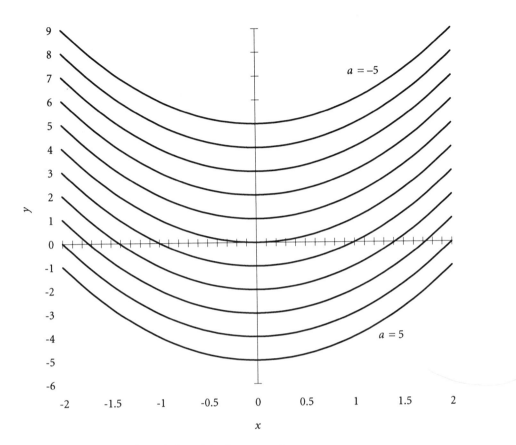

Figure A9. *A graph of parabolas of the form y = x2 – a*

pendulum, as used in some clocks, has two equilibrium positions: one at the bottom of its swing ($\theta = 0°$), which is stable, and one (less well-known, perhaps) vertically above its point of suspension ($\theta = 180°$), the latter being unstable against small displacements, and of course not used in clocks!

A roulette wheel provides far more complicated dynamics, approaching chaotic behaviour, and being a case with many bifurcations, where infinitesimal changes in initial conditions lead to devastating differences in outcomes, as some have learned to their cost! Yet another (relatively) common experience that gives a clue to how chaos arises is playing a pinball machine in an amusement arcade. Similar to the roulette wheel, it suggests, perhaps, a more intuitive analogy to the evolution of a system via bifurcations towards chaotic behaviour.

Another way of thinking about bifurcations is to consider the simplest quadratic equation, $y = x^2 - a$, which represents a parabola in the (x, y) plane (see Figure A9), commonly studied in so much detail in school. The roots are obtained by setting $y = 0$.

If a is negative, there are no real solutions (i.e. the parabola does not cross the x-axis), only horrible imaginary ones involving the square root of minus 1; if a is zero, there is one solution ($x = 0$); and if a is positive, there are two solutions ($x = \pm\sqrt{a}$). Thus, as the parameter a increases from a negative value through 0 to positive values, the number of real solutions goes from none to one to two, and we have an example of a bifurcation at $x = 0$.

When there is a qualitative change like this in the dynamics as a system parameter alters, a bifurcation is said to occur. Bifurcations encapsulate in their vividly expressive names a conceptual picture of the immanent dynamic behaviour of systems as a parameter is modified. For example, flip bifurcations, in which period doubling of the solutions occurs at certain values of a parameter and systems can 'flip' between states, are characteristic of the logistic difference equation, well known for its application to models of growth with constraints. As we have seen in this case, as the growth parameter increases, there is a transition to chaos at a certain parameter value, beyond which there are very narrow windows of parameter values in which (predictable) period-doubling behaviour returns. In fact, the logistic difference equation is none other than the iterative function for the numbers game with which we began this section in another guise.

That such complexity can occur in the solutions of what appears to be a simple one-dimensional equation with a single parameter is a clear warning to users of this type of model when they draw conclusions about growth in competitive and bounded environments. It will be recalled that the logistic differential equation is

$$dx/dt = ax - bx^2 \tag{1}$$

and its difference version is

$$x_{n+1} = x_n(1 - x_n) = F(x_n, a). \tag{2}$$

Since it is the equilibrium solutions of these equations that are often of most interest, we seek turning-points where $dx/dt = 0$ or, equivalently, fixed points where $x = F(x, a)$. The flip bifurcations of the set of fixed points as the parameter a passes certain thresholds are like those illustrated schematically in Figure A7. At each flip, two new curves of fixed points appear (so-called period doubling) to replace each former trajectory; both the new ones are stable in the sense that the system keeps returning to them.

Thus the bifurcation pattern contains the essential information about equilibrium states and their stability with respect to small perturbations or changes in initial conditions. The difference equation formulation rather than the differential one is the form usually used in computation. The difference equation gives an iterative function system, in which on each iteration we put the current value of x (and of course a) into the function on the right-hand side of eqn. (2) and calculate a new value of x to insert into the next iteration; that is, we map x from one iteration to the next using the function F.

To summarize, what happens is as followings. To begin with, as before, we organize things so that x lies in the range [0,1]; this can always be done and is only a kind of normalization, like using percentages of a maximum value. If the growth factor a also lies in the range [0,1], irrespective of the initial value x_0 to start the iteration, as the computation proceeds, the value of x is irresistibly *attracted* to the fixed value of zero, i.e. the continuous line between 0 and 1 on the horizontal axis in Figure A7.

If the growth parameter is larger, in the range $(1 < a \leq 3)$, then, no matter what initial value x_0 is taken, the successive values of x_n tend to the value $(a-1)/a$, given by the continuous curve AB (Figure A7), which arches up to the right. Within a certain number of iterations the value $(a-1)/a$ is reached. The points on this curve are stable fixed points just like those on the line that corresponds to the a-axis between 0 and 1. When the growth parameter is increased still further, beyond $a = 3$, bifurcations start to happen and, after $a = 3.57$, the world of predictable phenomena, where we feel safe and sound, caves in, and chaos reigns.

In the intermediate zone $(3 < a < 3.57)$, as we have seen, a sequence of ever closer-together flip bifurcations occurs, creating first 2-cycles, then 4-cycles, ... 2P-cycles, etc., until, at $r = 3.57$, there is no longer a cycling through iterate values because they become random. At this stage the set of x_n (i.e. the successive iterates of x) can be shown to have non-integer dimension and therefore is a so-called fractal. If you have a PC and a language compiler or interpreter for, say, FORTRAN or BASIC, you could write a program to carry out the iterations for values of a between 1 and 4 and see for yourself the marvels of period-doubling bifurcations and the onset of chaos. You can pick any value between 0 and 1 for the starting value of x, and must sometimes allow for several hundred iterations before a steady state is reached. If, on the other hand you are not too keen on programming and debugging, then you can very easily do these iterations with a spreadsheet package, such as Lotus 1-2-3 or Microsoft Excel.

Another type of bifurcation is the pitchfork, which often shows up in systems that have symmetry when the symmetry is broken. Typically, the solution of a differential or difference equation representing the symmetrical system will switch from one to two branches when a parameter goes through some critical value. A pitchfork bifurcation occurs for the equation

$$dx/dt = ax - bx^3. \tag{3}$$

The pitchfork bifurcation crops up in the stability of steady flow in fluid dynamics; it has an inversion symmetry because if we make the transformation $x \to -x$, the equation remains the same. It can be seen from inspection that $dx/dt = 0$ (i.e. x does not change with time: steady state) if $x = 0$ or $x = \pm\sqrt{(a/b)}$. Although equation (3) is symmetric under $x \to -x$, each of these two non-zero solutions breaks the symmetry, because $ax - bx^3 \neq ax + bx^3$ in general.

To sum up, it is amazing how complex the stability of the solutions is, even for a seemingly innocuous equation. A system is stable if small initial disturbances do not cause its final state to wander off to infinity. Many physical and other systems exhibit symmetry-breaking, unstable equilibria and chaotic behaviour. In so doing, their static and dynamic states show qualitative differences, they are attracted to new and sometimes unexpected steady states, and they can oscillate and fluctuate in, if not totally mysterious, at least unpredictable ways.

GLOSSARY

algorithm A procedure for solving a problem, often a mathematical problem (e.g. finding the greatest common divisor), in a finite number of steps that frequently involves repetition of an operation.

artificial intelligence (AI) is, in the most general sense, the capability of a machine to imitate intelligent human behaviour, such as reasoning, learning or the understanding of speech and symbols. Expert systems (q.v.) are often cited as examples of artificial intelligence, which, however, also encompasses pattern-recognition, probabilistic optimization, heuristics and natural-language analyses. AI is not to be confused with artificial life (q.v.).

artificial life is a computer-based paradigm for life based on self-organizing automata that may compete and/or cooperate, according to specific rules. This metaphor for lifelike behaviour holds that however puzzling and complex life seems, it is in fact the result of a few simple rules unfolding spontaneously from the bottom up. Rather than replicating the evolution of plants or reptiles, as classical biologists do, artificial life researchers use computer simulation to deduce an abstract model of evolution and play with it iteratively and by varying its parameters. Thus, they attempt to explore all forms of life 'as it could be', not just as we know it.

attractor is the central point or the overriding pattern (set of points) towards which dynamic systems such as oscillations, or orbits of moving bodies (e.g. pendulum swings, planetary orbits), and likewise, stock-exchange fluctuations, are irresistibly pulled ('attracted'). In other words, all motion tends to return to its underlying attractor, which, in a simple case, can be just a fixed point or a limit cycle. On the other hand, so-called strange attractors are non-periodic and non-repetitive, and are germane to chaotic dynamics.

bifurcation A simple concept, namely division into two branches, is an erudite term. It crops up all over the place in the study of the dynamics of systems where the variables are related in a non-linear way. Bifurcation can lead to chaotic behaviour or, on the contrary, herald the return to a known repeat pattern. The notion of bifurcation in chaotics is closely linked to the concept of (strange) attractor (see ATTRACTOR).

biological evolutionism see Darwinism.

brainstorming is a group technique by which members of the group attempt to find a solution to a specific problem by amassing all the ideas spontaneously put forward, however paradoxical they might sound at first. Although based on the rule of unimpeded freewheeling thoughts, a brainstorming session often produces a genuine framework for a converging, real-life, scenario and/or alternatives to it.

butterfly effect is a metaphor designed to illustrate what theorists and technicians call sensitivity to initial conditions. The term was invented by MIT's Edward Lorenz and was initially contained in his 1979 address to the annual meeting of the American Association for the Advancement of Science in Washington, DC, entitled 'Predictability: does the flap of a butterfly's wing in Brazil set off a tornado in Texas?' Intended as an example of the unpredictability of weather forecasting, the notion spilled over to many fields of human endeavour and business operations.

chaos implies a state of disorder, with no deterministic measurement of state being possible. In everyday parlance, chaos has no precise meaning, as can be seen from its many synonyms, e.g. disturbance, turbulence, chasm, abyss, disorder, confusion, upheaval, catastrophe and so on. Chaos theorists stress the ubiquity of chaos as a dynamic phenomenon that permeates our physical and social environment and affects nearly all systems, whether natural or of human origin. See also CHAOS THEORY; CHAOTICS; COMPLEXITY THEORY.

chaos theory A set of concepts, axioms and hypotheses concerned with the irregular, unpredictable behaviour of non-linear dynamic systems. It started from the observation that simple deterministic systems can at some stage breed random, unpredictable behaviour recurrently—complexity and chaos. Those who participate come from all fields. Physicists, mathematicians, ecologists and many others have made important contributions. Of late, social workers, business decision-makers and engineers have increasingly come to rely on its ideas and methods. Technologists and physicists in mechanics, astronomy, telecommunications and weather forecasting have been among the first adopters. See also LINEARITY; COMPLEXITY.

chaotics (from French *chaotique*). A reference framework encompassing a comprehensive corpus of concepts, methodologies and practical tools from chaos theory and complex systems theory. Their application is to business management, distribution of wealth, social and natural environments. See also CHAOS; CHAOS THEORY; COMPLEX SYSTEMS; COMPLEXITY THEORY.

complex systems (as defined by complexity theorists) are networks of myriads of independent agents interacting with each other, without any central control, in a multitude of ways. Thus we cannot see a clear simple mechanism, theory or theme. The result is apparent confusion. So we cannot understand complexity from its first appearance, but can only note general trends and behaviour. Examples range from cells to brains to bees and ants, from markets to industries to firms and to communities and societies. However diverse, these entities all display certain cardinal properties. Each agent is part and parcel of an environment produced by the interactions, multidirectional and multilevel. Whatever coherence there is (or appears to be) in the system, it is due solely to the competition and/or cooperation among the agents. Such self-organizing systems are often highly adaptive. They can also be stratified into levels of increasing complexity, with agents at one level serving as building-blocks for those at a higher level. Following Steven Wolfram, the behaviour of cellular automata can bring a more logical insight into complexity in living systems by formulating four states—completely rigid, no chaos; some movement, which dies away; complete chaos in which any life-supporting order is too unstable; sustained interactive movement—equivalent to life.

complexity theory The most radical proponents of the theory aim to create a new science, based on a unified way of thinking about nature and the universe, which touches on our changing station in society, by adopting a new philosophy of living. We would add those implications for business and the conduct of public affairs. Strictly speaking, complexity theory is concerned with the behaviour of systems with seemingly irresistible escalation in their intricacy and the cumulative impacts of this evolution—usually expressed in terms of multiple autonomous agents with individual behaviour patterns.

cost–benefit analysis is a particular kind of evaluation that assigns a numerical value, in monetary terms, to the cost-effectiveness of a programme, a procedure or an operation. The aim is to assess the desirability of an ongoing, or a new, project or policy within a specified time horizon. This has been the basic method used by private corporations and some public utilities to determine investments, and by governments to assess large-scale technological ventures. The methodology however is open to criticism. Selection of the contributory factors may be highly subjective, often too short-term, and the problems of weighting may be insuperable.

Darwinism is the theory of the origin and perpetuation of species of animals and plants, asserting that organisms tend to produce offspring that vary slightly from their parents. Darwinism holds that the process of natural selection favours the survival of individuals that are best adapted to their milieu and that by the continuous operation of these factors new species are being produced, possibly quite different from their common ancestors. Darwinism is often equated with biological evolutionism. Neo-Darwinism holds natural selection to be the chief factor in evolution, and specifically denies the possibility of inheriting acquired characters. Modern theories of complexity have their roots in Darwinism, with the notable addition of the principle of self-organization, of which Darwin was probably unaware.

Delphi techniques were named after ancient Greece's Oracle. The Delphi technique is a family of methods whose goal is to ensure group participation in the preparation of forecasts using panels of experts. The experts are invited to comment, usually in writing, on a number of future technologies and their likely date of occurrence, and then review their initial answers in the light of the panel's aggregate views. Its chief weakness is in yielding a result of the middle-of-the-road consensus type (and sometimes in excessive conditioning of panellists).

determinism (1) The theory that all occurrences in our universe are determined by previous causes and are governed by natural laws. Thus new events can be determined from history and their causes are always known. (2) The theory that regards a certain order of phenomena (e.g. economic, geographical, social, etc.) as the primary or determining causes for cultural change, social evolution, or the appearance of certain culture traits or patterns.

economies of scale are deemed to reflect the gains in output or savings on costs resulting from increasing the size of plant, firm or industry. Economies of scale may be internal or external. The former were traditionally attributed to imperfect divisibility of the factors of production, which used to come in large chunks. External economies presumably resulted from expansion of the industry as a whole. The present trend is rather towards smaller-sized production units, many of which have no difficulty outperforming the larger plants.

ecosystem An ecological community considered together with the inanimate elements of its environment as a whole or a unit. A distinction is often made between real ecosystems and ecosystem models, used in computer simulation. In the latter case, one usually starts by figuring out an ecosystem where species are free to mutate and evolve by natural selection, but where they can interact with each other only in arbitrarily specified ways. The concept has been applied in particular to an economy where each firm is free to organize itself as it sees fit internally, but where its relation to other firms is fixed by contract or by regulation. Natural selection is supposed to ensure that the average motion is always uphill toward greater fitness or performance.

'edge of chaos' An expression from complexity and chaos theory, designating the twilight zone lying on the border between order and disorder, and possibly exhibiting a blend of both without the distinctiveness of either. Some complexity theorists believe that life itself originated at the edge of chaos. Synonyms include: boundary of chaos; onset of chaos; transition to chaos.

entropy A measure of the order (or disorder) of a system. For instance, a completely regular matrix of atoms at zero degrees Kelvin exhibits zero entropy with everything frozen into a perfectly aligned set. A natural system's entropy generally increases with temperature. Going from a solid to a liquid to a gas represents major step changes in entropy at the transition points between the phases, for single elements or simple compounds. The Second Law of Thermodynamics formalizes this trend to increasing entropy, or increasing disorder, for any system.

expert systems Broadly speaking, expert systems are custom-made, complex computer programs designed to mimic the process of deductive/inductive reasoning of a human specialist. They can be broken into two parts. First, there is a database containing recorded and categorized knowledge about a specific field of expertise, e.g. medical, industrial, etc. in a narrow speciality. Then, there is a set of rules for making inferences, plus a kind of *vade mecum* for interpreting the reasonings and the findings. Expert systems belong under the label artificial intelligence (q.v.).

extrapolation is a statistical method of drawing inferences from known data or experience and/or of projecting the trend into an area not known or into the future. Extrapolation is widely used—and abused—in many fields, particularly for predicting future growth patterns of some discrete variable. This is too often done on the basis of unwarranted assumptions or speculations. The longer the future time-frame, the riskier the methodology.

feedback In engineering and science, feedback means adding a small part of the output of a machine, system, or process to the input. An electronic amplifier furnishes a simple illustration. Adding some fraction of the amplifier output to its input circuit is used either to obtain amplification of voltage or power ('positive feedback') or conversely, to restrict the amplification and reduce distortion ('negative feedback'). Feedback has found dozens of applications, not just in engineering and physics, but also in biology and medicine, even in population studies. In business, the controversy over positive versus negative feedback has revived the age-old argument about increasing and diminishing returns, resulting from changes in the proportions in which factors of production are combined.

fractal Pioneered by its inventor, Benoit Mandelbrot, the term refers to geometrical shapes that, unlike those of Euclid, are not regular at all. Fractal geometry began with the observation of all sorts of odd-looking shapes in nature (e.g. broccoli, coastlines, distribution of galaxies, forest foliage) whose shapes turned out to be recurrent, irrespective of size or distance. On the other hand, manmade fractals are geometrical idealizations, constructed by carrying out iteratively a geometrical operation on a line, a triangle, a cube or some other initial shape. Fractals have revolutionized computer graphics and data-compression techniques, and have opened the way for high-definition television.

game theory is a method of applying mathematical logic to determine which of several possible strategies is likely to increase/maximize one's gain, or to minimize one's loss, typically in a business situation or a military problem in which one's opponent or opponents can also choose between several strategies. A most important game for Chaotics is the 'Game of Life', due to John Conway, an English mathematician. In the game, which is played on computers, self-organizing automata live together according to set rules. Survival of in this artificial life universe depends on the choice of the rules. The set 'tit for tat', with some cooperation as well as competition, has been shown to be optimal.

globalization The catch-all word 'globalization' is being used in a number of different ways to cover trends in commerce and government. Examples include the globalization of corporate activity and of such environmental dangers as global warming and ozone depletion. Globalization is equated with the emergence of worldwide financial markets, and of free flows of information across national borders. It is most often understood to refer to a multilateral lowering of the barriers to the free movement of goods and services between countries—the process known as multilateralism.

heuristic research approach In the 19th century, the term 'heuristic' was defined by the Scottish philosopher Sir William Hamilton (1788–1856) as that branch of logic that treats the 'art' of discovery and invention. The heuristic approach to research is based on using past experience with inductive reasoning to guide, reveal or discover. The term refers to arguments, notions and methods that assume or postulate what remains to be proven, when no algorithm exists. The approach is especially valuable for conducting or stimulating empirical research that is so far unproved and/or unprovable.

holism teaches that the determining factors in nature are wholes (as organisms) that are irreducible to the sum of their parts inasmuch as the whole is greater than the sum of its parts. Advocates of holism believe that the evolution of the universe is the record of the activities carried out by these wholes. In many ways, holism is the opposite of reductionism, in that to divide a system into its components destroys part of it.

identity crisis is a state of confusion or uncertainty about our role, function or goals. More specifically, the term reflects introspective interrogations about our station in life, group and community affiliations, the minority syndrome, unease about the work location, vacillating corporate loyalty, the generation gap and other existential worries.

industrial Darwinism By a loose analogy, the expression 'industrial Darwinism' refers to a model of unconstrained (or less constrained) economic take-off, in which the stronger firms win, inspired by artificial life, and applicable to developing economies.

linearity The notions of linearity and non-linearity have been used in a variety of contexts and for a variety of purposes. In mathematics and in chaotics, however, the expression 'linear function' refers to a very precise concept. Simply put, it means that variables appear only to the power of one in the equation, i.e. there are no squares, cubes, etc. Another, more physical way of grasping linearity is to consider a system with inputs and outputs, e.g. an electrical circuit or a production process. Assuming that input A_1 gives rise to output B_1, and input A_2 produces output B_2, then if the combined input $(A_1 + A_2)$ gives rise to output $(B_1 + B_2)$, the system is said to be additive. If, in addition, when we multiply the input by a constant, K, the output is increased/decreased by the same K, then we say the system is homogeneous. If a system is both additive and homogeneous, then it is a linear one. All other systems, represented by other equations that do not have this property, are called non-linear.

maximum entropy A system whose state of entropy is maximized has been used as a mathematical identification technique, originally used by J. P. Burg for seismic analysis in oil prospecting. The principle is that the solution with the highest entropy will be the most accurate, since natural systems tend to seek a state of most disorder.

non-linearity Systems that do not obey superposition (adding or multiplying inputs has unexpected results on the system output: see LINEARITY) are said to be non-linear. For instance, they do not preserve the frequency characteristics of the input signals. Most natural systems are non-linear, including most systems in our bodies, population growth, fluid turbulence, etc. Common non-linearity types are saturation, dead-space, rate or acceleration limiting, POWER LAWS (square and cube laws and higher), memory and reluctance.

phase space A description of a dynamic system by plotting the first differential of some parameter (that is, its rate of change) against the value of that parameter changing with time. This is commonly performed for position, along a line x, against velocity (or momentum), on two scales at right angles, to produce a phase-space diagram of the movement.

power laws A power law is one in which the dependent variable is proportional to a power (other than 1) of the independent variable. The power may be integral or fractional, positive or negative (e.g. $y = kx^\lambda$ when $\lambda = -0.6$).

reductionism is a procedure or theory of reducing complex phenomena, or complex data, to simple terms. Reductionism stands in sharp contrast to the theory of holism. Reductionists hold that a whole can be understood completely if one understands its parts and the nature of their sum.

response time in a physical system is the delay between exciting the input and seeing the output response. The definition for a computer system is similar and is usually taken as the time to reply in transaction processing to a command entered at the user's terminal. In a business, response time is the interval from the reception of a purchase order to the delivery to the final consumer at whatever destination. Traditionally, only about 15 per cent of the production cycle used to be spent on dedicated working on the customer's orders. The remaining 85 per cent was actually taken up by backlog order clearance, waiting for semi-finished products and components, temporary storing pending delivery of complementary items, quality control, testing, etc. Nowadays, keeping the response time to a minimum has become a 'must' for any business faced with increasing competition worldwide.

scenario A logical sequence of future, projected or imagined events and the descriptions of the forces giving rise to them. Scenario-writing is commonly resorted to wherever forecasting is attempted and the technique is meant to ensure internal consistency of the exercise.

scientific management In 1911, the American industrial engineer Frederick W. Taylor invented the phrase and codified the concept, with the advent of mass production. It was first really exemplified by Henry Ford. The book *Principles of Scientific Management* by Taylor was a primary text for American business schools for some decades. It appears increasingly anachronistic in the light of today's sociomanagerial context, and of business notions using chaos and complexity.

stochastic process A dynamic process, usually a time-series such as an electrical signal, whose previous samples can only predict its future value with a given probability or level of uncertainty.

technological forecasting A technological forecast is usually taken to mean a prediction of the future characteristics of a new or upgraded technology, device, procedure or technique. Key parameters are the time-frame and level of confidence of the forecast.

technology assessment is a term for a certain form of policy research aimed at the provision of a balanced appraisal for decision-makers of potential dangers, as well as the benefits, inherent in new untried technology. Ideally it identifies policy issues and assesses impacts of alternative courses of action while leaving the final decision to policy-makers and executives. Simultaneously it should inform the general public of what is in store.

thermodynamics—and the second law A branch of physics that deals with the mechanical action or relations of heat. In particular, the second law of thermodynamics asserts that the universe is governed by an inexorable tendency toward disorder, dissolution and decay. In practice, this means that if unchecked, the forces of decay result in near-depletion of, say, energy resources of one kind or another. Chaotics shows, among other things, how the second law of thermodynamics can be reconciled with the opposite principle of self-organization and self-preservation characteristic of most non-linear dynamic systems.

trade-off is a technique of balancing desirable considerations or goals all of which are not attainable at the same time. Generally, it involves giving up one thing—an advantage or a plus—in return for an equally valuable compensation. Trade-off is common practice in system design, engineering and many other fields. A specific example used increasingly in our world is the space–time trade-off.

unemployment—new and old definitions Usually understood to mean involuntary idleness of workers seeking work at prevailing wages. In contrast, Lord Beveridge, the father of the British welfare system (1942), defined full employment as a situation in which the number of vacancies exceeded the number of people unemployed, so that the demand for labour was larger than the supply. Economists tend to distinguish between several types of unemployment, i.e. seasonal, frictional, cyclical, structural.

uniqueness theorem A mathematical theorem that applies to problems that have at most one solution.

virtual corporations, communities and other entities (e.g. virtual networks) are modern forms of association, alliance or partnership that are bound together functionally or effectively by some common interest, yet, as a general rule, only informally. Thus, members are free to change allies, partners, associates, as they see fit, or disengage altogether.

Weltanschauung (German) (1) worldscape, outlook on the world, worldview; (2) philosophy of life; (3) a cosmological conception of a society and its institutions held by its members.

BIBLIOGRAPHY

Anderla, Georges and Anthony Dunning, *Computer Strategies 1990–9* (Chichester & New York : John Wiley & Sons, 1987).

Arthur, W. Brian, 'Positive feedbacks in the economy', *Scientific American*, February 1990.

Barnsley, Michael, *Fractals Everywhere* (San Diego: Academic, 1988).

Boulding, Kenneth E., *Economic Analysis*, rev. edn. (New York: Harper & Brothers, 1948).

Cambel, A. B., *Applied Chaos Theory: A Paradigm for Complexity* (San Diego, CA: Academic Press, 1993).

Casti, John, *Complexification* (New York: HarperCollins, 1995).

Cohen, Jack and Ian Stewart, *The Collapse of Chaos: Discovering Simplicity in a Complex World* (London & New York: Viking, 1994).

Coveney, Peter, and Roger Highfield, *Frontiers of Complexity.* (London: Ballantine Books and Faber & Faber, 1995).

Ford, Joseph, 'What is Chaos that we should be mindful of it?', ch. 12 in Paul Davies (ed.), *The New Physics* (Cambridge and New York: Cambridge University Press, 1989)

Gell-Mann, Murray, *The Quark and the Jaguar* (London: Little, Brown and Company, 1994).

Gleick, James, *Chaos: Making a New Science* (London: Sphere Books, Penguin Group, 1988).

Hofstadter, Douglas R., *Gödel, Escher, Bach: An Eternal Golden Braid* (London: Penguin Books, 1979).

Hutton, Will, *The State We'ere in* (London: Vintage, 1996).

Jantsch, Erich, *Technological Forecasting in Perspective* (Paris: OECD, 1967).

Kahn, Hermann, 'On alternative world futures: issues and themes' (New York: Macmillan, 1967).

Kauffman, Stuart, 'Antichaos et adaptation', in *Pour la Science* (Scientific American), Paris, January 1995, pp. 104–10.

Kennet, Wayland (ed.), *The Futures of Europe* (Cambridge: Cambridge University Press, 1976).

Laskar, Jacques. 'La stabilité du système solaire', in *Pour la Science* (Scientific American), Paris, January 1955, pp. 45–7.

Lewin, Roger, *Complexity: Life at the Edge of Chaos* (London: Dent, 1993).

Lorenz, E. N., 'Deterministic non-periodic flow', *Journal of Atmospheric Sciences*, vol. 20 (1963), pp. 130–41.

Mandelbrot, Benoit, 'Fractals: a geometry of nature', *New Scientist*, 15 September 1990.

Martino, Joseph P, *Technological Forecasting for Decision-Making* (New York: Elsevier, 1972).

Merry, Uri, *Coping with Uncertainty: Insights from the New Sciences of Chaos, Self-Organization, and Complexity* (Westport : Greenwood Publishing Group, 1995).

OECD, *Managing the Environment: The Role of Economic Instruments* (Paris: OECD, 1994).

——*The OECD Jobs Study: Facts, Analysis, Strategies* (Paris: OECD, 1994).

——*Project and Policy Appraisal: Integrating Economics and Environment* (Paris: OECD, 1994).

——*Globalization and Regionalization: The Challenge for Developing Countries* by Charles Oman (OECD: Paris, 1994).

Ott, Edward, *Chaos in Dynamical Systems* (Cambridge, Cambridge University Press, 1993).

Peitgen, Heinz-Otto, Jürgen Hartmut and Saupe Dietmar, *Chaos and Fractals: New Frontiers of Science* (New York and Berlin: Springer Verlag, 1992).

Penrose, Roger, *Shadows of the Mind* (first published in Great Britain by Oxford University Press, 1994).

Peters, Tom, *Thriving on Chaos* (New York: Pan Books, 1987).

Romer, Paul, 'Increasing returns and long-run growth', *Journal of Political Economy* 1986.

Rosen, Joe, *The Capricious Cosmos: Universe Beyond Law* (New York: Macmillan, 1991).

Ruelle, David, *Hasard et chaos* (Paris: Editions Odile Jacob, 1991).

—— 'Où le chaos intervient-il?', in *Pour la Science* (Scientific American), Paris, January 1995, pp. 6–13.

Russel, Bertrand. *History of Western Philosophy*, new edn. (London: George Allen & Unwin, 1961).

Samuelson, Paul A. *Economics*, 5th edn. (New York: McGraw-Hill, 1961).

Shinbrot, Troy and Celso Grebogi, 'Using small perturbations to control chaos', *Nature* 363 (3 June 1993).

Waldrop, M. Mitchell, *Complexity: The Emerging Science at the Edge of Order and Chaos* (New York: Simon & Schuster, 1992).

Wills, Gordon, Richard Wilson, *et al.*, *Technological Forecasting* (London: Penguin Books, 1972).

INDEX

About the Authors

GEORGES ANDERLA, an economist by training, was head of the EC Information Technology Directorate, where he set up Euronet, an early European academic forerunner of the Internet. He is the coauthor, with Anthony Dunning, of *Computer Strategies, 1990–1999* (1987).

ANTHONY DUNNING, a mathematician by training, is Information Resources Manager in the office of the Directorate-General for Telecommunications, Information Market and Innovation of the European Commission.

SIMON FORGE is a director of the Cambridge Strategic Management Group, a telecommunications and information technology consultancy, and is on the board of *Futures*.

ISBN 0-275-95691-1

HARDCOVER BAR CODE